Child Maltreatment Solutions Network

More information about this series at http://www.springer.com/series/15457

Douglas M. Teti

Editor

Parenting and Family Processes in Child Maltreatment and Intervention

 Springer

Editor
Douglas M. Teti
Human Development & Family Studies
The Pennsylvania State University
University Park, PA, USA

ISSN 2509-7156   ISSN 2509-7164   (electronic)
Child Maltreatment Solutions Network
ISBN 978-3-319-40918-4   ISBN 978-3-319-40920-7   (eBook)
DOI 10.1007/978-3-319-40920-7

Library of Congress Control Number: 2016957840

Printed on acid-free paper

This Springer imprint is published by Springer Nature
The registered company is Springer International Publishing AG
The registered company address is: Gewerbestrasse 11, 6330 Cham, Switzerland

To Mark Chaffin 1952-2015
Scholar, colleague and friend
And a leader in the field of child
maltreatment research

Preface

This volume is the direct outgrowth of a recent meeting, held at Penn State University on May 5–6, 2014, entitled "The role of parenting and family processes in child maltreatment and intervention." This meeting's and this volume's central purpose was to bring together internationally renowned scholars to address child maltreatment in terms of the roles that family processes, and in particular parent–child processes, play in the etiology, impact, treatment, and prevention of maltreatment. The hope was and is to push family science toward the development of innovative approaches in the study of the etiology of maltreatment, a broader understanding of the transmission of child maltreatment and/or parenting-at-risk across generations, and new ideas on how best to treat and, ideally, prevent maltreatment. The conference was the third conference on the overall topic of child maltreatment organized by Penn State's Network on Child Protection and Well-Being and was supported by many sponsors within and external to Penn State.

Like the meeting, this volume is organized into four main parts. The first part, **Child Maltreatment and Family Processes**, addresses child maltreatment in the context of the broader family system. Sherry Hamby's lead-off chapter emphasizes the point that child maltreatment frequently occurs as part of a larger "web-of-violence," with multiple forms of maltreatment (physical abuse, sexual abuse, neglect) commonly co-occurring in multiply-stressed families. The high frequency and overlapping causes of poly-victimization emphasize the need for child- and family-centered approaches to the study and treatment of maltreatment. Hamby further argues against unidimensional treatment approaches that purport to remediate a specific child problem and for more resilience-based approaches that are more likely to provide the kinds of comprehensive, multilayered, developmentally informed treatments needed for maltreated children and their families.

Margaret Wright addresses the complex role of social supports in the short- and long-term impact of maltreatment. She calls attention to the fact that children's informal social networks, which include but can extend beyond the immediate family, may not be consistently supportive and could even be hostile and rejecting. Wright advocates that an important part of treatment is to provide "corrective relationship experiences" for the child and to bring in formal supports to assist families attempting to cope with the realities of maltreatment disclosure.

In the final chapter in this part, Nancy Kellogg addresses the specific supportive roles that clinicians can play when disclosure takes place. These are many and varied and tied to the specific circumstances in each family. Clinicians can, for example, help families understand the various ways children disclose maltreatment; that disclosure is rarely a single event but can unfold over months and even years; that sexual abuse is not necessarily associated with prototypical physical, behavioral, or emotional symptoms; and that children may disclose, later recant, and then re-disclose, depending on their beliefs in the level and quality of support they receive from the non-offending parent. Kellogg notes that a critical factor in the child's well-being following disclosure is the child's belief that he or she is believed and supported.

The second part, **Intergenerational Transmission of Child Maltreatment**, leads off with Laura McCloskey's chapter addressing the intergenerational (IG) cycle of abuse. She notes that whereas a cycle of abuse is borne out by evidence, IG transmission is complex and moderated by many risk and protective factors, that maltreatment's impact may vary as a function of the nature and severity of the maltreatment and the gender of the victim, and that specific linkages are elusive. She points out that prospective designs are far superior to retrospective designs in describing the probabilistic transmission of maltreatment from one generation to the next, but that prospective designs are challenging in their own right in terms of maintaining connections with participants, obtaining adequate sampling of historical moderators of maltreatment–outcome relations, and selecting the right points in the life span to assess maltreatment's impact.

In the second chapter of this part, Jennie Noll notes that IG transmission estimates are primarily based on the transmission of physical abuse and that very little data is available on IG transmission of other forms of maltreatment. Further, it is likely that mechanisms underlying IG transmission are quite distinct for different types of maltreatment. She puts forth an important premise that whereas the search for IG linkages that are specific to particular forms of maltreatment may be elusive, parents who were maltreated as children, in whatever form(s), are more likely to fail to protect children, either in the context of their own caregiving or the caregiving of others, and/or they may create conditions for their children in which maltreatment from others is enabled. Such maladaptive parenting patterns can be internalized by the children of maltreated parents, putting them at risk for protection failures of their own offspring and for a variety of negative developmental and psychosocial sequelae.

Judith Cohen and Anthony Mannarino kick off Part III of this volume, **Intervening with Maltreated Children and Their Families**, with a detailed overview of Trauma-Focused Cognitive Behavioral Therapy (TF-CBT), one of the most well-established, evidence-based treatments for child maltreatment in the field. Cohen and Mannarino describe the principles of TF-CBT, which include whenever possible the involvement of non-offending parents and/or caregivers in the treatment, and its major components. They emphasize that parental involvement in treatment has many advantages. It promotes better parental understanding of the details underlying the child's trauma and of child behavior problems that may have surfaced as a result of trauma, better communication between the parent and the child about the trauma and its effects, and greater capacity to cope with their own distress over the trauma and to take on a more supportive role.

Carisa Wilsie and her group, led by the late Mark Chaffin, follow with a chapter describing Parent–Child Interaction Therapy (PCIT), an evidence-based treatment that is geared more toward preschool and school-aged children. As its name implies, the parent who is at risk for abuse, and that parent's relationship with the child, is the central focus of PCIT, whose goal is to promote the use of positive parenting, promote consistent and developmentally appropriate strategies for behavioral management, and reduce child behavior problems. As the authors note, PCIT has been shown to improve mental health and behavior in children, and its benefits extend to parents as well by reducing recidivism abuse rates among offending parents. PCIT can be delivered to parents in the home and has been adapted for use with foster parents and for parents involved in child welfare services.

Sheree Toth ends this part with a chapter that presents Child–Parent Psychotherapy (CPP) intervention, an evidence-based program originally developed by Alicia Lieberman that draws heavily from attachment theory and research on the effects of maltreatment on attachment processes. The aim of CPP is to break the intergenerational cycle of abuse by focusing on issues in the relationship in the child–parent dyad, helping the parent (typically the mother) recognize how her own prior histories of trauma and neglect could be impacting the parent's perceptions of her child, her interpretation of specific child behaviors, and her interactions with her child. Through weekly sessions, the aim of CPP is to promote more positive, sensitive, and emotionally attuned parent–child interactions, a more secure child–parent attachment, and a reduction in child internalizing and externalizing behavior problems. Of the three treatments discussed in this part, CPP perhaps most strongly qualifies as a prevention program. It is an appropriate segue to the next and final part of this volume.

Preventing Child Maltreatment: Current Efforts, Future Directions

The final part turns to new approaches in preventing child maltreatment—not simply preventing its recurrence (i.e., secondary prevention), but preventing it from occurring at all (primary prevention). In the absolute, this is, of course, a practically unreachable goal, but given what is now known about parenting competence, which is considerable, this part addresses how can this knowledge be brought to bear to reduce, significantly, the incidence of child neglect, physical, and sexual abuse.

Guastaferro and Lutzker address this question with a broad-based, detailed discussion of scaling up the use of evidence-based programs, such as SafeCare®, a well-known parenting program that has shown particular success for parents who have been referred to child protective services for neglect. Scaled-up SafeCare® is now in widespread use, and this chapter calls attention to the challenges pertaining to the implementation and dissemination of evidence-based programs to the public at large. They note that, happily, reports of child maltreatment are in decline but still occur at unacceptably high rates. Dissemination of evidence-based programs that are specifically designed to reduce the risk for maltreatment must continue by ongoing solicitation of feedback from providers and clients and adapting implementation strategies to meet continually changing needs and circumstances.

Charles Wilson and Donna Pence further develop this premise by systematically addressing what "risk reduction" actually entails. They note that child maltreatment prevention requires a broad array of risk reduction strategies that target both distal and proximal influences. These include creating economic opportunities and providing parents with affordable child care; promoting parents' knowledge of child developmental milestones, in particular knowledge about what a typically developing child can reasonably be expected to do and not do at a given point in development; knowledge about the basic components of competent parenting, particularly in response to child provocations; promoting family supports for parenting; and connecting parents to external resources to further support parenting efforts.

Lastly, Sharon Wasco introduces the concept of "practice-based evidence," which she argues must be a critical component of efforts to reduce child maltreatment risk. This is information that practitioners can share with researchers in the implementation of evidence-based programs that can be used in a variety of ways to adapt and tailor the program more effectively to particular constituents. She argues that the collection of PBE should be incorporated into the fabric of scaled-up evidence-based programs, which should help program staff adjust program delivery to be of better use to individual groups. PBE can be used to answer or raise questions about what program elements appear to be particularly useful, what particular data should be examined to determine whether a program is successful or not, what and what are not program elements that are cost-effective, etc.

It is hoped that this volume will promote a more integrative understanding of the role of family processes in the etiology, impact, treatment, and ultimate prevention of child maltreatment, and as such be useful to researchers and practitioners alike.

University Park, PA, USA   Douglas M. Teti

Contents

Contributors

Michelle E. Alto, B.A. Mt. Hope Family Center, University of Rochester, Rochester, NY, USA

Heather Bensman, Psy.D. Division of Behavioral Medicine and Clinical Psychology, Cincinnati Children's Hospital Medical Center, Cincinnati, OH, USA

UC Department of Pediatrics, The University of Cincinnati, Cincinnati, OH, USA

Christopher Campbell, Ph.D. College of Education and Psychology, East Central University, Ada, OK, USA

Mark Chaffin Department of Pediatrics, Child Study Center, University of Oklahoma Health Sciences Center, Oklahoma City, OK, USA

Judith A. Cohen, M.D. Department of Psychiatry, Allegheny Health Network, Drexel University College of Medicine, Philadelphia, PA, USA

Susan F. Folger, M.A. Department of Psychology, Miami University, Oxford, OH, USA

Beverly Funderburk, Ph.D. Department of Pediatrics, Child Study Center, University of Oklahoma Health Sciences Center, Oklahoma City, OK, USA

Katelyn Guastaferro, M.P.H. Mark Chaffin Center for Healthy Development, School of Public Health, Georgia State University, Atlanta, GA, USA

Danielle J. Guild, M.A. Mt. Hope Family Center, University of Rochester, Rochester, NY, USA

Matthew Hagler University of Massachusetts Boston, Boston, MA, USA

Sherry Hamby Life Paths Appalachian Research Center and University of the South, Sewanee, TN, USA

Wojciech Kaczkowski Georgia State University, Atlanta, GA, USA

Nancy D. Kellogg, M.D. Division Chief of Child Abuse, University of Texas Health Science Center at San Antonio, San Antonio, TX, USA

John R. Lutzker, Ph.D. Mark Chaffin Center for Healthy Development, School of Public Health, Georgia State University, Atlanta, GA, USA

Anthony P. Mannarino, Ph.D. Department of Psychiatry, Allegheny Health Network, Drexel University College of Medicine, Philadelphia, PA, USA

Laura Ann McCloskey Center for Research on Health Disparities, School of Public Health, Indiana University, Bloomington, IN, USA

Jennie G. Noll Department of Human Development and Family Studies, The Pennsylvania State University, University Park, PA, USA

Network on Child Protection and Wellbeing, The Pennsylvania State University, University Park, PA, USA

Donna M. Pence Pence-Wilson Training & Consulting, Inc., San Diego, CA, USA

Jonathan M. Reader Department of Human Development and Family Studies, The Pennsylvania State University, State College, PA, USA

Lindsey T. Roberts Bowling Green State University, Bowling Green, OH, USA

Elizabeth Taylor University of the South, Sewanee, TN, USA

Sheree L. Toth, Ph.D. Mt. Hope Family Center, University of Rochester, Rochester, NY, USA

Sharon M. Wasco, Ph.D. 142 North Hayden Parkway, Hudson, OH, USA

Carisa Wilsie, Ph.D. Department of Pediatrics, Child Study Center, University of Oklahoma Health Sciences Center, Oklahoma City, OK, USA

Charles A. Wilson Chadwick Center for Children & Families, Rady Children's Hospital, San Diego, CA, USA

Margaret O'Dougherty Wright, Ph.D. Department of Psychology, Miami University, Oxford, OH, USA

Part I
Child Maltreatment and Family Processes

Families, Poly-victimization, & Resilience Portfolios: Understanding Risk, Vulnerability & Protection Across the Span of Childhood

Sherry Hamby, Lindsey T. Roberts, Elizabeth Taylor, Matthew Hagler, and Wojciech Kaczkowski

A Need for a Paradigm Shift

In the last half century, remarkable progress has been made toward the goal of making families safer. However, to build on existing progress, a paradigm shift is needed. This chapter identifies three primary shifts that have the potential to further advance our understanding of family violence and to enhance our ability to prevent violence and promote resilience when violence does occur. The first shift is to encourage researchers and providers to adopt a more integrated framework for violence and victimization. All forms of violence and victimization are interconnected and treating them as discrete phenomena has been a major obstacle to progress in reducing the burden of violence on children, families and on society. The second shift is to focus more on mechanisms and less on correlates, especially static correlates such as demographic characteristics. The third shift is to promote a strengths-based

S. Hamby (✉)
Life Paths Appalachian Research Center and University of the South, Sewanee, TN, USA
e-mail: sherry.hamby@lifepathsresearch.org

L.T. Roberts
Bowling Green State University, Bowling Green, OH, USA
e-mail: thomala@bgsu.edu

E. Taylor
University of the South, Sewanee, TN, USA
e-mail: entaylor@sewanee.edu

M. Hagler
University of Massachusetts Boston, Boston, MA, USA
e-mail: matthew.hagler001@umb.edu

W. Kaczkowski
Georgia State University, Atlanta, GA, USA
e-mail: wkaczkowski1@student.gsu

© Springer International Publishing Switzerland 2017
D.M. Teti (ed.), *Parenting and Family Processes in Child Maltreatment and Intervention*, Child Maltreatment Solutions Network,
DOI 10.1007/978-3-319-40920-7_1

approach to working with families, children, and parents. No one thinks of their life goals as simply avoiding psychological distress or trauma. People are motivated to pursue happiness and well-being for themselves and their loved ones. Using a framework called "Resilience Portfolios" (Grych, Hamby, & Banyard, 2015) we present a way to shift science, prevention and intervention to a family-centered approach that better aligns with the goals that most people have for their families.

Building on Prior Progress

To understand the need for new conceptual shifts, it is helpful to understand the first dramatic shift in our understanding of family and other forms of violence. Our earliest surviving writings and other artistic mediums are filled with depictions of violence. For millennia, however, violence was considered an inherent part of existence, not something that could be studied scientifically, much less reduced. That began to change in the nineteenth century and shifted in earnest in the second half of the twentieth century.

The twentieth century was a period of tremendous change and innovation. People began to apply the tools of social science to the issue of violence, revolutionizing our understanding of violence. By simply asking people about issues, even very private issues, a subject that was thought of as private, rare, and taboo transformed into a question to which the scientific method could be applied. Alfred Kinsey was one of the first scientists to cross these frontiers and collected the first systematic data on child sex offenders (Kinsey, Pomeroy, & Martin, 1948). Another breakthrough occurred when physicians began to inquire about the nature of suspicious pediatric injuries (Kempe, Silverman, Steele, Droegemueller, & Silver, 1962). In the 1970s, the first national survey on family violence was conducted in the United States (Straus, Gelles, & Steinmetz, 1980). These efforts transformed the understanding of family violence. It was no longer seen as a rare problem affecting a deviant few, but a huge social problem that touched the lives of many. Largely as a result of these efforts, healthcare, schools, criminal justice institutions, social services, and policymakers invest far greater resources in family violence than was formerly the case. Despite these significant social changes, in some respects we have become too wedded to some of the conventions established in these early years. This is keeping us from making further progress.

Conceptual Shift #1: From Disciplinary Siloes to the Web of Violence

The first major shift that needs to occur is to move away from the hyper-specialization that has developed (Hamby & Grych, 2013). There has been a huge proliferation of research on all different types of child and family violence. However, these lines of research have largely emerged in isolation from each other. Researchers studying sexual abuse are a different group than those who study rape; scientists who study exposure to domestic violence are different from those who study dating violence; experts who study adolescent dating violence are often different from those who study bullying and other peer victimizations. This separation limits the potential of the field, as those are not independent phenomena; they are all closely interrelated. Similarly, prevention and intervention efforts have tended to focus on a single problem.

Fortunately, this siloed approach to violence has started to shift and it is increasingly recognized that most people who are victimized have experienced multiple forms of victimization. Labels such as "victim of child abuse" or "victim of bullying" miss critical elements of many children's experiences. For the last decade, the National Survey of Children's Exposure to Violence (NatSCEV; Finkelhor, Turner, Ormrod, & Hamby, 2009) has monitored youth victimization in the United States. NatSCEV is an ongoing survey, with each wave including more than 4000 families with children between the ages of 1 month and 17 years old. Surprisingly, until NatSCEV, there was no systematic attempt to measure (at a nationally-representative level) crimes against children under the age of 12 that were not reported to authorities. One of the primary insights from NatSCEV—and what sets it apart from other surveys that focus solely on one specific domain of victimization—is that children's lives are neither organized by our research disciplines nor by our social institutions.

Poly-victimization

Unlike many studies on child victimization, which often focus on a single type of abuse or closely related set of types, NatSCEV assesses more than 40 different types of victimization. This has enabled us to see the close interrelationships among all forms of victimization. For example, children who are victims of maltreatment are more than four times as likely to also be victims of sexual victimization by a non-caregiving offender (Finkelhor et al., 2009). Maltreated children are also almost twice as likely to be the victim of non-familial assault and more than twice as likely to witness violence. Perhaps especially surprisingly, they are even about twice as likely to experience a property crime. Seemingly unrelated offenses are not unrelated at all but rather are closely intertwined.

David Finkelhor and Heather Turner coined the term "poly-victimization" to capture these relationships (Finkelhor, Ormrod, & Turner, 2007; Turner, Finkelhor, & Ormrod, 2010). Poly-victims are people who experience multiple, different types of violence and represent the children with the greatest victimization burden. Children who are getting exposed to abuse in the home are often the same children who are being bullied at school and witnessing gang violence in the community. These are not independent populations. Rather, many children are getting victimized in multiple settings by multiple perpetrators and have no safe haven.

The Over-reliance on Formal Similarities in Studies of Interconnections

When thinking about these interconnections, the field, often without seeming to realize it, has emphasized isomorphic similarities instead of studying the mechanisms underlying these connections (Hamby & Grych, 2013). For example, dozens of studies link exposure to domestic violence and child physical abuse (for a review, see Holt, Buckley, & Whelan, 2008). Although that is an important link, the emphasis on this particular interconnection misses something crucial. Exposure to domestic violence and child physical abuse are not linked simply because perpetrators enjoy hitting multiple targets. Instead, multiple, complex problems lead to multiple violations.

Recognizing these shared vulnerabilities begins to shed light on findings such as one from NatSCEV showing that exposure to domestic violence is *more closely related to other forms of maltreatment than it is to child physical abuse*. Children who grow up in domestically violent homes are about 5 times more likely to experience physical abuse by a caregiver (odds ratio = 4.99; Hamby, Finkelhor, Turner, & Ormrod, 2010). However, the odds ratios for neglect and sexual abuse by another known adult are as high or higher at 6.2 and 5.2, respectively (adjusting for several demographic characteristics). Exposure to domestic violence is also more closely related to other forms of victimization, including some that might not be expected, such as custodial interference (taking and keeping a child in violation of a custody agreement), which was more than 9 times as common in domestically violent homes as it was in other homes. In fact, custodial interference was extremely rare in non-domestically violent homes and almost 3 out of 4 cases (72 %) occurred in homes where children had also been exposed to domestic violence.

Another example is exposure to domestic violence and teen dating victimization. Although these two forms of victimization are significant related, they are related to many other forms of youth victimization as well. It is not as simple as one dysfunctional romantic relationship producing another dysfunctional romantic relationship. In NatSCEV, teen dating violence is more closely related to bias-motivated assaults (hate crimes), internet harassment, and statutory rape/sexual misconduct than it is to exposure to domestic violence, for example (Hamby, Finkelhor, & Turner, 2012). It is also closely related to poly-victimization. Multiple types of dysfunction are bleeding into all of the relationships in a child's life. They are so interconnected that in NatSCEV, there was not a single victim of teen dating violence who did not report at least one other form of victimization, although "mono-victimization" does occur (isolated incidents of violence; Hamby & Grych, 2013). The complete picture is not a simple mirroring phenomenon, but is instead a tangled web of dysfunction.

Taking a Child-Centered Approach

Another way that past research has missed important aspects of children's vulnerabilities is in taking an adult or parent-centered approach, rather than a child-centered approach to the assessment of violence. A distinctive feature of NatSCEV (Finkelhor et al., 2009) is its child-centered approach. Unlike much of the family research that has been done, NatSCEV's child-centered focus means that the research is based on the child as the frame of reference. This might sound similar to other child abuse research, but a child-centered approach produces insights that are not well recognized in the field. An example best illustrates the differences in methodology. As is well known, in the United States Census there has been a decline in two-parent households (Vespa, Lewis, & Kreider, 2013) and household structure has been a topic of considerable interest. However, this Census statistic is parent-centered data, and it does not accurately reflect children's experiences. Simply surveying current two-parent households misses important aspects of many families and—surprisingly given the widespread recognition of the decline of the traditional "nuclear" family—is based on untenable assumptions about the homogeneity of two-parent families.

Consider the example of a man who gets married multiple times and starts multiple families. If he responds to the Census while currently married, he will appear to be part of a two-parent household. His current marital status does not, however, capture the fact that he could have biological children living in single-parent households (maybe even multiple single-parent households.) It could also be possible that he is parenting step-children and not all of the children living in his "two-parent" household are living with their biological parents. A child-centered approach, however, accounts for these possibilities. It is surprisingly difficult to find child-centered data on household structure, but a study using National Survey of Family Growth data showed that even by age 10, 29 % of children born in the U.S. to married parents are not living with both biological parents. For children born outside of marriage, the figure is more than twice as high. Two out of three (66 %) of children born to unmarried parents do not live with both biological parents by the age of 10 (Manning, 2004).

This different focus is the crucial difference between an adult-centered and child-centered perspective. A child-centered approach gives a very different picture of children's vulnerabilities. Children who are living in single-parent households are at greater risk of victimization, probably due to the increased financial strain and reduced ability to provide close supervision that are common in many single-parent homes (Turner et al., 2010). Although the situation of adoption (but not foster care) complicates the picture somewhat, other children experience increased vulnerability because they live with non-biologically related adult males. These children are at higher victimization risk too, in part because of "discriminative parental solicitude" (favoring biological children over non-genetically related children, whether step, foster, or adoptive) and also because antisocial individuals are over-represented in the population of individuals with multiple marriages. As a result of both processes, fathers are twice as likely to physically abuse step-children as genetically related children (Hilton, Harris, & Rice, 2015).

In the study of family violence, a child-centered approach requires assessing family violence among all of the caregivers to whom the child is exposed. This approach, however, is surprisingly uncommon. Most domestic violence studies only assess a single caregiver, often the mother, and her current relationship.

That approach does not accurately represent the number of caregivers who are often responsible for children, particularly following divorce or other relationship termination. Huge numbers of children follow joint custody schedules and shuttle back and forth between households. For example, these schedules might involve spending Wednesdays and every other weekend with their father's family. The lack of two parents in either household could mean that other caregivers are commonly present too. Of course, this is just one example of many patterns that occur. Given the variety of situations in which children might be under the supervision of other caregivers, when researchers measure domestic violence exposure in the traditional way by only asking one parent (usually the mother) about their current relationship, they may not be capturing all of the child's exposure to victimization. This is exactly what we found in NatSCEV. Children are in fact getting exposed to violence by a wide variety of caregivers. About 1 in 4 DV perpetrators are not mothers or fathers, but are other caregivers. The single biggest category in this "other" group is mothers' boyfriends (Hamby, Finkelhor, Turner, & Ormrod, 2011). By only talking to one parent, researchers miss much of the domestic violence to which children are exposed.

Missing the Sources of Psychological Trauma due to the Overly Siloed Approach

A final important insight from NatSCEV (Finkelhor et al., 2009) regards the source of trauma symptoms and the ways that "siloed" approaches miss important aspects of mental health symptoms (Hamby & Grych, 2013). Researchers studying a specific area of violence, such as exposure to domestic violence or sexual assault, often assume that the specific types of violence they study are responsible for any trauma symptoms that are reported. Although all of these separate forms of victimization are certainly traumatic and toxic events, this bivariate approach is missing important connections. Researchers, although they may have the best of intentions, tend to focus on and attempt to artificially carve out a single causal factor that realistically cannot be separated from a complex system of causal factors. Bivariate approaches, at least in violence research, do not represent the reality of victimization experiences. In the population, children are not *only* victims of exposure to domestic violence or child sexual abuse, but are often victimized across many domains of their lives. This is especially true for children who have experienced more severe forms of victimization.

Not surprisingly, there is a linear relationship between the number of exposures for different victimization types and mean trauma scores on the Trauma Symptom Checklist (Briere, 1996; Turner et al., 2012). Like many other studies, NatSCEV finds that at the bivariate level, all forms of victimization are associated with trauma symptoms (Finkelhor et al., 2009). However, with poly-victimization introduced into the equations first as a score that measures the total number of *different* ways that a child has been victimized, the statistical contribution of any single form of

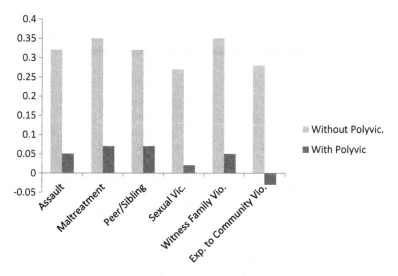

Fig. 1 Mean Trauma Symptom Checklist scores for individual effects compared with effects of poly-victimization

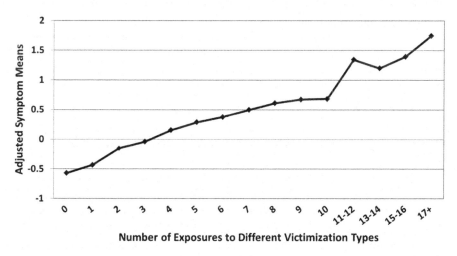

Fig. 2 Mean standardized trauma symptom levels by total number of victimization types, after controlling for demographic variables

victimization, over and above poly-victimization, drops to zero (statistically) (Finkelhor et al., 2007). Figure 1 illustrates the effects of each type of victimization on trauma symptoms both before and after the introduction of poly-victimization into the equation, while Fig. 2 shows the increase in trauma symptoms as types of victimization increase. Even victimizations that are commonly thought of as driving forces behind children's symptomatology (e.g., maltreatment, assault) are reduced to having statistically no effects after the introduction of poly-victimization. Current trauma symptoms are more tied to the *number and variety* of exposures than to specific victimization types. These findings have been replicated in NatSCEV 2 (Turner et al., 2010).

Researchers often wonder about confounding poly-victimization with frequency and chronicity of abuse. One way this has been explored is by dividing children into four groups: non-victims, mono-victims who report a low frequency, mono-victims who report a high frequency of incidents but only for one type of victimization, and poly-victims (Turner et al., 2010). As one would expect, the non-victims score low on trauma symptoms and the low and high frequency mono-victims are notably higher than non-victims. However, even mono-victims who experienced a high frequency of violence do not score nearly as high as the poly-victims, who are highest in symptomatology. This is true for all of our major victimization domains, including exposure to domestic violence, maltreatment, sexual victimization, and peer victimization. It is also interesting to note the low and high frequency victims score fairly similarly on symptomatology for each of these domains.

Another way we have explored the intersections between severity and frequency is by trying a number of combinations of weights and other scoring alternatives, to see if there is any advantage to, for example, weighting sexual victimizations more heavily than verbal aggressions (Finkelhor, Ormrod, Turner, & Hamby, 2005). Surprisingly, this also turns out not to be the case. This result parallels studies of dating violence—frequency is a better measure of the problem than severity (Hamby, Poindexter, & Gray-Little, 1996) and poly-victimization scores—number of different types—have better psychometrics than other measures of frequency or severity (Shorey, Brasfield, Febres, Cornelius, & Stuart, 2012).

Beyond Poly-victimization: Reinventing the Web of Violence

Thinking about violence in the poly-victimization framework has many implications for prevention and intervention. Poly-victimization is not the only type of interconnection that has been studied and, remarkably, even the study of interconnections has become fragmented (Hamby & Grych, 2013). Several disciplines describe similar phenomena that also refer to types of interconnections among forms of violence, but they often do so using terminology that obscures the similarities. For example, in criminology, researchers have been studying "criminal generalists" for decades (e.g., Chamelin, Fox, & Whisenand, 1979). However, this pattern of "poly-perpetration" conceptually overlaps with poly-victimization, and those two concepts could (and should) inform each other. Further, poly-perpetration and poly-victimization have been studied in isolation from re-victimization or perpetrator-victimization patterns such as the intergenerational transmission of violence. Other similarly overlapping concepts exist, such as "trauma-informed care" (e.g., Hodas, 2006), which also reflects interconnections between perpetration and victimization, and "complex trauma" (e.g., Spinazzola et al., 2005), which is similar to the concepts of poly-victimization and re-victimization. This large number of terms impedes scientific progress. Many of these terms do not lend themselves to recognizing similarities in these patterns or the development of an internally consistent terminology. By studying related concepts in isolation from each other, much of psychologists' work has ended up in silos, and as a result, the field as a whole spends too much time reinventing the wheel. Because of these artificial siloes, psychologists do not fully benefit from insights in closely-related fields. One such place this occurs is in the study of mechanisms.

Conceptual Shift #2: Understanding the Mechanisms of Violence and Victimization

There are etiological processes that affect many different forms of violence (Hamby & Grych, 2013). Because of these overlapping causal agents, the insight that interconnections among violence are not simple, unitary links becomes even more important. Arguably, our job as researchers would be far simpler if these relationships were unitary. However, sexual victimization does not simply beget more sexual victimization. The first instance of sexual victimization probably occurred because of vulnerabilities that leave children open to many types of victimizations. Indeed, 50 % of child sexual abuse victims are poly-victims, the most highly victimized segment of the population. Further, prior sexual victimization is not the best predictor of risk of later sexual victimization—poly-victimization is (Finkelhor, Shattuck, Turner, & Hamby, 2014). The total burden of victimization both signals extensive vulnerabilities and also can create additional vulnerabilities, such as dissociative symptoms, that increase the risk for further victimization.

Why One Form of Violence and Not Another?

Psychologists need to better understand these processes. The field has already made significant progress in identifying a large number of causal factors. For example, identified factors at the individual level include affective processes, self-regulation, cognitive processes such as beliefs about aggression and schemas, and personality factors such as impulsivity and narcissism (Sampson & Lauritsen, 1994). At the situational level, factors such as environmental conditions (heat, overcrowding, etc.), substance use, social integration, family context, and behavior of others are important. Although these discoveries are promising in some sense, that same list of etiological factors could potentially describe the risks of almost all forms of victimization and even perpetration. All too often, they have been "discovered" multiple times in multiple sub-disciplines of violence research (Hamby & Grych, 2013).

The interconnection among forms of violence is evidenced by the fact that any list of etiological factors drawn from any sub-discipline of violence research can be applied to almost any other form of violence. To advance the scientific knowledge on the subject, researchers need to identify and understand both the common mechanisms and the unique ones. For example, on some occasions, a perpetrator might hit his dating partner and on other occasions bully a peer in the classroom. Further research is needed to investigate the difference between these two types of perpetration and victimization. Why does it emerge as dating violence in one scenario and as bullying in another? At least part of the answer can be found in situational characteristics. This is one more area that would greatly benefit from interdisciplinary communication. Psychologists tend to focus more on individual characteristics, while criminologists excel at studying situational characteristics. Criminology knows far more about how situational factors can trigger violence than psychology does, despite the fact that these factors almost always work in conjunction and that both fields might benefit from collaboration. Yet, we often do not take advantage of the hard-earned insights that others have already learned. There are relational and other factors that probably influence these patterns too, although we know relatively little about them. For example, a woman who might hit her child may never hit her boss, co-worker, or her own parent. Psychology has largely neglected the study of inhibiting factors in individuals who commit violence in some settings but not others, but this is one avenue that holds promise for understanding variation in the behavior one individual (Finkel, 2007, 2008).

Understanding Direct Versus Indirect Mechanisms

In addition to the proliferation of terms for the web of violence, other terminology problems also hold us back. When talking about mechanisms, researchers often reference "direct" and "indirect" mechanisms. Unfortunately, these terms have different meanings depending on whether the context is theory or statistics and this has created considerable confusion. Oftentimes, testing a "direct" statistical relationship does not mean that a direct, bivariate relationship exists in the real world. What is the difference? There are some real-world causal relationships that are best described as direct. For example, imagine a person is incapacitated in a fight, and the perpetrator leaves the scene with the unconscious victim still on the ground. Then, a second perpetrator spots an easy target and steals the wallet of the victim. In this direct relationship, the actions of the first perpetrator rendered the victim defenseless in a scenario where he might otherwise have been able to keep his wallet (had he been conscious). For a non-violent example of a direct relationship, consider substance abuse. Being intoxicated is another immediate situational characteristic that creates a direct vulnerability or risk for perpetration in the moment.

Some longer term factors can also have direct relationships, speaking conceptually. For example, persistent poverty can create long-term direct vulnerabilities, such as living in unsafe neighborhoods.

However, many factors studied by psychologists represent theoretically indirect relationships, regardless of how they are tested statistically. Psychologists are typically trying to understand how people's experiences, often events that happened years or even decades ago, affect and change their lives (e.g., Felitti et al., 1998). How can long ago events increase the long-term risk for becoming a victim or a perpetrator? It is because these events change people, and people carry traces of their experiences with them into later relationships long after the situation changes. Victims are still affected, sometimes very deeply, by their experiences long after they have moved to a new house in a new city and the perpetrator is no longer anywhere nearby. Some of these changes are direct consequences of the victimization, such as persistently heightened anxiety, dissociative symptoms, poor emotional regulation, or other mental health symptoms that might put someone at risk (Jouriles, Simpson Rowe, McDonald, & Kleinsasser, 2014; Noll & Grych, 2011). Unfortunately (and so unjustly), such changes can make people look like "easy marks" to future would-be perpetrators. Other effects can create cascading chains of risk—for example, victimization can interfere with the ability to work (Browne, Saloman, & Bassuk, 1999) and that can lower socioeconomic status, which increases vulnerability to other crimes.

When studying risk and protective factors, it is important not to confuse direct and indirect mechanisms. However, this is not uncommon in the language of some empirical articles. For example, when testing a mediational model between a victimization and a long-term consequence, if the mediator is not statistically significant, it is often said that the relationship between the original variables is "direct." However, this is theoretically incorrect unless the factors are the sort of immediate situational characteristics that do produce direct vulnerabilities. A more accurate way to present the findings would be to say that the study failed to identify the mediator of the victimization-consequence relationship, or perhaps even that the tested mediator is ruled out. This is very different from saying that there is no mediating mechanism. The relationship between past victimization and later functioning is always indirect, because it is always about some consequence that the victim is carrying into later interactions. It is important to note that this does not make the victim responsible—this cascade of negative consequences is the perpetrator's fault (Hamby & Grych, 2013). However, we must understand how these consequences operate if we are to successfully interrupt these trajectories and reduce the risk of re-victimization and poly-victimization.

This is one conceptual problem with existing research on risk and protective factors. In the next section we take up further limitations of current knowledge and propose a new conceptual framework, Resilience Portfolios, to address these limitations.

Conceptual Shift #3: From A Fragmentary Mélange of Risk & Protective Factors to Resilience Portfolios

In the foregoing we have shown how disciplinary siloes have impeded the scientific study of patterns of victimization and perpetration and the mechanisms responsible for both. The lack of appreciation for poly-victimization and other interconnections from the web of violence has limited our ability to recognize the many shared mechanisms that exist across forms of violence. A regrettable focus on isomorphism when interconnections are studied has likewise hampered progress. Further, there is confusion in the study of mechanisms and an inattention to the conceptual elements of direct and indirect relationships. In this section of the chapter, we add to the analysis of conceptual limitations that are holding the field back and present a new strengths-based model, the Resilience Portfolio Model.

Key Limitations of Existing Research on Resilience

Too much focus on risk and harm. Another problem in the existing literature is too much emphasis on problems and deficits rather than strengths. This deficit orientation, however, does not reflect the way people think about their own lives. The vast majority of people want to thrive; they do not simply hope to be "not dysfunctional." In the clinical arena, Ticho (1972) nicely captured this concept in his distinction between "treatment goals" and "life goals." However, this insight has remained at the periphery of most work. Surprisingly, even when studying resilience, researchers often do not move beyond deficit-focused conceptualizations (Grych et al., 2015). In much of the protective factors literature, scholars have simply studied the reverse of well-known risk factors. Indeed, one review found this accounted for fully 75 % of publications using a protective factors framework (Houston & Grych, 2015).

For example, instead of measuring school drop-out rates, a study on protective factors might measure school retention. Other well-established risk factors include *poor* self-regulation (at the individual level), *inconsistent* parenting (at the family level), and *unsafe* neighborhoods (at the community level). The complementary protective factors include *good* self-regulation, consistent parenting, *higher* socioeconomic status and *safe* neighborhoods. Although it might be preferable to discuss these concepts in positive terms, doing so does not actually add anything scientific to the conversation. Simply reversing the scoring on indicators of risk does not add new scientific information, because mathematically those are the same findings (Grych et al., 2014). The solution to this problem is to identify truly new factors that really are strengths that people have and not just the absence of problems.

Too much focus on relatively static characteristics as risk factors. Much of the risk factors literature also focuses on relatively static characteristics such as age, gender, race, and socioeconomic status. These are important contextual factors and research is needed on *why* these sociodemographic markers affect vulnerability to victimization, risk for perpetration, and differences in outcomes (Hamby, 2015).

However, it is not always widely recognized that these are not mechanisms themselves; they are markers for other processes, such as differences in roles, differences in access to services, differences in the experience of discrimination and other elements that explain the variations in these groups. A more developmentally attuned approach is needed too; one that does not simply include age but explores developmental trajectories. Further, not only are these factors not mechanisms themselves, also they are not ready targets for intervention or prevention. They range from difficult to change (socioeconomic status) to impossible to change (age). In this regard, it is even somewhat regrettable how many scholarly resources have been devoted to simply identifying group differences. The solution to this problem is to shift focus to more malleable factors.

A piecemeal approach. There are a very large number of risk or protective factors that might be studied. Indeed, one criticism that we have heard of the discipline of positive psychology is that it is the study of "all the adjectives in the dictionary." To date, even those papers that have adopted a clearer focus on true, malleable protective factors have tended to pick and choose which factors to study in a rather unsystematic fashion (Sabina & Banyard, 2015). Although there are many, many individual, family, and community strengths, it is not likely that all of them are equally relevant for understanding and facilitating resilience. We need to move beyond simply exploring whether a factor has a non-zero relationship with an outcome or whether a program is better than no treatment at all. Instead, we should be engaging in head-to-head comparisons of both mechanisms and programs to see which are the most promising. Time and other resource limitations will always mean that tough choices have to be made and these should be more scientifically informed.

Challenges in Shifting to a Strengths-Based Framework

We recognize that there are challenges in overcoming these limitations and share an example from NatSCEV to illustrate some of these challenges. One important effort to develop a resilience and thriving framework for children is the Centers for Disease Control and Prevention (CDC) concept of "essentials for childhood." They identified safe, stable and nurturing relationships as key elements necessary for healthy children (CDC, 2013). Operationalizing these concepts, however, has proven complex for several reasons, several of which would pertain to any effort to shift to a more strengths-based approach. One issue is that each protective construct has a number of potential indicators. Another issue is that switching from a risk factor to a protective factor framework can be more difficult than it might at first seem. A higher order construct such as "safety" will have many dimensions, some of which might be best conceptualized as protective or desirable factors and others which are more readily conceptualized as risk or negative factors. For example, monitoring and supervision are desirable, protective aspects of safety that are readily conceptualized as actions that parents do. Conceptualizing these as protective factors makes sense because the risk "side" of the construct is the absence of behaviors (lack of monitoring). Higher scores = more supervision = protective factor. On the other hand, corporal punishment can also be considered an element of safety and is also clearly comprised of parental behaviors, but in this case the parental actions add to risk, not protection. Although not impossible, it is not conceptually elegant to think of high scores as representing the "lack of corporal punishment." To craft a single indicator of safety, some compromises must be made.

NatSCEV operationalized each of these constructs (safety, stability, nurture) (Turner et al., 2012). As expected, we found a linear relationship between the number of different protective factors and trauma symptoms. However, disentangling the effects proved to be complex. The strongest unique association was with inconsistent and hostile parenting. For an example of inconsistent parenting, consider a moody parent who is too tired to punish the child one day, but then inflicts a severe punishment for the same offense on a different day. Other strong associations were found for parental psychiatric diagnoses and parental substance abuse. Initially, it seemed that these factors might make parents less available for nurturing, but results showed that they actually affected all three domains. Not only did these problems make parents less nurturing, these factors also incapacitated parents' ability to promote safety and stability as well. Despite significant efforts to develop positively framed indicators of safety, stability, and nurture, problem behaviors such as parental substance abuse showed the strongest associations with trauma and victimization. By and large, it was not possible to statistically demonstrate that parents who excelled in the three domains produced children with significantly fewer trauma symptoms than parents who provided merely adequate care (Turner et al., 2012). In the end, the results seemed to lend credence to Winnicott's idea of a "good enough" parent (Winnicott, 1960). The results were frustrating in terms of an effort to shift towards a more positive approach to understanding parent-child relationships, but offered several lessons for future research, including the need to experiment with different constructs and different operationalizations, because the protective factor literature is not as well-developed as the risk factor literature.

Resilience Portfolios: Advancing Our Understanding of Resilience

Despite the aforementioned limitations and challenges, the potential to advance research and programming through a stronger focus on protective factors exists and several of the solutions to some challenges can be readily implemented. Resilience Portfolios provide a path to strengthening the science and practice of resilience (Grych et al., 2015). Resilience Portfolios both expand and organize an approach that emphasizes protective factors over risk factors and thriving over the avoidance of clinically significant distress.

From re-packaged risk factors to true protective factors. To move beyond simply re-framing well-studied risk factors, Resilience Portfolios make use of the positive psychology literature. Although that literature has limitations as well, such as an excessive reliance on main effects (McNulty & Fincham, 2012), the positive psychology literature has introduced a new realm of strengths that are not simply the inverse of risk factors. For example, forgiveness is an important strength in that literature (e.g., Gordon, Hughes, Tomcik, Dixon, & Litzinger, 2009) and there exists no large literature on vengefulness in the study of children's and families' responses to adversity. Gratitude is another major protective factor in that sub-discipline (Layous, Chancellor, Lyubomirsky, Wang, & Doraiswamy, 2011), and we do not have dozens of studies on ingratitude.

From static to malleable. Another advantage of many of the protective factors that are emphasized in the positive psychology literature is that virtually all of them are malleable. There may yet be unrecognized challenges in making long-term shifts in characteristics such as forgiveness or gratitude (some of the programs developed to target these attributes are fairly simple and short term and may not produce long-term change) (Bolier et al., 2013). Nonetheless, they are at least more malleable than age or gender. They are potential targets for prevention and intervention programs and hence potentially more productive targets for research as well.

From demographic differences to ecological niches. Although simply examining group differences based on demographic characteristics is limited, we are not suggesting that demographic characteristics are unimportant. Rather, the recognition that they are not mechanisms and not likely programming targets calls for a shift in conceptualization. Fortunately, such a framework already exists, social ecology (Bronfenbrenner). However, although social ecology is an increasingly popular framework, the full implications of adopting an ecological approach are not always well understood.

From an ecological point of view, it would be more helpful to study the ways these variables might intersect with prevention or intervention efforts (Sabina & Banyard, 2015). In some cases, that would mean a shift to conceiving of demographic factors as potential moderators, in terms of a research and statistical framework. For example, would some programs work better for girls than boys? Is there a developmental stage that is ideal for some prevention messages? In others, attention to these aspects of social identity could be built directly into programs. For example, are there culturally specific strengths that could be incorporated into programs so that they would be more effective in diverse settings? Finally, this framework also calls for more explicit study of the mechanisms that are related to these social identities, such as social roles, the burden of discrimination, and other factors that might explain any observed group differences (Hamby, 2015).

The Elements of Resilience Portfolios

Resilience Portfolios focus on three core domains of individual strengths: regulatory, meaning making, and interpersonal. These three domains were identified through a review of the literature and especially the existing (limited) literature that has examined multiple strengths and thus identifies not only ones that might have a non-zero relationship with resilience but might be especially good predictors of it (Grych et al., 2015). Regulatory strengths are the ability to control impulses, manage difficult emotions, and persevere in the face of setbacks and are some of the individual strengths that have long been singled out as particularly important (Fosco & Grych, 2013; Gottfredson & Hirschi, 1990). Meaning making is another heavily siloed area in psychological research, too often relegated only to the specific topic area of the psychology of religion. However, meaning making, including religious and spiritual meaning making, is a key way that many, many people cope with family violence and other victimization (Hamby, 2014). Interpersonal strengths, the third domain, bring in the outer layers of the social ecology and show how both the presence of good relationships and the ability to initiate and maintain strong relationships among families, friends, and communities supports resilience and thriving. Furthermore, we believe these fit into a broader system of personal, family, and community resources that improve well-being (beyond just a lack of symptoms).

The largest psychological study, to our knowledge, ever conducted in rural Appalachia addressed many of these research goals. The survey included a wider range of positive strengths—more than 20—than are commonly studied in victimization research. Most of them have a significant, positive outcome with measures of well-being, but some were more strongly associated than others with thriving after adversity (Grych et al., 2015; Hamby, 2015). It also has various other unique features worth mentioning. The community sample includes both adolescents and adults. There is often an artificial break where researchers focusing on children study participants up until age 17, and researchers studying adults start sampling at age 18. This set up, however, does not accurately represent adolescence. There is no magical transformation that happens on an eighteenth birthday. Because of this artificial and arbitrary distinction between adolescence and adulthood, scientists know very little about the transition between the two. A few longitudinal studies exist, but the field in general does not sufficiently track how these cohorts change across late adolescence and early adulthood. This allowed us to explore age as a moderator in greater detail than prior studies.

Preliminary Findings on Resilience Portfolios

In our analyses, we were looking at predictors of several indicators that promoted well-being even after accounting for poly-victimization and other adversities. The set of predictors were remarkably successful at explaining current levels of well-being. For psychological forms of well-being (subjective well-being, spiritual well-being, posttraumatic growth, mental health), we explained 42–58 % of the variance in scores with a combination of strengths, poly-victimization, and other adversities (improving notably over the earlier effort in NatSCEV to operationalize the CDC's Essentials for Childhood) (Hamby, Banyard, & Grych, 2015). Even for physical health in this relatively young sample, these factors explained 24 % of the variability in physical health reports (Banyard, Hamby, & Grych, 2015). Our analyses of these data have identified key constructs in each of the Resilience Portfolio domains. In Regulatory Strengths, some key constructs appear to be: emotional awareness, emotional regulation, and endurance. In Meaning Making, key strengths were optimism, purpose, and religious meaning making. In interpersonal strengths, some key strengths were compassion, generativity, and community support.

Conclusion

Three conceptual shifts hold promise for advancing our abilities to understand and promote resilience after family violence. The first of these is the furthest along—the field increasingly recognizes the web of violence and the importance for understanding poly-victimization to truly understand the burden of violence among children and families. A child-centered and family-centered approach—versus a discipline-centered or institution-centered approach—is needed. The second shift requires extending this understanding to the causes and consequences of violence and realizing that they, too, are largely overlapping processes affecting many forms of violence. The final shift involves a further step in adopting a family-centered approach and realizing that past efforts have been too focused on pathology and sociodemographic markers of vulnerability. What is needed is a more positive and integrated approach that identifies the best and most malleable targets for intervention. Resilience Portfolios offer promise for integrating multiple lines of research and taking the field to the next level of understanding and ability to impact resilience. Instead of having individual programs that focus on a specific problem, the field of psychology and the communities in which it works would benefit from a more developmentally-informed and coordinated offering of prevention curricula.

References

Banyard, V., Hamby, S., & Grych, J. (2015). *Health effects of adverse childhood events: Identifying promising protective factors at the intersection of mental and physical well-being*. Sewanee, TN: Life Paths Appalachian Research Center.

Bolier, L., Haverman, M., Westerhof, G. J., Riper, H., Smit, F., & Bohlmeijer, E. (2013). Positive psychology interventions: A meta-analysis of randomized controlled studies. *BMC Public Health, 13*(1), 119.

Briere, J. (1996). *Trauma symptom checklist for children* (pp. 00253–00258). Odessa, FL: Psychological Assessment Resources.

Browne, A., Saloman, A., & Bassuk, S. S. (1999). The impact of recent partner violence on poor women's capacity to maintain work. *Violence Against Women, 5*(4), 393–426.

CDC. (2013). *Essentials for childhood: Steps to create safe, stable, and nurturing relationships and environments for all children.*

Chamelin, N. C., Fox, V. B., & Whisenand, P. M. (1979). *Introduction to criminal justice*. Upper Saddle River, NJ: Prentice-Hall.

Dong, M., Dube, S. R., Felitti, V. J., & Giles, W. H. (2003). Adverse childhood experiences and self-reported liver disease—New insights into the causal pathway. *Archives of Internal Medicine, 163*, 1949–1956.

Dube, S. R., Anda, R. F., Felitti, V. J., Croft, J. B., Edwards, V. J., & Giles, W. H. (2001). Child abuse tends to be highly interrelated with other adverse childhood experiences. *Child Abuse & Neglect, 25*, 1627–1640.

Dubowitz, H., Papas, M. S., Black, M. M., & Starr, R. H. (2002). Child neglect: Outcomes in high-risk urban preschoolers. *Pediatrics, 109*, 1100–1107.

Felitti, V. J., Anda, R. F., Nordenberg, D., Williamson, D. F., Spitz, A. M., Edwards, V., et al. (1998). Relationship of childhood abuse and household dysfunction to many of the leading causes of death in adults: The Adverse Childhood Experiences (ACE) study. *American Journal of Preventative Medicine, 14*(4), 245–258.

Finkel, E. (2007). Impelling and inhibiting forces in the perpetration of intimate partner violence. *Review of General Psychology, 11*, 193–207.

Finkel, E. (2008). Intimate partner violence perpetration: Insights from the science of self-regulation. In J. Forgas & J. Fitness (Eds.), *Social relationships: Cognitive, affective, and motivational processes*. New York: Psychology Press.

Finkelhor, D., Ormrod, R., & Turner, H. (2007). Poly-victimization: A neglected component in child victimization. *Child Abuse and Neglect, 31*, 7–26.

Finkelhor, D., Ormrod, R., Turner, H., & Hamby, S. (2005). Measuring poly-victimization using the Juvenile Victimization Questionnaire. *Child Abuse & Neglect, 29*(11), 1297–1312.

Finkelhor, D., Shattuck, A., Turner, H., & Hamby, S. (2014). La polyvictimisation comme facteur de risque de revictimisation sexuelle [Poly-victimization as risk factor for sexual revictimization]. *Criminologie, 47*(1), 41–58.

Finkelhor, D., Turner, H., Ormrod, R., & Hamby, S. (2009). Violence, abuse, and crime exposure in a national sample of children and youth. *Pediatrics, 124*(5), 1411–1423.

Fosco, G. M., & Grych, J. H. (2013). Capturing the family context of emotion regulation a family systems model comparison approach. *Journal of Family Issues, 34*(4), 557–578.

Gordon, K. C., Hughes, F. M., Tomcik, N. D., Dixon, L. J., & Litzinger, S. C. (2009). Widening spheres of impact: The role of forgiveness in marital and family functioning. *Journal of Family Psychology, 23*(1), 1.

Gottfredson, M. R., & Hirschi, T. (1990). *A general theory of crime*. Palo Alto, CA: Stanford University Press.

Grych, J., Hamby, S., & Banyard, V. (2015). The Resilience Portfolio Model: Understanding healthy adaptation in victims of violence. *Psychology of Violence, 5*(4), 343–354.

Hamby, S. (2014). *Battered women's protective strategies: stronger than you know*. New York: Oxford University Press.

Hamby, S., Grych, J., & Banyard, V. (2015). *What's in your resilience portfolio? Identifying character strengths associated with thriving after adversity*. Sewanee, TN: Life Paths Appalachian Research Center.

Hamby, S. (2015). On the use of race & ethnicity as variables in violence research. *Psychology of Violence, 5*(1), 1–7. doi:10.1037/a0038470.

Hamby, S., & Grych, J. (2013). *The web of violence: Exploring connections among different forms of interpersonal violence and abuse*. New York: Springer.

Hamby, S., Finkelhor, D., & Turner, H. (2012). Teen dating violence: Co-occurence with other victimizations in the National Survey of Children's Exposure to Violence (NatSCEV). *Psychology of Violence, 2*(2), 111–124.

Hamby, S., Finkelhor, D., Turner, H., & Ormrod, R. (2010). The overlap of witnessing partner violence with child maltreatment and other victimizations in a nationally representative survey of youth. *Child Abuse and Neglect, 34*(10), 734–741.

Hamby, S., Finkelhor, D., Turner, H., & Ormrod, R. (2011). *Children's exposure to intimate partner violence and other family violence*. US Department of Justice, Office of Justice Programs, Office of Juvenile Justice and Delinquency Prevention.

Hamby, S., Poindexter, V., & Gray-Little, B. (1996). Four measures of partner violence: Construct similarity and classification differences. *Journal of Marriage and the Family, 58*, 127–139.

Hilton, Z. N., Harris, G. T., & Rice, M. E. (2015). The step-father effect in child abuse: Comparing discriminative parental solicitude and antisociality. *Psychology of Violence, 5*(1), 8–15.

Hodas, G. R. (2006). Responding to childhood trauma: The promise and practice of trauma informed care. *Pennsylvania Office of Mental Health and Substance Abuse Services, 1*–77.

Holt, S., Buckley, H., & Whelan, S. (2008). The impact of exposure to domestic violence on children and young people: A review of the literature. *Child Abuse & Neglect, 32*(8), 797–810.

Houston, J., & Grych, J. (2015). *Resilience in youth exposed to violence: Protective factors and underlying mechanisms*. Milwaukee, WI: Marquette University.

Jouriles, E. N., Simpson Rowe, L., McDonald, R., & Kleinsasser, A. (2014). Women's expression of anger in response to unwanted sexual advances: Associations with sexual victimization. *Psychology of Violence, 4*(2), 170–183.

Kempe, C., Silverman, F. N., Steele, B. F., Droegemueller, W., & Silver, H. K. (1962). The battered-child syndrome. *JAMA, 181*(1), 17–24. doi:10.1001/jama.1962.03050270019004.

Kinsey, A. C., Pomeroy, W. B., & Martin, C. E. (1948). *Sexual behavior in the human male*. Bloomington, IN: Indiana University Press.

Layous, K., Chancellor, J., Lyubomirsky, S., Wang, L., & Doraiswamy, P. M. (2011). Delivering happiness: Translating positive psychology intervention research for treating major and minor depressive disorders. *Journal of Alternative and Complementary Medicine, 17*(8), 675–683.

Manning, W. D. (2004). Children and the stability of cohabitating couples. *Journal of Marriage and Family, 66*(3), 674–689.

McNulty, J. K., & Fincham, F. D. (2012). Beyond positive psychology? Toward a contextual view of psychological processes and well-being. *American Psychologist, 67*(2), 101–110.

Noll, J. G., & Grych, J. (2011). Read-react-respond: An integrative model for understanding sexual revictimization. *Psychology of Violence, 1*(3), 202–215.

Sabina, C., & Banyard, V. (2015). Moving towards well-being: The role of protective factors in violence research. *Psychology of Violence, 5*(4), 337–342.

Sampson, R. J., & Lauritsen, J. L. (1994). Violent victimization and offending: Individual-, situational-, and community-level risk factors. *Understanding and preventing violence, vol. 3. Washington, DC: National Research Council*.

Shorey, R. C., Brasfield, H., Febres, J., Cornelius, T. L., & Stuart, G. L. (2012). A comparison of three different scoring methods for self-report measures of psychological aggression in a sample of college females. *Violence and Victims, 27*(6), 973–990.

Spinazzola, J., Ford, J. D., Zucker, M., van der Kolk, B. A., Silva, S., Smith, S. F., & Blaustein, M. (2005). Survey evaluates complex trauma exposure, outcome, and intervention among children and adolescents. *Psychiatric Annals, 35*, 433–439.

Straus, M., Gelles, R., & Steinmetz, S. K. (1980). *Behind closed doors: Violence in the American family*. New York: Doubleday.

Ticho, E. A. (1972). Termination of psychoanalysis: Treatment goals, life goals. *The Psychoanalytic Quarterly, 41*, 315–333.

Turner, H., Finkelhor, D., & Ormrod, R. (2010). Poly-victimization in a national sample of children and youth. *American Journal of Preventative Medicine, 38*(3), 323–330.

Turner, H., Finkelhor, D., Ormrod, R., Hamby, S., Leeb, R., Mercy, J., & Holt, M. (2012). Family context, victimization, and child trauma symptoms: Variations in safe, stable, and nurturing relationships during early and middle childhood. *American Journal of Orthopsychiatry, 82*(2), 209.

Vespa, J., Lewis, J., & Kreider, R. (2013). *America's family and living arrangements: 2012 Current population reports* (pp. 20–570). Washington, DC: U.S. Census Bureau.

Winnicott, D. W. (1960). The theory of the parent-infant relationship. *International Journal of Psychoanalysis, 41*(6), 585–595.

Creating a Safe Haven Following Child Maltreatment: The Benefits and Limits of Social Support

Margaret O'Dougherty Wright and Susan F. Folger

The interpersonal nature of child maltreatment, particularly abuse and neglect originating within the family, presents particular challenges to recovery and the subsequent establishment of healthy, supportive personal relationships (Cicchetti & Toth, 2013). Quality of attachment has long-lasting implications for relational interactions across the life span (Sroufe, 2005), as it impacts internal working models of self, others, and self-in-relation to others (Bowlby, 1988). When a child's attachment to the parent is secure, the child can turn to the parent in times of danger, uncertainty, or distress and find the parent available, responsive, and able to provide comfort in a way that is reassuring and helps the child re-stabilize. Over time, following repeated supportive interactions with one's parent(s), the child learns to internalize adaptive emotion regulation strategies and also develops confidence that others will respond in a helpful way when distress is experienced or the child is unable to cope (Bowlby, 1988; Cloitre, Stovall-McClough, Zorbas, & Charuvastra, 2008). Thus, attachment security is significantly associated with a child's ability to regulate negative mood and the development of interpersonal expectations of support when it is needed.

There is now substantial research evidence that attachment security can be negatively impacted by experiences of child maltreatment and the impact of this can be long lasting (Cicchetti & Toth, 2013). Familial child abuse and neglect have the potential to significantly disrupt the development of secure attachment because in such families the child's source of safety and protection is also a source of danger and distress (Charuvastra & Cloitre, 2008). Following child maltreatment experiences, survivors report struggling with feelings of betrayal, mistrust of others,

M.O. Wright, Ph.D. (✉) • S.F. Folger, M.A.
Department of Psychology, Miami University, 90 North Patterson Ave,
Oxford, OH 45056, USA
e-mail: wrightmo@miamioh.edu; folgersf@miamioh.edu

© Springer International Publishing Switzerland 2017
D.M. Teti (ed.), *Parenting and Family Processes in Child Maltreatment and Intervention*, Child Maltreatment Solutions Network,
DOI 10.1007/978-3-319-40920-7_2

23

intense shame, low self-worth, insecurity in relationships, powerlessness, and a stigmatized identity (Briere, 2002; Courtois, 2010). Safety and trust in interpersonal relationships have often been severely damaged (Herman, 1992) and survivors can have difficulty maintaining close and safe intimate partner relationships later in life (Davis, Petretic-Jackson, & Ting, 2001). Some adults who have been sexually victimized as children report more loneliness, withdrawal, and a tendency to isolate themselves from friends, family, and co-workers (Courtois, 2010). Past research has also revealed a subsequent risk for revictimization (Messman-Moore & Long, 2003; Widom, Czaja, & Dutton, 2008) and/or perpetration of abuse of one's partner or child (Berlin, Appleyard, & Dodge, 2011; Kwong, Bartholomew, Henderson, & Trinke, 2003). All of these painful sequelae can intensify disconnection and/or alienation from others and may be linked to difficulty accessing much needed social support.

Prior research in this area has found that survivors of child maltreatment tend to have smaller social networks, lower levels of social support, and report less satisfaction and more distrust with these networks (Gibson & Harshorne, 1996; Sperry & Widom, 2013). More severe, chronic, and multi-type maltreatment has also been associated with increased psychological and interpersonal difficulties and lower levels of support from one's social network (Finkelhor, Ormrod, & Turner, 2007; Folger & Wright, 2013; Pepin & Banyard, 2006; Salazar, Keller, & Courtney, 2011; Vranceanu, Hobfoll, & Johnson, 2007). Posttraumatic sequelae of abuse, such as PTSD symptoms, depression and anxiety, and anger, hostility, and aggression, can also exhaust supportive friends and family and may be an additional reason why there is an erosion of social support over time and increased isolation (Charuvastra & Cloitre, 2008; Clapp & Beck, 2009; Norris & Kaniasty, 1996).

Social Support as a Promotive and/or Protective Factor

Many individuals are resilient following child maltreatment experiences and some studies have explored positive social relationships and social support as promotive and/or protective factors in overcoming the negative effects of abuse. Access to and perceptions of social support may be important factors contributing to variability in long-term outcome. Social support is theorized to shield child maltreatment survivors from the development of symptoms by attenuating the stress appraisal response (Cohen & Wills, 1985). An individual may evaluate his or her maltreatment experience as less stressful if he or she perceives that others will provide the resources needed to cope. This is why the initial response to a child's disclosure of child sexual abuse is so critical. Being believed by the parent disclosed to, and having confidence that action will be taken to protect the child from further abuse, have been strongly linked to positive outcome (Elliott & Carnes, 2001). Research findings indicate that parent support following disclosure may be a better predictor of the child's later adjustment than abuse-related variables (Tremblay, Hébert, & Piché, 1999).

Social support has been proposed to impact later well-being following abuse in two different ways: (1) as a *promotive* (compensatory) factor that positively impacts outcome regardless of the severity of abuse (typically identified as a statistical main effect); and (2) as a *protective* factor that has a differential impact on outcome depending on the severity of the abuse exposure (identified as a moderator in a statistical interaction effect). To date, past research exploring social support as a protective factor following child maltreatment has yielded mixed and conflicting findings. In part this may be because the process of providing and receiving social support is complex and many factors influence the positivity or negativity of this interpersonal exchange (Clapp & Beck, 2009; Cohen, 2004). Studies vary significantly in the way that they define and assess the beneficial or detrimental impact of social support. For example, supportive people in an individual's life may directly provide actual assistance (received social support is high), but the manner in which this support is provided (e.g. too controlling or intrusive) may not be perceived in a positive way by the individual. Or, an individual may not perceive that he or she has many people to rely on in his or her support network (low perceived network support), and so does not seek out or utilize resources that actually are available. Clearly, perceptions of the type of social support that is available, desired, and received play a crucial role in determining whether social support has a buffering or an aggravating impact. In addition, social interactions and relationships within one's network are not always or consistently supportive, and consequently, some individuals can be both a source of stress or distress, as well as a resource and comfort (Cohen, 2004). This possibility seems particularly likely in the context of child maltreatment, in which the child can be exposed to or experience conflict, abuse, neglect, and/or exploitation from attachment figures, but may also experience loving care, interest, and positive attention.

This chapter reviews recent research that examines when, how, and what types of social support might foster resilience among survivors of child maltreatment. Promotive (main) effects of social support are highlighted, followed by studies that demonstrate a buffering or protective (moderating) role of support. Finally, studies illustrating significant limits to the beneficial effects of social support are reviewed, particularly in the context of more severe child maltreatment experiences.

Benefits of Social Support: Main Effects

The benefits of social support have been documented for a number of outcomes in different samples in which at least a portion of individuals reported experiencing childhood maltreatment. For young adult men and women in college, perceived support from family and from friends predicted lower levels of depression/anxiety and anger/hostility (Folger & Wright, 2013). In Wilson and Scarpa's (2014) sample of college women, greater perceived support from friends and family was associated with fewer posttraumatic stress symptoms, but only for those with physical abuse, not sexual abuse, histories. In a sample of 17–18 year old young adults who recently transitioned out of foster care, Salazar et al. (2011) assessed for types of maltreatment experienced before entering foster care and subsequently assessed maltreatment experienced while in the foster care system, as well as perceived social support (i.e., availability of social support and sufficiency of social network), and depressive symptoms. Results indicated that higher levels of perceived social support predicted fewer depressive symptoms approximately two years later. In a different sample of adults, a small number of whom reported child maltreatment before age 15, a composite variable of family support in adolescence predicted lower risk of being diagnosed with a psychiatric disorder or engaging specifically in antisocial behavior in adulthood (Feldman, Conger, & Burzette, 2004). Finally, mediational analyses in a prospective study by Sperry and Widom (2013) demonstrated the benefits of total and specific kinds of perceived social support on depression and anxiety symptoms in adults who either had a substantiated history of childhood physical abuse, sexual abuse, or neglect or were in a matched control group.

Significant gender effects regarding the impact of social support have sometimes been found. Evans, Steel, and DiLillo (2013) reported that 54 % of a sample of recently married men and women endorsed experiences that met criteria for at least one form of child maltreatment. Perceived friend support predicted less trauma symptomatology for women, whereas both perceived friend and family support predicted less trauma symptomatology for men. In the study by Sperry and Widom (2013), men were found to be more affected by higher levels of social support than women, which was counter to their prediction. Powers, Ressler, and Bradley (2009) found that friend support (i.e. emotional support, advice or guidance, practical assistance, financial assistance, and socializing) predicted fewer depressive symptoms in their highly traumatized sample of adults, in which 15–32 % of individuals reported moderate to severe levels of various forms of childhood maltreatment. When exploring this finding by gender, the main effect of friend support was significant for women but not men.

Some studies have explored the impact of social support in samples comprised of women only. Murthi and Espelage (2005) found that perceived family support was related to lower levels of loss of sense of self in their sample of young women who reported at least one experience of childhood sexual abuse. In another sample of women, of whom 85 % reported at least one instance of child maltreatment, less satisfaction with and perceived availability of social support predicted higher levels of PTSD severity (Vranceanu et al., 2007). Finally, Crouch, Milner, and Caliso (1995) reported that in their sample of young women, half of whom experienced some instance of childhood physical abuse, individuals with high perceived support availability before age 13 had fewer depressive symptoms, lower trait anxiety, and lower physical child abuse potential than those with low support.

Overall, these studies highlight the promotive effect of social support for samples in which at least a portion of individuals experienced childhood maltreatment. As expected, higher levels of social support generally had a beneficial impact on emotional functioning and, occasionally impacted behavioral functioning as well.

Inconsistencies regarding gender effects indicate the complicated nature of these relationships for men and women, as well as the importance of examining different types and sources of social support over time and across various types of outcomes.

Benefits of Social Support: Moderating Effects

The buffering hypothesis purports that support will have a greater positive impact as maltreatment experiences worsen. Some support has been found for this hypothesis regarding social support as a truly protective factor for adolescents and adults who are at risk because of child maltreatment or exposure to violence in their home. For example, in a sample of adolescent boys and girls, Levondosky, Huth-Bocks, and Semel (2002) demonstrated that perceived social support from friends moderated relations between both domestic violence experienced by their mothers and their own childhood abuse with satisfaction in a best friend relationship. While support was generally promotive, these relationships were stronger for the groups who reported higher levels of child abuse or domestic violence. Muller, Goebel-Fabbri, Diamond, and Dinklage (2000) assessed witnessing violence in the family in a sample of adolescents hospitalized in a psychiatric unit. For those with low received social support, high exposure to family violence was related to greater overall psychopathology in comparison to those with low violence exposure. However, there was no difference in outcome between violence exposure groups when social support was high.

Sperry and Widom (2013) found that women with a history of maltreatment reported more symptoms of depression than women in a matched control group when tangible social support was low. However, there was no difference in depressive symptoms between these groups when tangible support was high. Although the nature of the maltreatment variable in this study (i.e., substantiated history of maltreatment versus matched control group) did not allow for exploration of the impact of support at varying levels of maltreatment, the fact that the abuse or neglect was substantiated suggests the maltreatment was likely more severe in nature. Folger and Wright (2013) found that men with higher levels of childhood maltreatment and lower perceived friend support reported more depression/anxiety symptoms than men with higher levels of childhood maltreatment and higher friend support, suggesting a protective impact of friend support for these men. Murthi and Espelage (2005) found that perceived family and friend social support moderated the impact of childhood sexual abuse on loss-related outcomes (e.g., loss of self, loss of childhood) for women. More specifically, those with more severe child sexual abuse experiences reported greater loss of childhood and loss of self when they reported less family support, and also greater loss of self when they reported less friend support.

Similar findings have been documented for other individuals with adult abuse-related experiences, but who have not experienced childhood maltreatment specifically. For example, Babcock, Roseman, Green, and Ross (2008) demonstrated support for the buffering hypothesis in a sample of women in physically or emotionally abusive romantic relationships. Perceived social support moderated the impact of psychological abuse on PTSD symptomatology. A significant positive correlation was obtained between psychological abuse and PTSD symptoms for those in the low support group and no association was found in the high support group. Overall, these studies provided some support for the buffering hypothesis that social support would be especially protective for those with more extensive histories of childhood maltreatment or exposure to violence in their home environment.

Limits of Social Support: Failure to Find Protective Effects at More Severe Levels of Maltreatment

Other research findings have not supported the buffering hypothesis. Rather, social support has demonstrated a positive impact in situations in which maltreatment experiences were less severe or frequent, or in which the individual experienced fewer types of maltreatment or maltreatment that was limited to a particular type. For example, Salazar et al. (2011) found significant interactions between maltreatment before foster care and social support, and between maltreatment during foster care and social support for youth exiting the foster care system. Having moderate to higher levels of social support was protective for those with fewer types of maltreatment experiences before and during foster care. Interestingly, for those who experienced more types of maltreatment during foster care, having moderate to higher levels of support was related to more depressive symptoms in comparison to those with low support. Wilson and Scarpa (2014) explored the impact of type of abuse on efficacy of social support for college women and found that family and friend support was protective against the development of posttraumatic stress symptoms for those who experienced physical abuse, but not for those who experienced sexual abuse. In addition, perceived support from a romantic partner was associated with increased posttraumatic stress symptoms for women with sexual abuse histories, suggesting that such support heightened rather than reduced risk.

Studies by Evans et al. (2013) and Folger and Wright (2013) explored the impact of perceived support from family and friends following childhood maltreatment for men and women. Evans et al. (2013) found that for women, family social support moderated the impact of physical abuse, emotional abuse, and emotional neglect on trauma symptomatology. For women with abuse experiences that were low to moderate in severity, greater social support was related to fewer symptoms. However, this effect lessened for those with more severe abuse histories. Folger and Wright (2013) found that family support moderated the impact of cumulative childhood maltreatment on dating abuse, aggressive behavior, and anger/hostility, such that for those with lower levels of maltreatment, higher support was related to better outcomes. Friend support was beneficial for women with lower levels of maltreatment, as those with higher support reported less aggressive behavior than those with low support. Similar to findings by Salazar et al. (2011), there were complicated effects of family support on dating abuse victimization for women. For women who reported fewer maltreatment experiences, higher levels of family support related to less dating abuse victimization, but for those with higher levels of child maltreatment, higher family support related to more dating abuse victimization (Folger & Wright, 2013).

Levondosky et al. (2002) demonstrated that perceived social support from friends moderated the relation between childhood abuse and satisfaction in a romantic relationship for adolescents. Support was positively associated with satisfaction for those with lower and higher levels of childhood maltreatment, but this relationship was stronger for those in the low maltreatment group. Friend social support also moderated the relation between mothers' report of domestic violence experiences and negative romantic relationship indicators for adolescents. For adolescents whose mothers reported low levels of domestic violence, higher support was related to less abuse experiences (i.e., perpetration and victimization) and less negative communication with partner. Importantly, higher support was related to more negative communication and abuse experiences (i.e., perpetration and victimization) for adolescents whose mothers reported high levels of domestic violence (Levondosky et al., 2002).

Appleyard, Yang, and Runyan (2010) explored concurrent and longitudinal mediated and mediated moderation pathways among early reports (i.e., before age 6) of child maltreatment, self-perception (i.e., loneliness and self-esteem), and social support and internalizing and externalizing problems. For both boys and girls, early allegations of child abuse or neglect made to Child Protective Services were related to later internalizing and externalizing problems indirectly through loneliness reported at age 6. For boys, low self-esteem at age 6 was also a mediator. However, contrary to expectation, more allegations of maltreatment, combined with high perceived social support, was associated with more negative self-esteem for boys and this was associated with more negative emotional and behavioral outcomes. While unexpected, these findings were consistent with some of the previously described findings indicating that social support does not always buffer against deleterious outcomes at high levels of child maltreatment. In the Appleyard et al. (2010) study, the child identified and reported on his or her three primary support people, which was likely comprised of parents and other family members. In the context of a maltreating family, these support figures may also have been the perpetrators of the abuse or neglect, which highlights the complexity of assessing perceptions of support in this context.

In a study focused on the role of social support in moderating parenting outcomes for child sexual abuse survivors, Seltmann and Wright (2013) explored whether mothers' depressive symptomatology mediated the relation between severity of childhood sexual abuse experiences and various parenting outcomes and if support from the women's partners moderated this hypothesized mediating relationship. Results of interest include that for women who reported low levels of depression, support from their partner was protective against particular parenting difficulties. Contrary to expectation, however, partner support was not found to be protective at high levels of depressive symptomatology. At high levels of partner support, women with high levels of depressive symptoms reported more problems communicating with and being involved with their children than survivors with low partner support. Survivors with high depressive symptomatology may rely on their partners to take over some of their parental duties, so that their partners spend more time with their children. While possibly helpful for the children and alleviating some stress for the survivor, it does not strengthen the survivor's parenting skills. It is also possible that while the partner is supportive in parenting the child, the interactions between the survivor and her partner may in fact be critical or con-flicted, and a source of stress for both members of the couple.

Similar findings have been documented for individuals with violent or abuse-related experiences, who have not experienced childhood maltreatment specifically. For example, Ceballo and McLoyd (2002) found that the beneficial impact of emotional and instrumental support on parenting behavior lessened as quality of neighborhood deteriorated. Carlson, McNutt, Choi, and Rose (2002) created a lifetime abuse variable based on recent intimate partner violence, past partner vio-lence, and childhood abuse in a sample of women, and measured a number of hypothesized protective factors, including partner support and non-partner support. Moderation analyses indicated that as the number of abuse experiences increased, the benefit of having multiple protective factors, with respect to anxiety symptoms, lessened. Similarly, Beeble, Bybee, Sullivan, and Adams (2009) found that per-ceived social support had a stronger positive impact on quality of life for women who experienced lower levels of psychological abuse by an intimate partner. Lastly, Scarpa, Haden, and Hurly (2006) found that while controlling for young adults' most traumatic experience, the positive relation between community violence vic-timization and PTSD symptom severity associated with the reference trauma was stronger for those who reported high perceived friend support. This is consistent with the previously described findings by Levondosky et al. (2002), which high-lighted possible risks associated with high levels of friend support in the context of a violent environment.

As these studies demonstrate, research exploring the impact of social support in the context of childhood maltreatment has also failed to support the buffering hypothesis. Instead, support had a positive impact for individuals with less severe or frequent childhood maltreatment, or those with fewer types of maltreatment experi-ences or maltreatment that was limited to a particular type. These findings suggest that, in some cases, its benefits may not sufficiently compensate for the negative sequelae of more extensive childhood maltreatment. Additionally, social support functioned as a vulnerability factor in certain samples in which individuals experi-enced higher levels, more types, or specific types of maltreatment. When support from an abusive or violent network is high, an individual may learn to normalize, internalize, or perhaps tolerate abusive behavior, placing him or her at increased risk for negative outcome.

Clinical Implications

While the construct of "social support" is typically associated with having a positive impact on health and well-being, the reviewed studies revealed that social support was not uniformly positive, and its impact was dependent upon many factors. This select review revealed both promotive (main) and protective (moderating) effects in the context of childhood maltreatment, but also suggested that there were limits to the degree that social support buffered against negative outcomes for individuals who experienced severe and persisting maltreatment. In some contexts and samples, social support was beneficial for individuals who reported more experiences of childhood maltreatment, which supported the buffering hypothesis. However, other results demonstrated that social support primarily had a positive impact for individuals with fewer, or less severe, or a particular type of maltreatment experience. In addition to these conflicting findings, a few studies suggested that the combination of more extensive maltreatment or violence exposure and greater social support was problematic and led to worse outcomes. The precise mechanisms involved are still not well understood, in large part because of the multidimensional nature of the construct which makes accurate measurement challenging (Spilsbury & Korbin, 2013).

It is important to note that how social support was conceptualized and measured varied considerably across studies. Although it was common to assess perceived support from family and/or friends, some studies did not identify a specific source of support, and others measured specific types (e.g., emotional, instrumental, tangible) or total amount of support received. Few studies exist that compare possible differences in outcome depending on the actual support that is received versus perceptions of the quality of support available. Taken together, substantial study differences in type, severity and duration of maltreatment experiences, variety of outcome measures, multiple types and sources of support, and differing time frames (e.g., support provided last week, last month, last year), made it difficult to identify the specific processes accounting for the contradictory findings. There are also sources of support not discussed in this brief chapter that might have an important impact (e.g., school support; Feldman et al., 2004). Regardless, existing literature demonstrates the importance of exploring social network support more closely in order to understand its differential impact on individuals with histories of childhood maltreatment. High perceived support from a dysfunctional and/or violent network can foster continued vulnerability and the likelihood of this occurring within maltreating families is high.

The findings from the reviewed studies have important implications for promoting resilience following child maltreatment experiences. While many empirically supported treatment protocols emphasize the importance of informal social support in recovery, it is critical for clinicians to assess the extent to which existing social networks have protective capacities or instead function to increase risk and heighten vulnerability (Folger & Wright, 2013; Spilsbury & Korbin, 2013; Wilson & Scarpa, 2014). Detailed inquiry about the availability, accessibility, and nurturing capacity of network members is crucial and caution is needed before advising adult survivors to seek support from family members who may have perpetrated or colluded in the abuse. In addition, careful assessment of the potential risk or protective nature of friendships and romantic relationships is particularly important when working with abuse survivors. While activating informal social support networks may be very helpful for those with less severe maltreatment experiences, this may not be the best course for those with sexual abuse histories or more complex and chronic histories of maltreatment who may need more formal intervention (Salazar et al., 2011; Wilson & Scarpa, 2014). Following a thorough assessment, the clinician can work collaboratively with the client and/or family to either improve existing network support or to develop alternative sources of support that are stable, safe, and nurturing (Center for Disease Control, 2014). If informal social networks are not safe or consistently reliable, or are unpredictable, hostile, or rejecting, formal support can be activated as a means to help families compensate. Specific types of home health visiting programs (e.g., Nurse-Family Partnership), parent education and support groups (e.g., Triple P Positive Parenting Program), and dyadic parent-child interaction therapies (e.g., PCIT, AF-CBT, and Child-Parent Psychotherapy) have documented efficacy in promoting well-being in maltreating families (Kolko, Iselin, & Gully, 2011; Macmillan et al., 2009). Variability in outcome following child maltreatment may well be accounted for in part by the extent to which corrective relationship experiences subsequently occur. Continued study of how best to promote socially supportive networks both within and outside of the home and family may be critical in facilitating recovery.

References

Appleyard, K., Yang, C., & Runyan, D. K. (2010). Delineating the maladaptive pathways of child maltreatment: A mediated moderation analysis of the roles of self-perception and social support. *Development and Psychopathology, 22*, 337–352. doi:10.1017/S095457941000009X.

Babcock, J. C., Roseman, A., Green, C. E., & Ross, J. M. (2008). Intimate partner abuse and PTSD symptomatology: Examining mediators and moderators of the abuse-trauma link. *Journal of Family Psychology, 22*, 809–818. doi:10.1037/a0013808.

Beeble, M. L., Bybee, D., Sullivan, C. M., & Adams, A. E. (2009). Main, mediating, and moderating effects of social support on the well-being of survivors of intimate partner violence across 2 years. *Journal of Consulting and Clinical Psychology, 77*, 718–729. doi:10.1037/a0016140.

Berlin, L. J., Appleyard, K., & Dodge, K. A. (2011). Intergenerational continuity in child maltreatment: Mediating mechanisms and implications for prevention. *Child Development, 82*, 162–176. doi:10.1111/j.1467-8624.2010.01547.x.

Bowlby, J. (1988). *A secure base: Parent-child attachment and healthy human development.* New York: Basic Books.

Briere, J. (2002). Treating adult survivors of severe childhood abuse and neglect: Further development of an integrative model. In J. E. Myers, L. Berliner, J. Briere, C. T. Hendrix, C. Jenny, & T. A. Reid (Eds.), *The APSAC handbook on child maltreatment* (2nd ed., pp. 175–204). Thousand Oaks, CA: Sage.

Carlson, B. E., McNutt, L., Choi, D. Y., & Rose, I. M. (2002). Intimate partner abuse and mental health: The role of social support and other protective factors. *Violence Against Women, 8*, 720–745. doi:10.1177/10778010222183251.

Ceballo, R., & McLoyd, V. C. (2002). Social support and parenting in poor, dangerous neighborhoods. *Child Development, 73*, 1310–1321. doi:10.1111/1467-8624.00473.

Center for Disease Control. (2014). *Promoting safe, stable and nurturing relationships: A strategic direction for child maltreatment prevention.* Retrieved from http://www.cdc.gov/violenceprevention/pdf/cm_strategic_direction--long-a.pdf

Charuvastra, A., & Cloitre, M. (2008). Social bonds and posttraumatic stress disorder. *Annual Review of Psychology, 59*, 301–328. doi:10.1146/annurev.psych.58.110405.085650.

Cicchetti, D., & Toth, S. L. (2013). Child maltreatment and attachment organization: Implications for intervention. In S. Goldberg, R. Muir, & J. Kerr (Eds.), *Attachment theory: Social, developmental, and clinical perspectives* (pp. 279–308). London: Routledge.

Clapp, J. D., & Beck, J. G. (2009). Understanding the relationship between PTSD and social support: The role of negative network orientation. *Behaviour Research and Therapy, 47*, 237–244. doi:10.1016/j.brat.2008.12.006.

Cloitre, M., Stovall-McClough, C., Zorbas, P., & Charuvastra, A. (2008). Attachment organization, emotion regulation, and expectations of support in a clinical sample of women with childhood abuse histories. *Journal of Traumatic Stress, 21*, 282–289. doi:10.1002/jts.20339.

Cohen, S. (2004). Social relationships and health. *American Psychologist, 59*, 676–684. doi:10.1037/0003-066X.59.8.676.

Cohen, S., & Wills, T. A. (1985). Stress, social support, and the buffering hypothesis. *Psychological Bulletin, 98*, 310–357. doi:10.1037//0033-2909.98.2.310.

Courtois, C. A. (2010). *Healing the incest wound: Adult survivors in therapy* (2nd ed.). New York: W. W. Norton & Company.

Crouch, J. L., Milner, J. S., & Caliso, J. A. (1995). Childhood physical abuse, perceived social support, and socioemotional status in adult women. *Violence and Victims, 10*, 273–283 Retrieved from http://www.ingentaconnect.com/content/springer/vav.

Davis, J. L., Petretic-Jackson, P. A., & Ting, L. (2001). Intimacy dysfunction and trauma symptomatology: Long-term correlates of different types of child abuse. *Journal of Traumatic Stress, 14*, 63–79. doi:10.1023/A:1007835531614.

Elliott, A. N., & Carnes, C. N. (2001). Reactions of nonoffending parents to the sexual abuse of their child: A review of the literature. *Child Maltreatment, 6*, 314–331. doi:10.1177/1077559501006004005.

Evans, S. E., Steel, A. L., & DiLillo, D. (2013). Child maltreatment severity and adult trauma symptoms: Does perceived social support play a buffering role? *Child Abuse & Neglect, 37*, 934–943. doi:10.1016/j.chiabu.2013.03.005.

Feldman, B. J., Conger, R. D., & Burzette, R. G. (2004). Traumatic events, psychiatric disorders, and pathways of risk and resilience during the transition to adulthood. *Research in Human Development, 1*, 259–290. doi:10.1207/s15427617rhd0104_3.

Finkelhor, D., Ormrod, R. K., & Turner, H. A. (2007). Poly-victimization: A neglected component in child victimization. *Child Abuse & Neglect, 31*, 7–26. doi:10.1016/j.chiabu.2006.06.008.

Folger, S. F., & Wright, M. O. (2013). Altering risk following child maltreatment: Family and friend support as protective factors. *Journal of Family Violence, 28*, 325–337. doi:10.1007/s10896-013-9510-4.

Gibson, R. L., & Harshorne, T. S. (1996). Childhood sexual abuse and adult loneliness and network orientation. *Child Abuse & Neglect, 20*, 1087–1093. doi:10.1016/0145-2134(96)00097-X.

Herman, J. L. (1992). *Trauma and recovery*. New York: Harper Collins.

Kolko, D. J., Iselin, A. R., & Gully, K. J. (2011). Evaluation of the sustainability and clinical outcome of Alternatives for Families: A Cognitive-Behavioral Therapy (AF-CBT) in a child protection center. *Child Abuse & Neglect, 35*, 105–116. doi:10.1016/j.chiabu.2010.09.004.

Kwong, M. J., Bartholomew, K., Henderson, A. J. Z., & Trinke, S. J. (2003). The intergenerational transmission of relationship violence. *Journal of Family Psychology, 17*, 288–301. doi:10.1037/0893-3200.17.3.288.

Levondosky, A. A., Huth-Bocks, A., & Semel, M. A. (2002). Adolescent peer relationships and mental health functioning in families with domestic violence. *Journal of Clinical Child & Adolescent Psychology, 31*, 206–218. doi:10.1207/s15374424jccp3102_06.

MacMillan, H., Wathen, C. N., Barlow, J., Fergusson, D. M., Leventhal, J. M., & Taussig, H. N. (2009). Interventions to prevent child maltreatment and associated impairment. *Lancet, 373*, 250–266. doi:10.1016/S0140-6736(08)61708-0.

Messman-Moore, T. L., & Long, P. J. (2003). The role of childhood sexual abuse sequelae in the sexual revictimization of women: An empirical review and theoretical reformulation. *Clinical Psychology Review, 23*, 537–571. doi:10.1016/S0272-7358(02)00203-9.

Muller, R. T., Goebel-Fabbri, A. E., Diamond, T., & Dinklage, D. (2000). Social support and the relationship between family and community violence exposure and psychopathology among high risk adolescents. *Child Abuse & Neglect, 24*, 449–464. doi:10.1016/s0145-2134(00)00117-4.

Murthi, M., & Espelage, D. L. (2005). Childhood sexual abuse, social support, and psychological outcomes: A loss framework. *Child Abuse & Neglect, 29*, 1215–1231. doi:10.1016/j.chiabu.2005.03.008.

Norris, F. H., & Kaniasty, K. (1996). Received and perceived social support in times of stress: A test of the social support deterioration deterrence model. *Journal of Personality and Social Psychology, 71*, 498–511. doi:10.1037//0022-3514.71.3.498.

Pepin, E. N., & Banyard, V. L. (2006). Social support: A mediator between child maltreatment and developmental outcomes. *Journal of Youth Adolescence, 35*, 617–630. doi:10.1007/s10964-006-9063-4.

Powers, A., Ressler, K. J., & Bradley, R. G. (2009). The protective role of friendship on the effects of childhood abuse and depression. *Depression and Anxiety, 26*, 46–53. doi:10.1002/da.20534.

Salazar, A. M., Keller, T. E., & Courtney, M. E. (2011). Understanding social support's role in the relationship between maltreatment and depression in youth with foster care experience. *Child Maltreatment, 16*, 102–113. doi:10.1177/1077559511402985.

Scarpa, A., Haden, S. C., & Hurley, J. (2006). Community violence victimization and symptoms of posttraumatic stress disorder: The moderating effects of coping and social support. *Journal of Interpersonal Violence, 21*, 446–469. doi:10.1177/0886260505285726.

Seltmann, L. A., & Wright, M. O. (2013). Perceived parenting competencies following childhood sexual abuse: A moderated mediation analysis. *Journal of Family Violence, 28*, 611–621. doi:10.1007/s10896-013-9522-0.

Sperry, D. M., & Widom, C. S. (2013). Child abuse and neglect, social support, and psychopathology in adulthood: A prospective investigation. *Child Abuse & Neglect, 37*, 415–425. doi:10.1016/j.chiabu.2013.02.006.

Spilsbury, J. C., & Korbin, J. E. (2013). Social networks and informal social support in protecting children from abuse and neglect. *Child Abuse & Neglect, 37S*, 8–16. doi:10.1016/j.chiabu.2013.10.027.

Sroufe, L. A. (2005). Attachment and development: A prospective, longitudinal study from birth to adulthood. *Attachment & Human Development, 7*, 349–367. doi:10.1080/14616730500365928.

Tremblay, C., Hébert, M., & Piché, C. (1999). Coping strategies and social support as mediators of consequences in child sexual abuse victims. *Child Abuse & Neglect, 23*, 929–945. doi:10.1016/S0145-2134(99)00056-3.

Vranceanu, A., Hobfoll, S. E., & Johnson, R. J. (2007). Child multi-type maltreatment and associated depression and PTSD symptoms: The role of social support and stress. *Child Abuse & Neglect, 31*, 71–84. doi:10.1016/j.chiabu.2006.04.010.

Widom, C. S., Czaja, S. J., & Dutton, M. A. (2008). Childhood victimization and lifetime revictimization. *Child Abuse & Neglect, 32*, 785–796. doi:10.1016/j.chiabu.2007.12.006.

Wilson, L. C., & Scarpa, A. (2014). Childhood abuse, perceived social support, and posttraumatic stress symptoms: A moderation model. *Psychological Trauma: Theory, Research, Practice, and Policy, 6*, 512–518. doi:10.1037/a0032635.

"Why Didn't You Tell?" Helping Families and Children Weather the Process Following a Sexual Abuse Disclosure

Nancy D. Kellogg

The Problem: Parent Responses to Disclosures of Abuse

Since most sexually abused children have no signs of injury or infection (Heger, Ticson, Velasquez, & Bernier, 2002; Shapiro & Makoroff, 2006), detection relies on the child disclosing that they have been abused. However, many children do not disclose their abuse (Finkelhor, Hotaling, Lewis, & Smith, 1990), and children who do disclose may give incomplete details about the abuse (Gonzalez, Waterman, Kelly, McCord, & Oliveri, 1993; DeVoe & Faller, 1999) or recant their history completely (Summit, 1983; Rieser, 1991). This process of disclosure is influenced by numerous factors, including the child's perception of consequences (Sauzier, 1989; Summit, 1983; Jensen, Gulbrandsen, Mossige, Reichelt, & Tjersland, 2005), family responses to disclosure (Lawson & Chaffin, 1992; Jensen et al., 2005), cultural factors (Kellogg & Huston, 1995; Shaw, Lewis, Loeb, Rosado, & Rodriguez, 2001), and investigation processes (Hershkovitz, Orbach, Lamb, Sternberg, & Horowitz, 2006). Factors associated with delayed, partial, and non-disclosures include family member perpetrator (Kogan, 2004), younger victim age (McElvaney 2013), male gender of victim (Goodman-Brown, Edelstein, Goodman, Jones, & Gordon, 2003), and Hispanic ethnicity (Shaw et al., 2001). However, many of these studies have been limited by small sample size (Jensen et al., 2005; Crisma, Bascelli, Paci, & Romito, 2004; Hershkowitz, Lanes, & Lamb, 2007; Jensen et al., 2005; McElvaney, Greene, & Hogan, 2014; Schaeffer, Leventhal, & Asnes, 2011; Sorsoli, Kia-Keating, & Grossman, 2008), recollection bias of adults abused during childhood (Alaggia, 2004; Arata, 1998) and select patient populations such as those in therapy (Shaw

N.D. Kellogg, M.D. (✉)
Division Chief of Child Abuse, University of Texas Health Science
Center at San Antonio, San Antonio, TX, USA
e-mail: kelloggn@uthscsa.edu

© Springer International Publishing Switzerland 2017
D.M. Teti (ed.), *Parenting and Family Processes in Child Maltreatment
and Intervention*, Child Maltreatment Solutions Network,
DOI 10.1007/978-3-319-40920-7_3

et al., 2001; Gonzalez, Waterman, Kelly, & Wood, 1996; Sorenson & Snow, 1991), those within a limited age range (McElvaney et al., 2014), or victims whose cases are going to trial (Goodman-Brown et al., 2003). Additionally, few studies (Kellogg & Huston, 1995; Schaeffer et al., 2011) have examined disclosure characteristics in children with contemporaneous disclosures of abuse. Understanding the barriers children confront during their initial disclosure may inform strategies for facilitating full disclosures and preventing recantations.

The medical assessment of children and adolescents who are suspected victims of sexual abuse is typically juxtaposed between investigative processes, including forensic interviews and victim statements, and the onset of therapy. While one purpose of the medical assessment is to gather forensically important information, a primary goal is to assess the medical and mental health needs of the child, and to devise a strategy for meeting those needs. This treatment plan for the child also entails assessment and treatment of the child's caregiver. At Center for Miracles in San Antonio, a licensed social worker assesses the parent's mental health, need for resources, and reactions to the child's abuse disclosure, focusing on factors that impact the parent's ability to support and believe their child. At the same time, medical professionals assess the child's emotional and behavioral health in addition to gathering information about the abuse. This assessment includes questions about family life, parent responses to abuse, and fears related to their abuse disclosure. After the psychosocial assessment, the child fills out the Trauma Symptom Checklist for Children (TSCC-A; Elliott & Briere, 1994), and the medical exam is conducted. The medical and social work staff confer following the exam and identify issues affecting the parent-child relationship that need to be addressed at the conclusion of the visit or in therapy. These issues commonly involve misunderstanding about how children disclose abuse and the lack of material evidence that abuse occurred.

Although parent support following disclosure reduces the likelihood of recantation (Elliott & Briere, 1994), little is known about the type of support needed, or how the child's need for support may change through the processes of disclosure, investigation and possibly trial. Following disclosure, children and families face various doubts and challenges that may threaten family integrity and the child's sense of security and well-being. Because parents are often warned by child protection and law enforcement investigators not to discuss the allegations of abuse with the child, these doubts and challenges are sometimes not addressed, causing serious rifts in the parent-child-family relationships. It is critical to understand and address these concerns soon after the disclosure is made in order to preserve these relationships, promote healing, and support the child's disclosure.

Parents typically have questions about the child's disclosure:

- Why did she wait so long to tell?
- Why didn't she tell her mom or dad?
- I've always told her to tell me right away if someone tries to touch her privates- and this was going on for 5 years?

Children are highly perceptive to the reactions of their parents (Jensen et al., 2005). The child sees their parent as angry, grieving, disappointed, disbelieving and sometimes supportive. There is often a mixture of strong emotions that is frightening and confusing to the child. A supportive parent can also be angry at the whole situation. Children may feel responsible for, and confused by, the emotional turmoil: "Is my parent upset because of me? Are they mad at me, or are they mad at the other person?" The child then blames herself for the consequences of her disclosure. Because many parents do not tell their child specifically why they feel the way they do, the child assumes the worst, and the parent-child relationship is often compromised.

Understanding reasons for disclosure and non-disclosure can provide insight into the specific types of support a child needs during and following a disclosure of abuse. The first time a child tells someone that she has been abused is a critical time for the child, as she carefully assesses the responses of others. Parental reactions of shock, anguish and anger can be misinterpreted by the child as disbelief and disappointment. These initial parent reactions also impact the child's trauma symptoms; in one study (Melville, Kellogg, Perez, & Lukefahr, 2014), children of parents who did not completely believe the initial disclosure of abuse were more likely to have abuse-specific self-blame which was associated with a greater number of trauma symptoms.

Patterns of Disclosure Among a Consecutive Sample of Children Presenting for Medical Evaluations

Once suspected abuse is reported, children are asked to talk to investigators, forensic interviewers, child protection workers, health care providers and mental health professionals about their abuse. Also during this initial phase following disclosure, family reactions tend to be emotional, volatile and fluctuating. Identifying the barriers and fears related to disclosure during this time period may enable parents to more effectively understand and support their child.

A consecutive sample of 221 children and adolescents who presented for medical evaluations acutely (within 5 days of initial sexual assault or abuse) and 440 who presented non-acutely (more than 5 days after the first abuse) answered questions about their sexual abuse disclosures. The average age was 11.6 years (range 3–17 years), 89% were female, and 71% were Hispanic. About one-third of the perpetrators were younger than 18, half of whom were family members. The average time to disclosure for the total sample was 1.5 years (median 90 days); the non-acute group waited an average of 2.3 years (median 18 months).

Disclosure questions were embedded within the medical form. Following their description of abuse, children were asked what kept them from wanting to tell right away, why they decided to tell, and how long they waited to tell based on their age at onset of abuse and at disclosure. Additionally, children were asked if anything was said to them about the consequences of telling.

Factors Impacting Time to Disclosure

Time to disclosure did not vary significantly by gender, abuse-specific self-blame or abuse severity (penetration with genitals vs none). Children (non-acute sample) abused by family members had longer average disclosure times than children abused by non-family members (37 months v. 13 months), and those abused by a biological parent waited the longest (43 months). The younger the child was at the onset of abuse, the longer they waited to disclose. Spearman's Rank Correlation for days to disclosure by age at onset of abuse was -0.49 ($p < 0.001$).

Consistent with the findings of a previous study (Shaw et al., 2001), Hispanic children waited an average of 13 months longer to disclose abuse than African American children ($p = 0.02$). Caucasian children waited an average of 8.7 months longer on average to disclose than African American children. About half of the African American children presented for medical care within 5 days of their assault. These differences raise questions about how family culture influences the tendency to disclose.

Reasons for Nondisclosure of Abuse

Utilizing recursive abstraction, five themes were identified based on children's responses to the question about why they delayed disclosure: fear of consequences, incapacitating feelings, lack of opportunity/ person to tell, told not to tell, and didn't know/think it was wrong at the time.

The most common reason children did not want to tell was fear of consequences (59 %). Children who feared adverse consequences had the longest average disclosure time among these 5 groups. Explicit threats by the abuser were reported by 29 % of children, but only 11 % indicated that threats by the perpetrator were a reason for their delay in disclosure. Overall, the consequences of disclosure that children feared more commonly concerned what others, particularly family members, would say or do rather than fear of personal harm. As one child said, "I thought it would hurt my mom. That's the only reason that I didn't tell, because if I let him do it to me, then he didn't hurt my mom." Others worry they will be punished, or that their parent won't believe them. Some children fear consequences to the abuser, and are ambivalent in that they want the abuse to stop but they still desire a relationship with the abuser. This ambivalence is often misunderstood by the non-abusive parent who may be angry and unforgiving towards the abuser, further compounding the child's feelings of guilt and concern for the abuser.

The second most common reason for non-disclosure was incapacitating feelings (29 %). These children have overwhelming feelings of shame, embarrassment and guilt. Speaking about the abuse is traumatic, and after they have made an initial disclosure, they sometimes refuse to talk about it again. Parents who want their children to give them lots of details about the abuse may become confused or skeptical when their child is reluctant to answer their questions. For children with incapacitating feelings, a parental response that praises the child's decision to disclose rather than probes for details is more likely to facilitate the child's disclosure of abuse.

Less common categories of why children delayed disclosure include lack of opportunity or person to tell (7 %). Responses that illustrate this category include: "I didn't know who to tell" and "I didn't know how to say it, how to tell Mom and Dad that a person we trusted, hurt me." Some children did not disclose because of doubts about their parent's protective response: "I didn't think mom would do anything. He would get drunk and beat her, and he would leave but she always took him back. What was the point?" Children are constantly weighing the pros and cons of disclosing their abuse. When they witness their mother's inability to effectively protect herself or her children, or see her continue to defend or defer to the abuser, children know that disclosure will not necessarily result in cessation of abuse. Because some children are looking for the right person and place to tell, efforts to develop rapport and trust and opportunities for safe disclosure may prompt some children to divulge their abuse.

Another group didn't tell simply because they were told not to (6 %). This group did not indicate that they felt threatened; rather they were simply obeying the adult. Previous studies (Piper & Wilson, 1994) have illustrated the tendency for children, particularly children between 5 and 7 years old, to keep a secret when an adult, even a stranger, asks them to. Finally, about 5 % didn't tell because they didn't know the abuse was wrong. Some in this group were young children who did not perceive the sexual acts as abusive, a situation not uncommon with children abused by an older sibling. Sometimes the child's realization that they were abused comes several years later: "I didn't tell because he told me not to, and my mother told me to trust him, so I did. I didn't know it was the wrong thing. In health class they told us it was the wrong thing and that it was important to tell." This child was 12 when she told and 7 when she was abused. Others in this group were adolescents, including a 15 year old girl who was in a sexual relationship with a 38 year old teacher and expected to marry him. Those in an abusive, but consensual relationship often do not disclose their abuse; their abuse is discovered when someone witnesses the abuse or they need help because they fear they are pregnant or infected with a sexually transmitted disease.

Reasons for Disclosure

There were 6 themes identified related to reasons for disclosure. These themes were further grouped into those derived from external influences (needing help from others or finding the right opportunity or person to get help from) and those based on internal factors (independent reactions to abuse). External factors, which are potentially modifiable, were more common (56 %) than internal factors. External factors or themes that depended on responses of others included: found opportunity or person to tell (18 %); abuse was witnessed, child was rescued or somebody else told (17 %); and needed help from others because of physical, psychological or behavioral symptoms or concerns (21 %). In this latter group are adolescents with responses such as: "I was crying all the time at home. I was upset at school. My friends were asking what was wrong, and I finally told." Being vigilant to these types of behaviors, asking about the possibility of abuse, and being supportive may provide the opportunity and impetus for victims to disclose. Sometimes the opportunity to tell arises because another person shares their abusive experience: "The night before, my grandmother was talking about something similar that happened to her when she was little." Sometimes simply being asked will prompt disclosure. Although few indicated they disclosed because a doctor or professional asked them, it is not known how often clinicians routinely ask children about abuse.

While internal factors were less common than external factors, the most common single reason children told was emotional pressure, accounting for about 29 % of the responses: "I wanted to get it out. It was like a soda can, just shaking and shaking." This is not the same group as those who did not tell due to incapacitating feelings. Others told because it was the right thing to do (13 %): "Just knowing that if I didn't tell other people would get hurt, and he would get away with it." The realization that an abuser could hurt, or may have hurt, another child can be an important motivator for disclosure. The least common reason children disclosed is because they felt safe (2 %): "I told because my mom left him." Children who told because "it was the right thing to do" had the shortest average disclosure time, 7.6 months. The children who told because they "felt safe" had the longest average disclosure time, 2.74 years.

Family Reactions Following Disclosure

Family reactions following disclosure may increase the child's tendency to recant: "I don't know if my mom believes me. At night everyone is crying. My mom doesn't know who to believe and my little sister and brother cry for their father." This paradoxical responsibility that a child feels for keeping her family together causes her to consider the risks of continuing her disclosure. Even when a mother says and does all the things she is supposed to do to protect and support her child, some children cannot bear the anguish of their family members.

When a child is abused by someone living in the home (as opposed to a person living outside the home), the mother's initial response to their child's disclosure is less likely to be supportive (Elliott & Briere, 1994). About 60 % of mothers believe and support their child, and report promptly to authorities, about 20 % don't believe the child and don't report, and about 20 % don't know who to believe (Kellogg & Menard, 2003). Some of the ambivalent and non-believing parents want irrefutable evidence that abuse has occurred: proof from the examination that there was penetration, DNA or a sexually transmitted disease. Other parents are ambivalent because of the apparent lack of behavioral indicators of abuse or because the child seems attached to the abuser. Explaining that responses to abuse are highly variable and that children often love their abuser but hate the abuse may help some parents reconcile their ambiguity and doubts.

About half of the children in the disclosure study had abuse-specific self-blame. Children with self-blame did not have longer disclosure times than children without self-blame, but their parents were more likely to have some doubt following the child's initial disclosure (Melville et al., 2014). Of those who reported self blame, most felt the abuse occurred because of something they did or did not do; for example, "I should never have gone to him when he called me." Others blamed themselves for the continuation of the abuse because they did not disclose after the first time. A third group indicated that they blamed themselves for all the consequences of their abuse disclosure.

Even when the parent response is supportive, there are several other events following disclosure and reporting of the abuse to child protection and law enforcement agencies that create stress and anxiety for the child and family. Every time a child tells someone, there is the stress of anticipating the other person's reaction. Confrontational or violent responses between the victim's and abuser's families may occur. Due to the nature of criminal investigations, child interviews are typically not empathetic or encouraging. In addition, most investigators withhold information from the family until the investigation is complete. This lack of communication is sometimes misinterpreted by the child or the family as lack of belief in the child's disclosure. Young children may feel they are in trouble because of the number of professionals involved and the sometimes repetitive questions that are asked. In urban areas, it is not uncommon for cases to take 2 or 3 years to go to trial. Families may receive 7 or 8 notices of trial date resets, each generating another surge of anxiety and anticipation. Some children recant their disclosures in an effort to stop the confusion and turmoil.

Weathering the Process of Disclosure: A Role for Clinicians

One important role for clinician is to clarify with families how children disclose abuse. There is no typical time to disclosure or single reason why children disclose or decide not to disclose as every child and situation is different. In addition, there are no typical behavioral, emotional or physical symptoms of sexual abuse. However, disclosure can take years, particularly for children whose abuse started when they were very young or whose abuse involved a family member. Ethnicity of the child also influences time to disclosure. Disclosure is a process, not an event. The same fears associated with disclosure continue beyond disclosure. The child's most common fear is the response of others, particularly her parents. Although threats by the abuser can prolong disclosure, most children are not threatened, nor do they fear personal harm as a result of their disclosure. As children perceive variances in support and belief from others, they may recant part or all of their disclosure. In one study (Sorenson & Snow, 1991), 92 % of children who recanted eventually reasserted their original disclosure of abuse. During the initial disclosure and the events that follow, parents should ensure their child knows she is believed and supported, leaving the questions of credibility to investigators. This is especially important for children with incapacitating feelings related to the abuse since they may require more time and patience to divulge their abuse. These incapacitating feelings do not always end with disclosure; depending on a number of factors, some of these children will continue to have trauma symptoms and difficulties with mental health issues following the abuse disclosure. Regardless of the criminal investigation or trial outcomes, it is critical that parents appropriately support their children through all these processes.

While delay in disclosure is common, that doesn't mean that children don't love and trust their parents. Parents may feel they failed to protect their child because she didn't tell sooner and she didn't tell her parent. Parents should understand that children are reluctant to risk family happiness and integrity, and for those reasons may first tell a non-family member.

In working with children to bridge gaps with parents, understanding the child's perception of the parent's belief and support is key. Children often misinterpret the parent's anger, despair or silence as disbelief or disapproval. Additionally, clinicians should assess the parent's belief about their child's abuse (Runyon, Spandorfer, & Schroeder, 2014). Parents should explain their feelings to their child. When parents cry, children need to know that they're crying because they hurt for their child. Children feel responsible for their parents' emotions following the disclosure of abuse.

While emotions are unavoidable, following normal routines at home can provide a sense of security for the child. Familiarity is comforting to children during times of stress, and parents should be encouraged to limit questions about the abuse and to not vary the amount of attention and nurturing the child usually gets. Parents should be aware that emotions and behaviors sometimes worsen or develop after disclosure, relating to the development of trauma symptoms and anxiety about events and reactions following disclosure.

In summary, the events following a child's disclosure of sexual abuse can be confusing, traumatizing, and disruptive to children and families. Clinicians have the opportunity to preserve and strengthen parent-child relationships by clarifying the processes of, and responses to disclosure, facilitating healing and recovery for children and their families.

References

Alaggia, R. (2004). Many ways of telling: Expanding conceptualizations of child sexual abuse disclosure. *Child Abuse & Neglect, 28*(11), 1213–1227.

Arata, C. (1998). To tell or not to tell: Current functioning of child sexual abuse survivors who disclosed their victimization. *Child Maltreatment, 3*, 63–71.

Crisma, M., Bascelli, E., Paci, D., & Romito, P. (2004). Adolescents who experienced sexual abuse: Fears, needs and impediments to disclosure. *Child Abuse & Neglect, 28*, 1035–1048.

Devoe, E. R., & Faller, K. C. (1999). The characteristics of disclosure among children who may have been sexually abused. *Child Maltreatment, 4*, 217–277.

Elliott, D. M., & Briere, J. (1994). Forensic sexual abuse evaluations of older children: Disclosures and symptomatology. *Behavioral Sciences and the Law, 12*, 261–277.

Finkelhor, D., Hotaling, G., Lewis, I. A., & Smith, C. (1990). Sexual abuse in a national survey of adult men and women: Prevalence, characteristics, and risk factors. *Child Abuse & Neglect, 14*, 19–28.

Gonzalez, L. S., Waterman, J., Kelly, R. J., McCord, F., & Oliveri, M. K. (1993). Children's patterns of disclosures and recantations of sexual and ritualistic abuse allegations in psychotherapy. *Child Abuse & Neglect, 17*, 281–289.

Goodman-Brown, T. B., Edelstein, R. S., Goodman, G. S., Jones, D. P., & Gordon, D. S. (2003). Why children tell: A model of children's disclosure of sexual abuse. *Child Abuse & Neglect, 27*(5), 525–540.

Heger, A., Ticson, L., Velasquez, O., & Bernier, R. (2002). Children referred for possible sexual abuse: Medical findings in 2384 children. *Child Abuse & Neglect, 26*, 645–659.

Hershkowitz, I., Lanes, O., & Lamb, M. E. (2007). Exploring the disclosure of child sexual abuse with alleged victims and their parents. *Child Abuse & Neglect, 31*(2), 111–123.

Hershkowitz, I., Orbach, Y., Lamb, M. E., Sternberg, K. J., & Horowitz, D. (2006). Dynamics of forensic interviews with suspected abuse victims who do not disclose. *Child Abuse & Neglect, 30*, 753–769.

Jensen, T. K., Gulbrandsen, W., Mossige, S., Reichelt, S., & Tjersland, O. A. (2005). Reporting possible sexual abuse: A qualitative study on children's perspectives and the context for disclosure. *Child Abuse & Neglect, 29*, 1395–1413.

Kellogg, N. D., & Huston, R. L. (1995). Unwanted sexual experiences in adolescents. Patterns of disclosure. *Clinical Pediatrics, 34*(6), 306–312.

Kellogg, N. D., & Menard, S. W. (2003). Violence among family members of children and adolescents evaluated for sexual abuse. *Child Abuse & Neglect, 27*(12), 1367–1376.

Kogan, S. M. (2004). Disclosing unwanted sexual experiences: Results from a national sample of adolescent women. *Child Abuse & Neglect, 28*, 147–165.

Lawson, L., & Chaffin, M. (1992). False negatives in sexual abuse disclosure interviews: Incidence and influence of caretaker's believe in abuse in cases of accidental abuse discovery by diagnosis of STD. *Journal of Interpersonal Violence, 7*, 532–542.

McElvaney, R. (2013). Disclosure of child sexual abuse: Delays, non-disclosure and partial disclosure. What the research tells us and implications for practice. *Child Abuse Review.* doi:10.1002/car.2280.

McElvaney, R., Greene, S., & Hogan, D. (2014). To tell or not to tell? factors influencing young people's informal disclosures of child sexual abuse. *Journal of Interpersonal Violence, 29*(5), 928–947.

Melville, J. D., Kellogg, N. D., Perez, N., & Lukefahr, J. L. (2014). Assessment for self-blame and trauma symptoms during the medical evaluation of suspected sexual abuse. *Child Abuse & Neglect, 38*, 851–857.

Piper, M., & Wilson, J. C. (1994). Cues and secrets: Influences on children's event reports. *Developmental Psychology, 30*, 515–525.

Rieser, M. (1991). Recantation in child sexual abuse cases. *Child Welfare, 70*(6), 611–621.

Runyon, M. K., Spandorfer, E. D., & Schroeder, C. M. (2014). Cognitions and distress in caregivers after their child's sexual abuse disclosure. *Journal of Child Sexual Abuse, 23*, 146–159.

Sauzier, M. (1989). Disclosure of child sexual abuse. for better or for worse. *The Psychiatric Clinics of North America, 12*(2), 455–469.

Schaeffer, P., Leventhal, J. M., & Asnes, A. G. (2011). Children's disclosures of sexual abuse: Learning from direct inquiry. *Child Abuse & Neglect, 35*(5), 343–352.

Shapiro, R. A., & Makoroff, K. L. (2006). Sexually transmitted diseases in sexually abused girls and adolescents. *Current Opinion in Obstetrics and Gynecology, 18*, 492–497.

Shaw, J. A., Lewis, J. E., Loeb, A., Rosado, J., & Rodriguez, R. A. (2001). A comparison of Hispanic and African-American sexually abused girls and their families. *Child Abuse & Neglect, 25*, 1363–1379.

Sorsoli, L., Kia-Keating, M., & Grossman, F.K. (2008). "I kept that hush-hush." Male survivors of sexual abuse and the challenges of disclosure. *Journal of Counseling Psychology, 55*(3), 335–345.

Sorenson, T., & Snow, B. (1991). How children tell: The process of disclosure of child sexual abuse. *Child Welfare, 70*, 3–15.

Summit, R. C. (1983). The child sexual abuse accommodation syndrome. *Child Abuse & Neglect, 7*(2), 177–193.

Part II
Intergenerational Transmission of Child Maltreatment

The Intergenerational Transmission of Child Maltreatment: Socio-ecological and Psychological Origins of Maternal Risk

Laura Ann McCloskey

The Scope of Child Abuse and Neglect

> Children are arguably the most criminally victimized people in society. (Finkelhor, 2008, p. 3)

Abuse and neglect in childhood pose an enduring risk to positive human development across the life-course. In 2012 there were an estimated three million reports of suspected child abuse and neglect throughout the United States.[1] One in five cases was "substantiated" or found to warrant further investigation and intervention. Cases are substantiated depending on whether prior reports on the family are found or whether the police rather than family members or neighbors submit the report; the under-reporting bias maybe even by a factor as large as ten (Trocmé, Knoke, Fallon, & MacLaurin, 2008). Child abuse fatalities are also grossly under-recorded in official statistics, with as many as 58 % of child abuse deaths confirmed by medical examiners *omitted* from the official child abuse fatality count (Herman-Giddens et al., 1999).

The economic toll of child maltreatment is estimated to be as much as $212,000 per maltreated child; over ten years 89–140 billion dollars were lost nationally due to associated costs (Fang, Brown, Florence & Mercy, 2012). Expenditures include hospitalizations, social services, and the criminal justice system, yet the heaviest losses are those imputed to the loss of human potential, accounting for fully 70 % of the economic burden (Fang et al., 2012). Abuse and neglect derail the formation of children's human capital in multiple domains from educational achievement to

---

[1] DSHS, Child welfare.gov "State statutes governing child abuse reporting" https://www.childwelfare.gov/pubPDFs/define.pdf#page=2&view=Types%20of%20abuse.

L.A. McCloskey (✉)
Center for Research on Health Disparities, School of Public Health, Indiana University, Bloomington, IN 47408, USA
e-mail: lmcclosk@indiana.edu

© Springer International Publishing Switzerland 2017
D.M. Teti (ed.), *Parenting and Family Processes in Child Maltreatment and Intervention*, Child Maltreatment Solutions Network,
DOI 10.1007/978-3-319-40920-7_4

socioemotional development. Dante Cicchetti alludes to such a derailment when he describes "pathogenic childhood experiences" launching an adverse trajectory for many although not all affected children (Cicchetti & Toth, 2005). The degree of unabated child abuse in a society lowers human capital formation in childhood and adolescence which in turn lowers adult earning potential, culminating in self-destructive avenues such as crime for some individuals (Currie & Tekin, 2012). There is consensus that the earlier child abuse occurs and the longer it lasts, the worse the outcome (Cicchetti & Toth, 1995; Perry, Pollard, Blakley, Baker & Vigilante, 1995). Consequently, intervening early with any at-risk child yields the largest economic return across the life-course (Heckman & Carneiro, 2003). In the United States, unfortunately, the largest share of expenditures occur late in an abused child's trajectory: the ballooning costs of criminal justice is one example of intervention occurring in the teenage years, far too late.

Parental neglect is the most prevalent expression of maltreatment comprising 68 % of all reports, with 40 % reflected in the first 3 years of life.[2] Parents are implicated in 82 % of all reports to Child Protective Services and mothers make up 76 % of all parent referrals.[3] Mothers, therefore, are the primary targets of investigation and intervention since they are mainly responsible for early childcare. The bulk of early reports pertain to maternal neglect. Child abuse and neglect before the age of three carries a heightened risk for fatality with half of *all* child abuse fatalities concentrated in the first year (Finkelhor, 2008). In fact, fatal child abuse cases have increased since 2000 from 1.6 to 2.2 per 100,000; in 2012 there were 1640 fatalities, a trend at odds with statistics showing an overall decline in physical and sexual abuse of older children (Finkelhor & Jones, 2006).[4] Although mothers are implicated in most child neglect cases, fathers or father figures are disproportionately represented in child fatality statistics (Herman-Giddens et al., 1999). The United States ranks close to the highest among high income countries in fatal child abuse rates, behind only Mexico and Portugal.[5]

Gender and Maternal Behavior

> Mother love is anything *other than* natural and instead represents a matrix of images, meanings, sentiments and practices that are everywhere socially and culturally produced. — Nancy Scheper-Hughes (1992, p. 341).

Mothers are at center stage in the study of child socioemotional development. They have been the recipients of innovative parenting interventions (Daro, 2010;

---

[2] Children's Bureau (Administration on Children, Youth and Families, Administration for Children and Families) of the U.S. Department of Health and Human Services. Child Maltreatment: 2012 report. http://www.acf.hhs.gov/sites/default/files/cb/cm2012.pdf.

[3] Bureau of Labor.

[4] UNICEF report, 2003 http://www.unicef-irc.org/publications/pdf/repcard5e.pdf.

[5] National Center for Injury Prevention and Control Ten leading causes of death, United States, 2002, all races, all sexes. Atlanta, GA: US Centers for Disease Control and Prevention, 2002. http://www.acf.hhs.gov/sites/default/files/cb/cm2012.pdf#page=54.

Olds et al., 2002) in the hope of breaking a cycle of maltreatment. Because women are usually primary caregivers they shoulder the blame for child endangerment despite the contributions made by fathers. Maternal behavior is situated at the nexus of gender roles and macro social forces. Individual maternal culpability is often subordinate to the multi-tiered failures in a complex system of caregiving. For instance, social forces contributing to the rise in female-headed households or teen-age pregnancy create unique economic obstacles for women engendering the "femi-nization of poverty" (Pearce, 1978). The reduction in welfare starting in the 1990's left thousands of single mothers without a safety net. Poverty is tied to diminished "capabilities," or the chance to "achieve" and reach one's human potential (Nussbaum, 2003). Reduced capabilities in women's lives are measured by low educational attainment, poor access to healthcare, high rates of teenage pregnancy, and gender-based violence such as sexual abuse or intimate partner violence (Nussbaum, 2003). Understanding how gender and macro-level pressures intersect within the family is critical to the study of maltreatment.

Gender roles play a developmental role in the origins of maternal abuse or neglect. There is a raft of adverse gender-related experiences in childhood which may affect a woman's later caregiver capacity. Such experiences, including sexual abuse, may trigger maladaptive coping such as excessive use of alcohol or drugs later leading to parenting breakdowns (Miller, Downs, Gondoli & Keil, 1987). Girls appear to be more adversely affected than boys by dysfunctional family dynamics (Davies & Lindsay, 2004; Davies & Windle, 1997; Werner & Smith, 1992) and the lingering effects of a chaotic home life are more pronounced in girls grown up than boys entering adulthood (Werner & Smith, 1992, p. 169). When exposed to parental conflict, maternal depression, and other family stressors in middle childhood girls are more likely than boys to show conduct problems and depressive symptoms, explained in part by the "gender role intensification" hypothesis of Davies and Lindsay (2004). Their hypothesis proposes that girls are stronger barometers in a sense of family dynamics than boys of the same age; their heightened sensitivity may make them vulnerable as they mature. In adult women what might look like immediate or proximal causes of maternal neglect such as adult depression or drug dependency often have distal origins in early responses to family dysfunction. While girls respond more acutely than boys to family adversity, they also are subject more often to sexual abuse within the family and outside, with the threat escalating as they mature. Child sexual abuse has been linked to an array of difficulties in ado-lescent girls and women, from post-traumatic stress to substance use disorder (Becker, Stuewig, & McCloskey, 2010; McCloskey, 2013; Miller et al., 1987; Noll, 2005). Alexander (1992) has argued that incest destabilizes a daughter's identity to such an extent that attachment relationships in the family of origin are permanently damaged. Incest survivors sometimes manifest as parents the mistrust and ambiva-lence they felt during their childhood. Child sexual abuse (CSA) is associated with addiction among adolescent and adult women (Miller et al., 1987). In a study of 1411 adult women twin pairs, sexual abuse increased the odds of alcoholism by 2.8, and 3.09 for drug addiction (Kendler et al., 2000). When the abuse includes forced sexual intercourse the odds catapult to 4 and 5.7 respectively. Child sexual abuse sets a trajectory of "self-medication" with alcohol and drugs, and excessive alcohol and drug use presents a major risk for child abuse (Kelleher, Chaffin, Hollenberg & Fischer, 1994; Unicef, 2003). In fact, parents who abuse drugs or alcohol are more likely to perpetrate abuse or neglect (Dube et al., 2001), and fully 61 % of infants placed in out of home care have parents with likely substance use disorders (Wulczyn, Ernst, & Fisher, 2011).

Motherhood introduces a pivotal role for most American women. Having a child launches the adult formation of most women's identity (Chodorow, 1999). In fact, becoming a mother shapes women's self-described identity more than marriage, education or occupation (Rogers & White, 1998). Not having a child, or experiencing infertility, is more likely to create a crisis for women than for men. In one qualitative study, African-American, Latina and Arab American childless women attending fertility clinics disclosed intense distress at failing to conceive or bring a pregnancy to term, and the authors concluded that "infertility tore at the very foundations of their sense of self and womanhood" (Inhorn, Ceballo, & Nachtigall, 2009, p. 186). Such narratives demonstrate the high priority women place on having a child, embodying the "motherhood mandate" against the backdrop of infertility (Russo, 1976). Appreciating the motherhood mandate is central to analyzing the enactment of gender (Russo, 1976). With motherhood so essential to women's self-valuation it is traumatic to be classified as unfit in that role.

Although most American women want children, they also choose to work outside the home. As of 2012 70 % of all mothers were in the workforce.[6] Despite changing gender norms and expanded educational and employment opportunities for women, working mothers face daunting responsibilities. The weak safety net for working mothers in the United States contrasts with other high income countries which provide extensive paid family leave, subsidized childcare, and health insurance to ease the burden of family formation. In France such accommodations for working mothers—including sliding-scale and high-quality universal infant and early childcare (crèche)—may account for the rise in birthrate which is substantially higher than the rest of Europe, paired with French women's rising participation in the workforce now at 83 % (Fagnani, 2012). In summary, American family policies show only a weak commitment to supporting women with children which carry long-term consequences for children's prosocial development and society.

Defining Child Maltreatment

> Research must continue to pursue increased specificity in the ways maltreatment is defined so that we can better understand the experience of maltreated children.—Dante Cicchetti and Sheree Toth (1995), p. 544.

The term "maltreatment" spans a broad map of caregiving deficiencies across children's timeline. Defining maltreatment relies on the context of the parenting

---

[6]Department of Health and Human Services (DHHS), Administration on Children, Youth, and Families. Understanding the effects of maltreatment on early brain development. Washington (DC): Government Printing Office; 2001. Available from URL: http://www.childwelfare.gov/pubs/focus/earlybrain/earlybrain.pdf [PDF 454 KB].

behavior, on the surrounding environment and on available resources. When making judgments of potential abuse, social workers balance the intentions of the parents against their competence. The relative impact of any abusive act depends on the child's age: infant neglect is more likely to result in an immediate medical emergency or fatality in contrast to the neglect of a school-aged child. When Kempe et al. (1962) published their seminal paper in *JAMA* identifying child abuse or the "battered child syndrome" as a problem warranting attention from pediatric medical specialists they addressed physical and medical signs of maltreatment (e.g., subdural hematoma, fractured bones) which, at the time, were unrecognized formally as signs of abuse in medical nosology. Since initial recognition of the "battered child syndrome" the field has generated a catalogue of both visible and hidden effects and forms of maltreatment beyond the overtly physical to include child sexual abuse and dimensions of emotional and psychological abuse. Exposure to domestic violence is now increasingly recognized as abusive in definitions of maltreatment and in policy (Hamby, Finkelhor & Turner, 2010; McCloskey, Figueredo & Koss, 1995; Wolfe & Jaffe, 1991).

There are four putative categories classified by statute in virtually all U.S. states: (1) neglect; (2) physical abuse; (3) emotional abuse; and (4) sexual abuse. These categories are measured differently in research studies, although a general framework stretches across operational definitions. Nevertheless, researchers in pediatrics and psychology continue to make the empirical case for divergent forms of neglect or abuse, with at least three distinctive forms of neglect for instance (Dubowitz, Pitts & Black, 2004). Despite the expanding view of what constitutes maltreatment, definitions reflect the childrearing standards of the community (Giovannoni, 1989). Attempts to define child abuse based on psychological evidence are sometimes in conflict with class and regional values. What professionals see as abusive some community members see as normative punishment. Moreover, the distrust of government intervention erects an impasse at the borders of family and society. Indeed secrecy is a common characteristic of abusive families and " (so) much violence remains hidden and justified in families viewed as precious" (Levesque, 2001, p. 5). The clash around parenting standards is especially seen in U.S. Southern states (Gershoff, 2002; Zolotof et al., 2011) where corporal punishment is still accepted as the main tool of discipline. Moreover, there is even stronger distrust of government intervention in the South (Cohen and Nisbett 1994). If using a switch or belt to hit a child is accepted by the community, is it nevertheless harmful to a child? Researchers have argued that it is tracing multiple adverse outcomes spanning depression and behavioral aggression from frequent exposure to the raised hand (Gershoff, 2002; Straus & Mouradian, 1998).

Different Types of Maltreatment Overlap

Many researchers and clinicians focus on a single and perhaps most apparent form of abuse. Yet frequently professionals fail to inquire about additional instances beyond the presenting incident. Yet it is likely that repeat and overlapping abuse, or "poly-victimization," occurs even when researchers fail to measure it (Hamby, Finkelhor, & Turner, 2010). As many as 34 % of adults recalling past abuse endorsed at least two distinct co-occurring forms (Edwards, Holden, Felitti, & Anda, 2003). Many youth and adults who disclose a history of maltreatment recount concurrent forms of abuse in tandem with other sources of stress (Dong et al., 2004; Edwards, Holden, Felitti, & Anda, 2003; Stevens, Ruggiero, Kilpatrick, Resnick, & Saunders, 2005). In a national survey of 831 adolescents, 17 % were multiply victimized, experiencing both sexual and physical assault as teens (Stevens et al., 2005).

Child abuse and intimate partner violence typically overlap in the same households. Nearly half of all domestic violence households had children under the age of seven according to a study of families in five cities (Fantuzzo et al., 1997). The median concordance of domestic violence with physical child abuse is .41 with correlations in some studies as high as .56 (Appel & Holden, 1998). In a study of 8600 adult patients seen in the Kaiser Permanente health maintenance organization in California patients were asked about ten traumatic or abusive experiences in childhood (Felitti et al., 1998). As many as 24 % recollected witnessing intimate partner violence against their mothers and, of those; 57.5 % also reported child physical abuse in contrast to 21.7 % of respondents who disclosed no exposure to domestic violence (Dong et al., 2004). More than one form of abuse in a family signals abiding and severe family dysfunction. The more chaos in a child's family life, the greater the threat to their long-term adjustment and mental health (Sameroff & Chandler, 1975). Girls multiply exposed are more likely to re-enact multiple forms as adults, exposing their children to the same damaging cycle of polyvictimization (Cort, Toth, Cerulli,& Rogosch, 2011).

Risk Factors for Child Maltreatment

It is usual for aetiology to be multi-factorially determined (Rutter, 1988, p. 1)

Adding to the complexity surrounding a mother's early history of maltreatment is her coterminous childhood exposure to various stressors engulfing her family of origin. Maternal abuse or neglect may serve as barometers of a woman's past history filtered through her current circumstances. Michael Rutter (1988) remarked that the aetiology of any disease is explained through multiple tributaries: In the case of tuberculosis, for instance, there are many ways to succumb to infection. The web of connections and influences leading to a cycle of violence are equally complex. Risk markers among parents include socio-demographics (e.g. age of the child and the mother, parity, family income, family composition and maternal marital status, paternal unemployment, maternal education, race and ethnicity), family functioning (e.g., domestic violence) and psychosocial characteristics of the parents (e.g., substance use disorder, mental illness, past history of abuse in childhood). Neighborhood and community violence are also associated with an elevated number of maltreated children (Herrenkohl et al., 2008). More complexity is introduced when we analyze the relationship of different sources of risk to different forms of maltreatment. A prospective study of the determinants of different forms of maltreatment in a population-based sample ($N = 7000$) revealed that parents' physical abuse and neglect had different, non-overlapping risk factors. The circumstances that give rise to abuse or neglect therefore may be distinct (Chaffin, Kelleher, & Hollenberg, 1996).

Cumulative risk factors in a child's environment may contribute to psychopathology extending to a cycle of abuse in the next generation (Appleyard, Egeland, van Dulman, & Sroufe, 2005). Furthermore, characteristics of the child may interact with parental risk factors as in the case of child disability (Sullivan & Knutson, 2000). Risk factors have a compounding influence, pushing a mother into the realm of neglectful, abusive, or inadequate caregiving. In one study reports of child abuse or neglect showed a linear increase as a function of the sheer number of eco-social risk factors: when no risk factors were present only 3 % of parents were abusive in contrast to 24 % when there were four or more stressors present (Brown, Cohen, Johnson, & Salzinger, 1998). In a seminal test of Bronfenbrennner (1979) theory as applied to child abuse reports Garbarino (1976) coded New York counties for family income levels and for economic and community resources. He found that more than twice the variance (38 %) in child abuse reports was explained by the low resources of the county rather than the individual family income, demonstrating that where someone lives exerts even more influence than their personal income and resources.

Poverty

The measurement of poverty refers to a standard based on the fulfillment of basic needs or three times a family's food allowance (Orshansky, 1965). Forty-five million or 14.5 % of Americans fall below that figure (U.S. Census, 2013), and at least 22 % of children live below the standard. More women are poor than are men, and more women heading households with children are poor (31 %) than married couples (6.3 %) or single fathers (16.4 %) (U.S. Census). Family structure and single parenthood pave the way for economic disadvantage (McLanahan & Kelly, 2006). Building on the notion of the growing male:female ratio in poverty (Pearce, 1978), McLanahan and Kelly (2006) contend that "it is women's exclusive burden of childcare that creates the feminization of poverty." The growing gender disparity in U.S. poverty rates derives in part from the inadequate social safety net, rise in divorce and single-parent households, and gender disparities in earned income (McClanahan & Kelly, 2006). And poverty imposes its own stigma engendering social isolation among parents. Low family income is associated with poor child mental and physical health outcomes (Aber, Bennett, Conley, & Li, 1997). The association of poverty with maltreatment partially explains the delayed trajectory of low-income children (Aber et al., 1997; Lee & Goerge, 1999). Although correlational data may not always support strong causal inferences, there is evidence from a natural experiment that men's job loss results in a spike in child abuse. Steinberg, Catalano and Dooley (1981) found that a factory closing in the community with subsequent unemployment of fathers resulted in a sharp rise of child abuse reports within 3 or 4 months, rising throughout the year of the study. This prospective study does support a potentially causal link between fathers' unemployment, economic strain and child abuse perpetrated by either parent. Longitudinal research also illuminates potentially causal mechanisms. For instance, economic strain or being unable to cover the bills and the heightened stress poverty increased over time paternal aggression towards children (Simons, Whitbeck, Conger, & Wu, 1991).

Early Age of Childbirth and Teenage Pregnancy

One well-recognized risk factor for child maltreatment is the relatively young age of the mother. The U.S. prevalence of teenage births far outstrips any other high income country, although the national rates have been falling for two decades. Actually between 1990 and 2008 the rate fell 42 % among women aged 15–19 (Kost and Henshaw, 2012). Seventy-five percent of teenage births are to minority youth in the U.S. (mainly Latina, African American). Having a child during adolescence is one risk factor for child neglect and abuse (Brown et al., 1998; Goerge & Bong, 1996; Stier et al., 1993). In one large-scale study in Illinois women's young age interacted with low-income to increase the odds of substantiated child abuse reports (Goerge & Bong, 1996), predicting any form of abuse from neglect to sexual abuse. Early childbearing introduces a spiral of cumulative disadvantage that threatens adjustment and economic well-being of the mother and her child (Maynard, 1996) with girls pregnant in their teens less likely to finish high school; only 11 % marry (Haveman, Wolfe, & Peterson, 2008). Incest or child sexual abuse predicts teenage pregnancy (Boyer & Fine, 1992; Roosa, Tein, Reinholtz, & Angolini, 1997). Women whose mothers had an early birth often follow the same pattern (Kahn & Anderson, 1992). Not everyone agrees that teenage pregnancy is a culprit for child abuse. Geronimus, Korenman & Hillemeier (1994) analyzed a large NYLS dataset and found that the children of young mothers were no less developed than those of older women who were related to the index adolescent mothers. In other words family background rather than maternal age per se affected child adjustment.

Young mothers show unique patterns of interaction compared to older mothers. Single primiparous mothers in their teenage years talk less to their 4-month olds, smile less, and develop more hostile attributions as the infants grow older in contrast to mothers over 20 (Barratt & Roach, 1995). Mothers under 19 years of age misconstrue infant cries of distress or the vocalizations of infants who are physically compromised or disabled (Lester, Garcia-Coll, & Valcarcel, 1988). Adolescent mothers of infants born 2 months premature express unrealistic expectations and attributions which adversely affect the healthy development of their infants in contrast to older mothers with premature newborns who are more attuned to the infant's developmental stage (Field et al., 1980). Although it appears that teens are less sensitive to their infants, there may be a threshold after which age of the mother is irrelevant. Comparisons between primiparous mothers who ranged from 23 to about 33 yielded no age-related differences in sensitivity their infants (Belsky, Hancox, Sligo, & Poulton, 2012). Older mothers with abusive childhoods were as likely to reproduce some elements of dysfunctional parenting or maltreatment as mothers in their early twenties. It appears that the age effect in maternal sensitivity applies mainly to those in their teens.

The availability of birth control and abortion services is central to understanding early childbearing. Child abuse reports are more numerous in those states that restrict access to abortion (Bitler & Zavodny, 2002). Moreover, there are pronounced income disparities in access to reproductive health services, including birth control pill prescriptions and even emergency contraception (Hall, Moreau & Trussell, 2012). Policies which limit girls' access to birth control increase the number of unwanted and poorly timed pregnancies which in turn place offspring at risk.

In addition to the age of the mother at first birth, parity in excess of one increases the risk of child maltreatment (Brown et al., 1998; Zuravin, 1988). Having more than two children at home interacts with maternal youth, poverty and smoking to increase the risk of low birthweight in subsequent newborns (Wua et al., 1994). Caring for several children at home is related to post-partum depression in women from developing countries and is a strong potential factor in high income countries (Yargawa & Leonardi-Bee, 2015). Results of a study of urban mothers identified through Child Protective Services compared to controls showed that close spacing of births increased the odds of maltreatment (Zuravin, 1988). Multiple births (e.g., twins, triplets, etc.) combined with maternal age (younger) were the contributed to fatal or near-fatal inflicted traumatic brain injuries of children under 2 years of age admitted to intensive care or who died before receiving treatment in North Carolina (Keenan et al., 2003). Some anthropologists view closely spaced births as divergent from the birth patterns of our human ancestors. Consistent with a biosocial theory, mothers from the !Kung bushmen of the Kalahari Desert arranged 4 years birth spacing to ensure better child survival (Blurton Jones, 1986).

Marriage and Household Structure

Since the 1960's there has been a radical transformation of what constitutes a family and who "heads" the household. Women have increasingly entered the "public" sphere of work although men remain disengaged from the "private" sphere of the household (Chodorow, 1999). Despite the slow catch-up of men to assume domestic responsibilities, women have increased external labor force participation largely to their own advantage. Yet with expanded job opportunities come more overall paid and unpaid work hours (Craig, 2007). Married women with jobs work more hours than their husbands, spending nearly 50 % more time with their children and more than double the hours for household chores (Bianchi, Sayer, Milkie, & Robinson, 2012). Those husbands endorsing traditional gender roles spend less time with their children and on housework than husbands who endorse gender equality (Coltrane & Ishii-Kuntz, 1992), although Arlie Hochshild's (1992) ethnographic study of working couples suggest that feminist ideology is less related to how domestic chores are divided than one might expect.

Household family structure and the marital status of the mother contribute to the risk of child maltreatment. The highest risk profile for child maltreatment according to the National Incidence Study is a single mother with a live-in partner (Sedlak et al., 2010). Based on the National Incidence Study substantiated child abuse reports are 10 per 1000 among married couples, 50 among single mothers without a partner, and 75 among unmarried women with a live-in partner (Sedlak et al., 2010). Paxson and Waldfogel (1999) found that family structure, parental employment and income—especially below the poverty line—were highly related to child abuse reports. Furthermore, co-residing with a man who is not a woman's husband significantly increases the potential for intimate partner violence (Magdol, Moffitt, Caspi, & Silva, 1998). In the worst case scenario, a child is eight times more likely to be killed in a household when there is an unrelated man co-residing with the mother (Stiffman et al., 2002). Approximately 65 % of all child homicides are committed by a father or stepfather (Herman-Giddens et al., 1999), despite men spending less time as caregivers than women. Paternal neglect through abandonment falls outside the scope of Child Protective Services. Yet father absence should not be underestimated as a risk factor for children's adjustment: Father absence alone predicts a 150 % high school drop out rate for Anglo American youth, with elevated rates for African American (75 %) and Latino youth (96 %) (McLanahan, 1999).

Domestic Violence

As many as 30 % of American children who reside with two parents witness intimate partner violence (McDonald, Jouriles, Ramisetty-Mikler, Caetano, & Green, 2006). Children who witness such incidents are estimated to be under the age of seven in half of all cases (Fantuzzo, Boruch, Beriama, Atkins, & Marcus, 1997). Nine percent of adolescents report exposure to domestic violence (Zinzow et al., 2009), indicating that violence persists or is initiated for a significant number of families even with teenage children. Intimate partner violence sometimes shows a "spillover" effect onto the abuse of children. In a recent study of men referred to batterer intervention programs, the majority of fathers endorsed the use of corporal punishment and lacked empathy (Burnetta, Ferreira, & Buttell, 2015). Violent fathers or stepfathers are prone to violence against all members of the household, and the co-morbidity of physical abuse and domestic violence is high (Appel & Holden, 1998). Physical abuse of children also appears to be a tactic of control of wives in some cases—in one study two out of three abused women received a threat from their partner that he would harm or kill the children, and one in five discovered that he had killed their pet (McCloskey, 2001). These behavioral patterns reveal a strategic use of children to manipulate mothers.

Another spillover of domestic violence is seen in maternal caregiving. Women exposed to domestic violence as children or to physical abuse were at greater risk of neglecting or abusing their child according to one population-based survey of 6000 parents (Heyman & Slep, 2002). Moreover, there was an interaction effect for mothers who experienced two or more forms of child abuse (including exposure to domestic violence) showing the highest propensity towards re-enactment of abusive practices. The strain of relationship violence undermines women's sense of control, resulting in feelings of powerlessness and depression. Women in abusive relationships are indeed more likely to be depressed (Banyard, Williams, & Siegel, 2003) and depression jeopardizes healthy parenting (Cicchetti, Rogosch, & Toth, 1998). Impaired psychological functioning in response to partner violence diminishes parenting attitudes and behavior—as in the expression of warmth, effective child management and child-centeredness—which in turn results in adverse effects on children (Levendosky & Graham-Bermann, 2000). Women in abusive relationships rate themselves as having more parenting stress than non-abused women (Holden & Ritchie, 1991) and they have significantly lower social support (Thompson et al., 2000), which is in turn related to caregiving effectiveness (Bartlett & Easterbrooks, 2012). They also show hostile attributional biases towards even their unborn infants (Huth-Bocks, Levendosky, Theran, & Bogat (2004). Domestic violence interferes with a child's secure attachment formation (Levendosky, Lannert, & Yalch, 2012), with as many as 56 % of toddlers exposed to domestic violence showing insecure attachments according to the Ainsworth classification (Levendosky, Lannert & Yalch, 2012). Abused women's internal working models of attachment, crucial for establishing a secure attachment with their children, are sometimes poorly developed even before she has delivered her child as expressed during the prenatal period (Huth-Bocks, Levendosky, Theran, & Bogat, 2004). Ultimately intimate partner violence isolates women (Thompson et al., 2000), damaging their self-esteem which in turn curtails their parenting self-efficacy (Gelfand & Teti, 1990).

Substance Use: Alcohol and Drugs

Parental substance use is often linked to child abuse reports. Women who drink habitually are twice as likely to be reported to Child Protective Services in Ontario (Walsh, MacMillan, & Jamieson, 2003). Alcohol abuse was the strongest predictor for any form of abuse by any perpetrator in a population-based survey (Chaffin, Kelleher, & Hollenberg, 1996). Among children removed from the home to become wards of the Court in Massachusetts 67 % of the custodial parents had a substance use disorder, most commonly cocaine or alcohol (Famularo, Kinscherff, & Fenton, 1992). In a Canadian study of 20,000 parents reported for maltreatment 24 % of all "repeat offenders" had substance use disorders; fully 84 % of parents in the system with an addiction had more than one report over the 5-year study period (Laslett, Room, Dietze & Ferris, 2012). Heavy drinking instigates child maltreatment and prolongs its duration. At a population level does a presumed reduction in drinking predict subsequent declines in child abuse reports? Economists performed a prospective test of whether rising beer prices reduced child abuse reports over time (Markowitz & Grossman, 2000). Beer is the most widely used alcohol product, especially among low-income drinkers. Mothers but not fathers reduced their beer consumption in response to the beer tax. Fathers may draw upon reserves to cover their drinking costs which mothers may not have. The study confirmed a causal relationship of maternal alcohol consumption and child maltreatment relevant to policy and the prevention of maternal drinking.

Maternal Psychopathology

Women abused during childhood potentially are at risk for adopting unhealthy lifestyles in adolescence and adulthood due in part to the long-lasting effects of toxic stress on physiological systems (Danese et al., 2009; Shonkoff & Garner, 2012). Cumulative adverse events impose a "dose-response" effect on childhood health and adult disease, even shortening the lifespan (Felitti et al., 1998). Different psychiatric disorders may be linked to maltreatment at different stages of child development. For instance, maternal depression is associated with child maltreatment before the age of three (Dubowitz, Papas, Black & Starr, 2002; Kotch et al., 1995). Post-partum depression affects about 13 % of American women increasing the chance of maternal neglect of neonates and infants (O'hara & Swain, 1996). Women in high-income countries are prone to post-partum depression if they have a prior history of abuse, a strained relationship with their partner, or stress during late pregnancy (McDonald et al., 2012). In a meta-analysis of post-partum depression in developing countries researchers found that mothers were less likely to develop depression if their husbands participated in caring for them before and after the delivery, and if they were involved in caregiving post-natally (Yargawa & Leonardi-Bee, 2015). Having four or more children at home increases the chances of developing depression with subsequent births (Yargawa & Leonardi-Bee, 2015). These findings highlight the importance of the quality of marriage and the social support women receive surrounding pregnancy and birth. Maternal depression is actually implicated in a range of adverse child outcomes from insecure attachment to internalizing disorders, yet it develops out of experiences of stress and conflict. Women's depression is often a barometer of the quality of their relationships, and relationship conflict is a primary source of their self-reported stress (Hammen, 2012). Maternal depression among married women, for instance, is strongly tied to marital conflict (Cummings & Davies, 1994). Understanding the role fathers have in their wives' depressive symptoms is crucial for intervention. Mothers with severe mental illness struggle to meet the demands of childcare. However impaired mothers might be from mental illness even mothers with the diagnosis of schizophrenia, certainly among the most challenging of disorders, met the demands of caregiving more often than not as reported in a classic study of nearly 100 children of schizophrenic mothers who were indistinguishable on attachment indices from controls (Sameroff, Seifer, Zax, & Barocas, 1987).

In addition to having mental illness, women with intellectual disabilities are over-represented in child neglect cases (Azar, Stevenson, & Johnson, 2012). Intellectual disabilities are less related to overt child maltreatment than to the social information processing deficits resulting from impaired cognitive functioning. Social information processing biases of parents that are harmful to children include misattributions of blame, misinterpretations of infant behavior, insensitivity and parentification—when a child adopts the caregiving role in the parent-child dyad. Such biases also sometimes surface in depressed mothers of average intelligence (Gelfand & Teti, 1990). Furthermore, mothers' self-efficacy in their caregiving role correlates with their sensitivity to their infant. In other words, their self-image as a competent parent promotes their own responsiveness (Teti & Gelfand, 1991). Women's intellectual competence, their educational background, their social information processing biases and their self-efficacy are all individual attributes which promote or inhibit sensitivity to children. The failure of mothers to meet these social information processing demands can result in child maltreatment (Azar et al., 2012).

The Intergenerational Transmission of Maltreatment

The initial trauma of a young child may go underground but it will return to haunt us.—James Garbarino

Maltreating parents disclose traumatic and abusive childhoods more often than non-abusive parents (Egeland, Jacobvitz, & Papatola, 1987). In one of the earliest studies on this topic nine out of ten parents who abused or neglected their premature or otherwise medically compromised infants admitted to a childhood history of maltreatment themselves (Hunter & Kilstrom, 1979). As many as 70 % of mothers with childhood abuse histories displayed borderline or actual neglect and abuse of their toddlers when followed over 3 years (Egeland, Jacobvitz, & Papatola, 1987). Such high congruity between past history and current maltreatment is remarkable although the extent of the statistical association may be inflated. In retrospective research designs, when the participants are selected to express the risk outcome—in this instance perpetrating child maltreatment—the association between the predictors and outcome strengthens because there are too few people included with the risk variable who do not display the outcome of interest. The higher coefficients obtained through backward sampling based on the dependent variable are seen as resulting from "conditioning on the contingency" (Dawes, 1993). Kaufman and Zigler (1987), in their critique of the "cycle of violence" theory, rejected the findings from retrospective study designs, concluding that there is no credible cycle per se. Belsky (1993, p. 415) wrote that despite the widespread popular support in clinical circles for the notion of a cycle of violence "few in the scientific community would embrace such remarks." Yet the research performed since Belsky's remarks were made, including Belsky's own studies (Belsky, Hancox, Sligo, & Poulton, 2012) has made notable strides in methodology, sampling and in theory, engendering a spate of high quality longitudinal studies. These efforts do lend support for a cycle of poor parenting under certain conditions (c.f., Belsky, Conger & Capaldi, 2009). Maltreatment is *probabilistically* transmitted to the next generation of parents through transactional mechanisms between parent and child (Cicchetti & Toth, 1995).

Prospective designs improve on many clinical studies because at least one source of bias—the over-representation of the "outcome" or "contingency" in the sample—is eliminated. Nevertheless longitudinal studies have their own challenges because research participants are difficult to re-contact over the years and the optimal selection of measures may change. Another pitfall of longitudinal research on parenting is that the correlation between child abuse and later parenting often attenuates due to intervening life events. In other words, many "third" variable candidates accumulate during adulthood which overshadow the direct effect of childhood experiences. Additionally, the selected time point for measuring the outcome may fail to capture behavior that previously appeared though subsided, or, conversely, surfaced later after data collection ended (Rutter, 1988). Despite such conceptual and methodological challenges prospective studies have yielded convincing support for the intergenerational transmission thesis. In a longitudinal study of young mothers in Massachusetts child abuse history was strongly associated with the neglect of infants and toddlers (Bartlett & Easterbrooks, 2012). In the Iowa Youth and Families Project researchers early on assessed harsh parenting practices of three generations of parents within the same families in rural Iowa (Simons et al., 1991). Fathers rather than mothers were most likely to use corporal punishment with their sons across each generation in the extended family; the continuity of abusive practices was predicted mainly by the cross-generational transfer of poverty and resulting economic strain. Generally, low income rural families tend to condone corporal punishment, and these values sustain the use of physical tactics throughout the generations (Gershoff, 2002). The Iowa youth were followed into the next generation as new parents; those who received harsh parenting as adolescents showed similarly punitive and harsh physical punishment towards their preschool age children (Neppl, Conger, Scaramella, & Ontai, 2009). Parents who overcame their abusive histories were the ones who achieved the highest levels of education (e.g., college or more). The analysis of the Iowan families demonstrates the power of class and income mobility in sustaining or reversing abusive parenting scripts. Teenage youth in Seattle who received harsh discipline coupled with low parental monitoring exhibited the same tendencies 14 years later raising their 9-year olds (Bailey, Hill, Oesterle, & Hawkins, 2009). Pears and Capaldi (2001) found that mothers who reported a past history of abuse had sons who, when interviewed as teenagers, described their mothers as punitive and physically abusive. The effect was largest for mothers who reported their own childhood exposure to four or more different forms of abuse (i.e., poly-victimization). In a longitudinal study of 1116 families with twins based in the United Kingdom, approximately 15 % or more of the mothers disclosed at least "mild" maltreatment growing up (Jaffee et al., 2013).

Nearly half (46 %) of the formerly maltreated women showed abusive parenting with one or both of their twins in contrast to controls (OR = 3.55). Socioeconomic disadvantage, maternal psychopathology and low social support increased the odds of maltreatment by at least 2; domestic violence was also highly related (OR = 3.37). Researchers employing another longitudinal approach crossing child abuse records with subsequent interviews were able to identify substantiated cases of maltreatment (n = 908) and enlisted matched controls (n = 667) (Widom, Czaja, & DuMont, 2015). They discovered that 20 % of originally maltreated children were reported for child maltreatment in adulthood in contrast to 11 % of the controls; 4.8 % of parents with abuse histories lost custody of their children to the courts for neglect as opposed to the very few of the non-abused parents (1.3 %) (OR = 5.6). Most cases of maltreatment in the next generation were for sexual abuse and neglect rather than for physical abuse and the authors concluded that physical abuse is less likely to recur in the next generation.

The link between early exposure to domestic violence or child physical abuse and subsequent perpetration of violence as a romantic partner or spouse is fairly weak especially for men (Holtzworth-Munroe et al., 1997; Fergusson, Boden, & Horwood, 2006; Heyman & Slep, 2002). There is stronger empirical support for an intergenerational cycle of domestic violence among women (Ehrensaft et al., 2003; Heyman & Slep, 2002; McCloskey, 2013). Women exposed to domestic violence in childhood are susceptible to becoming victims in their adult relationships over and above exposure to other forms of childhood abuse (Ehrensaft et al., 2003; Mihalic & Elliott, 1997), although physical child abuse may also increase the risk (Heyman & Slep, 2002). The repeating cycle of partner violence has an early start in the life-course: In a 10-year longitudinal study adolescent girls who as children witnessed the abuse of their mother were more likely to enter abusive dating relationships (McCloskey, 2013). The nuances of gender are often overlooked in social science research on intimate partner violence (Kurz, 1989), yet clearly there are gender-differentiated patterns in both the determinants and the impact.

Child sexual abuse victimization sometimes re-surfaces across generations. Daughters of mothers who had been sexually abused were also more likely to experience sexual abuse compared to controls (Banyard, 1997). Banyard's (1997) study of 430 low-income, single-parent mothers further revealed that the mother's past history of child sexual abuse was associated with her use of physically abusive tactics to settle parent-child conflicts. The odds of the transfer of sexual abuse risk are magnified when the sexually abused mother uses illegal drugs (McCloskey & Bailey, 2000). Mothers with sexual abuse histories are more prone than non-abused mothers to a range of poor parenting practices including neglect and physical abuse (Alexander, 1992). Past sexual abuse also related to diminished feelings of satisfaction in parenting, after adjusting for other forms of past child abuse, depression, and demographics. In a similarly designed study researchers found a weaker overall association between child sexual abuse and subsequent abusive parenting, unless mothers recounted forced intercourse as a child (Zuravin, McMillen, DePanfilis, & Risley-Curtiss, 1996). Child sexual abuse involving intercourse was highly related to mothers' later documented abuse and neglect in Zuravin et al.'s study (1996).

Details about the severity and chronicity of sexual abuse are sometimes overlooked in research, and these results suggest that they may distinguish adverse trajectories for girls growing up to be mothers. In summary, the growing literature on intergenerational transmission, based on the collections of in-depth interviews across decades, point to the existence of a cycle of abuse in families. Such a cycle—propelled by so many forces within and outside the family—can also be interrupted. What mechanisms underlie the continuity or discontinuity of parenting deficiencies remain to be sorted out.

The Transmission of Risk Factors Within Families

All happy families are alike; each unhappy family is unhappy in its own way.—Leo Tolstoy

What follows is a brief overview of some of the evidence for the within-family transmission of several of the *risk factors* for child maltreatment described previously in the chapter, with a focus on poverty, teenage birth and single parenthood, domestic violence, substance use and psychopathology. Some of what gets transmitted in abusive families are the societal and psychosocial catalysts themselves such as poverty, drug addiction, psychopathology. It is worthwhile, therefore to synthesize risk factors which are associated with child maltreatment and which may be inextricably confounded with impaired parenting.

Poverty

About one in five (22 %) of American children lives below the poverty threshold and that statistic has seen little change over the past four decades.[7] Are children in individual families who grow up poor likely to remain poor in adulthood? One study followed 1000 American children between 1 and 4 years of age, starting in 1968 for 15 years with the aim of understanding the transmission of poverty (Boggess & Corcoran, 1999). Although poor children were at strong risk of remaining poor as young adults, more than half—whether African American or White—escaped poverty entirely as young adults (Corcoran & Chaudry, 1997). Some of the risk factors for a cycle of poverty included race (African American), education (less than high school), and family structure (single mother households during childhood). Child poverty is related to family structure: Among eighth graders 16.6 % without fathers in the home were poor in contrast to 9.9 % whose fathers lived with them (Ludwig & Mayer, 2006). Chronic poverty without relief is the strongest risk factor for children remaining poor in adulthood (Haveman, Wolfe & Peterson, 2008). Poverty is

---

[7] National Center on Children in Poverty, Mailman School of Public Health, Columbia University. http://www.nccp.org/topics/childpoverty.html.

not a unitary package, of course, and there are many ways to conceptualize what it means to be poor. Children from poor families have less access to material resources, safe neighborhoods and good schools than families with adequate incomes (Corcoran and Chaudry, 1997, p. 41). The "intensive parenting" visible today in middle and upper class families, with mothers managing an array of extra-curricular activities forges an ever more distant boundary between the achievement of lower and upper class youth in the United States (Romagnoli & Wall, 2012). Additionally mothers may be judged by rapidly rising childcare standards among the middle-class. Americans value the notion of upward mobility, and, indeed, historically, the country offered extensive opportunities to rise above one's class and income origins. Yet today the United States is among the most entrenched countries compared to others in the OECD for income or class mobility: Americans benefit more from their parents' wealth than Europeans, and are more likely to stay poor if their parents were poor than people growing up in Europe (Grusky & Hauser, 1984). Recent analyses of U.S. national administrative income data across several decades show no change in the rates of upward mobility or moving out of poverty since the 1970s (Chetty et al., 2014).

Teenage Pregnancy and Single Parenthood

Adolescent girls who give birth are likely to have mothers who also started families in their teenage years (Horwitz et al., 1991). Prospective studies also confirm the link between the early timing of motherhood in one generation and teenage pregnancy in the next across both African American and White women (Kahn & Anderson, 1992). Girls with sexual abuse histories including incest are also more likely to become pregnant and have a child as teens than non-abused peers (Boyer & Fine, 1992; Noll & Shenk, 2013). The transfer of teenage pregnancy from mothers to daughters for teenage pregnancy evolves from the continuity of social conditions and family dysfunction across the generations. There does not appear to be strong evidence for an intergenerational trend in single motherhood (Haveman et al., 2008).

Alcohol and Drug Use

The concentration of alcoholism in families is well-documented. In a 40-year longitudinal study of working-class families having an alcoholic parent was highly related in adulthood to alcohol dependence or alcoholism (Beardslee, Son, & Vaillant, 1986). Children of alcoholics died prematurely and had more contact with the criminal justice system. In a prospective study of at-risk youth parental alcoholism was the strongest determinant of developing alcohol problems as an adult, even beyond associated depression, anti-social traits of the parents, and harsh parenting

(Chassin, Pitts, DeLucia, & Todd (1999). Women who use drugs or alcohol during pregnancy are more likely to have been raised by parents who were substance abusers, particularly alcoholics (Hans, 1999). In a Swedish study men exhibit alcohol use disorders more than women although heritability is estimated to be the same at 55 % (Magnusson et al., 2012).

Psychopathology

Psychiatric disorders are more prevalent in adults whose parents and family members were also ill. In some cases the psychiatric illness transmitted matches that of the parent, and in other cases different disorders appear. For instance, bipolar disease (Type 1, 2) is highly heritable with concordance for the disorder as high as 40–70 % between monozygotic twins (Craddock & Jones, 1999). Depression is also a familial disorder. In a longitudinal study of women in California researchers found that not only were women more likely to develop major depressive disorder as adults if, in childhood, they experienced their mothers as depressed, and they faced more difficulty regulating their emotions in response to stress (Hammen et al., 2012). A recent study of depressed mothers and their young daughters found that although the daughters were not yet showing symptoms of childhood depression, there was concordance in the cortisol production of mother and child. Before psychological symptoms appear, therefore, an intergenerational synchrony in cortisol dysregulation appear uniquely among girls (LeMoult, Chen, Foland-Ross, Burley, Gotlib, 2015). Women with a history of abuse or current partner violence show elevated traumatic stress symptoms which could also adversely affect their ability to effectively parent (Becker, Stuewig & McCloskey, 2010).

Further Mechanisms in the Intergenerational Transmission of Child Maltreatment

Attachment Derailed

Attachment disorders emanating from neglectful parenting often have enduring effects on social development. Neglected children tend to lack basic social skills with peers (Youngblade & Belsky, 1989), show excessive anxiety in adult romantic attachments (Styron & Janoff-Bulman, 1997), and ultimately they are risk for neglecting their own children as parents (Egeland, Jacobvitz, & Papatola, 1987). Children with maltreatment histories are more likely to show "disorganized" ("D") attachment profiles (Cicchetti & Toth, 1995). Abused children show pronounced signs of clinical depression as early as the preschool years corresponding to insecure maternal attachment (Toth & Cicchetti, 1996). The effects of early attachment disruptions are complex but without a healthy attachment established by early childhood the formation of adult intimate relationships, including that with a child, may be compromised.

Neuroscience and Neurobiology

Children who are maltreated during infancy (birth to three) are more likely than controls to show neurocognitive deficits in middle childhood including impulsivity and poor attention spans (Cowell et al., 2015). The timing of maltreatment has a strong impact on neurobiological outcomes and the youngest children show the most serious decrements (Cicchetti & Toth, 1995; Perry, Pollard, Blakley, Baker, & Vigilante, 1995). Neurocognitive impairments starting in early childhood due to abuse, especially in the areas of language and executive processing, have also been measured (Hackman, Farah, & Meaney, 2010). Injuries to brain development undoubtedly contribute to failures in school performance (Eckenrode, Laird, & Doris, 1993). Arrested cognitive and socio-emotional development in childhood or adolescence may ultimately shape the capability of maternal sensitivity, limiting the flexibility and breadth of maternal responses to their infants. Researchers in neurobiology and developmental psychopathology have found that the earlier the exposure to abuse the more frequent the activation of the HPA axis, resulting in cognitive changes and altered profiles of the brain (Tarullo & Gunnar, 2006). Toddlers exposed to intimate partner violence show dysregulated cortisol production (Sturge-Apple, Davies, Cicchetti, & Manning, 2012). School-aged children exposed to physical or sexual abuse who show depressive symptoms also have disrupted cortisol rhythyms during the day (Cicchetti, Rogosch, Gunnar & Toth, 2010). Symptoms of emotional lability and PTSD have been observed in preschoolers exposed to domestic violence (Graham-Bermann & Levendosky, 1998). How children recover from major assaults on their developing brain is an important research question.

Genetic and Epigenetic Influences

While maltreatment affects children's neurocognitive development, there is mounting evidence that unique genes enhance the probability that child abuse will result in long-term damage to areas of the brain governing emotion self-regulation and reactivity. In a large-scale longitudinal study of maltreated boys, researchers identified the gene which governs activation of the enzyme monoamine oxidase A (MAOA) (Caspi et al., 2002). As it turns out, the boys who lacked this gene were more likely to grow up to become anti-social men than those whose genotype furnished MAOA in large amounts. Inner city women who described early child abuse showed higher levels of limbic dysfunction, notably irritability and depression, in contrast to controls if their karyotypes held one to two copies of the FK506 binding protein 5 gene (FKBP5) (Dackis, Rogosch, Oshri, Cicchetti, 2012) Despite the difficulties in distinguishing genetic from environmental influences these exciting data raise the question of what is being "transmitted" in families with chronic caregiving failures: Potentially a genetic profile which moderates the effects of environmental stress and abuse.

Emotion Regulation and Effortful Control (EC)

Another potential route by which child abuse practices recur in the next generation is through the general trait of impulsivity or low self-control. Effortful control develops in preschool children as they learn to resist temptation, inhibit otherwise primed responses, and self-regulate their behavior and emotions. Effortful control develops throughout childhood and adolescence as structures of the prefrontal cortex mature (Rothbart, 1995). Maltreated preschoolers display less emotion regulation and behavioral self-control than other children, which impedes their social adjustment as illustrated by their reactive aggression with peers (Shields & Cicchetti, 1998). In a prospective study of school-aged children, poor emotion regulation enhanced the risk for childhood depression in school-aged children (Kim-Spoon, Cicchetti, & Rogosch, 2013). Emotion lability-negativity impedes the child's ability to control emotional responses, which a year or two later manifests in childhood depression. Exposure to direct child abuse and domestic violence were equally damaging to children's emotion self-regulation (Maughan & Cicchetti, 2002).

There are also indications that at-risk mothers may be low in self-control. Some of the correlates of maternal child maltreatment (e.g., excessive drinking and drug use) derive from impulsivity. Mothers' failure to adjust their response to infant's crying was measured through skin conductance levels while listening to crying stimuli (Joosen, Mesman, Bakerman-Kranenburg & van Ijzendoorn, 2013). Those mothers who displayed over-reactive sympathetic nervous system responses to infant crying were more likely to show harsh parenting towards their 3-month old. Mothers with a history of child abuse show higher scores on impulsivity, and if they are elevated on impulsivity they achieve higher scores on child abuse potential (Henschel, de Bruin, & Möhler, 2014).

In turn, coercive and unpredictable parenting behavior affects the development of effortful control (EC) in children. Mothers whose children had ADHD were inconsistent in their discipline, less positive, and quick to threaten punishment if they themselves showed symptoms parallel to those of their children (Chronis-Tuscano et al., 2008). Moffitt et al. (2010) discovered links between early effortful control in youngsters and employment, smoking, healthy aging and many measures of adult adjustment at age 38. If impulsivity can be re-programmed and self-control cultivated at early stages of development there is a good chance such cycles could be offset (Moffitt et al., 2010).

Conclusions

It is clear that multiple forms of abuse and stress characterize abusive households. Gender is imbricated throughout the circumstances and attributes underlying maternal caregiving risk. The co-occurrence of child abuse with domestic violence highlights the hidden conflicts relating to power and gender. There is a cycle of child maltreatment, although not deterministic. The cycle of intimate partner violence is stronger for women as victims than it is explaining men's relationship violence. Although underlying psychological dynamics are often invoked to explain repetitions of abusive parenting the evidence suggests that other expressions of family pathology are also transmitted and which may trigger abuse in the next generation. Furthermore, poverty is inextricably associated with child abuse, and the political economy therefore has a part. How women are treated in the culture especially within their roles as mothers or wives is relevant to arriving at a comprehensive explanation of child maltreatment.

Therefore, different experiences, attributes, and genetic markers mitigate or amplify the perpetuation of abuse in families. Some of the areas of risk for child maltreatment may be shared by mothers and fathers, but many are unique to women's role as primary caregiver, especially of infants and young children. In this chapter some of the gender-based influences on women as caregivers have been presented. Poverty is associated with maternal abuse and neglect. The burden it inflicts is more entrenched and long-lasting in the lives of women than in men; there are gender-differentiated trajectories for men and women into and out of poverty that are associated with child abuse. Early childbearing is another widely cited risk for maltreatment, perhaps in part because of the immature response young women may have to children's needs, or because having a child without a partner at an early age generates long-term hardship and stress. Teenage motherhood is not a random event, and family characteristics—from the teenage parenting history of a girl's mother to abuse—increase its likelihood. It is possible that the family dynamics explanation would quickly become irrelevant if teenagers had free access to birth control throughout the country. Substance use and psychopathology are familial, and an abused daughter of an alcoholic parent faces a dual risk of transfer of risk for both alcohol dependence and abuse. Daughters are uniquely sensitive to their mother's depression and the route of transmission starts with the neurobiological synchronization of cortisol production. Finally, there are other characteristics of abused children grown up—dysregulated cortisol and mood lability, low self-control, neurocognitive deficits and poor school achievement—each posing unique territories of risk for parenting deficits. More work in the field is needed to elucidate exactly how and why maltreatment is repeated across the generations.

Women face many hurdles to equality in this country and their gender intersects with other identities including race and class. These experiences and circumstances culminate in their identity as a mother. Addressing the challenges women face because of their gender can elucidate the ways child abuse and neglect transects the generations; an examination of gender in light of social justice can inform interventions and policies surrounding maltreatment. Instead of focusing most efforts on a model of individual change it may be preferable to coalesce to transform policy and communities to eradicate the substrate of risk that gives rise to this costly and terrible human problem. Efforts to eradicate poverty, disseminate birth control to teens, extend support services to new mothers, strengthen battered women's programs, increase child care and provide infant care subsidies, expand access to drug and alcohol treatment could each make a dent in reducing child maltreatment. Each of these domains has special implications for women. More investment in girls and in babies is critical to eliminate child maltreatment whether the aim is ethical, political or economic. City by city, state by state—there is the chance to promote the best environment for childrearing and child development.

References

Aber, J. L., Bennett, N. G., Conley, D. C., & Li, J. (1997). The effects of poverty on child health and development. *Annual review of public health, 18*, 463–483.

Alexander, P. C. (1992). Application of attachment theory to the study of sexual abuse. *Journal of Consulting and Clinical Psychology, 60*, 185–195.

Appel, A. E., & Holden, G. W. (1998). The co-occurrence of spouse and physical child abuse: A review and appraisal. *Journal of Family Psychology, 12*, 578–599.

Appleyard, K., Egeland, B., van Dulman, M., & Sroufe, L. A. (2005). When more is not better: The role of cumulative risk in child behavior outcomes. *Journal of Child Psychology and Psychiatry, 46*, 235–245.

Azar, S. T., Stevenson, M. T., & Johnson, D. R. (2012). Intellectual disabilities and neglectful parenting: Preliminary findings on the role of cognition in parenting risk. *Journal of Mental Health Research in Intellectual Disabilities, 5*, 94–129.

Bailey, J. A., Hill, K. G., Oesterle, S., & Hawkins, J. D. (2009). Parenting practices and problem behavior across three generations: Monitoring, harsh discipline, and drug use in the intergenerational transmission of externalizing behavior. *Developmental psychology, 45*, 1214.

Banyard, V. L. (1997). The impact of childhood sexual abuse and family functioning on four dimensions of women's later parenting. *Child Abuse & Neglect, 21*(11), 1095–1107.

Banyard, V. L., Williams, L. M., & Siegel, J. A. (2003). The impact of complex trauma and depression on parenting: An exploration of mediating risk and protective factors. *Child Maltreatment, 8*(4), 334–349.

Barratt, M. S., & Roach, M. A. (1995). Early interactive processes: Parenting by adolescent and adult single mothers. *Infant Behavior and Development, 18*, 97–109.

Bartlett, J. D., & Easterbrooks, M. A. (2012). Links between physical abuse in childhood and child neglect among adolescent mothers. *Children and youth services review, 34*(11), 2164–2169.

Beardslee, W. R., Son, L., & Vaillant, G. E. (1986). Exposure to parental alcoholism during childhood and outcome in adulthood: A prospective longitudinal study. *The British Journal of Psychiatry, 149*, 584–591.

Becker, K. D., Stuewig, J., & McCloskey, L. A. (2010). Traumatic stress symptoms of women exposed to different forms of childhood victimization and intimate partner violence. *Journal of Interpersonal Violence, 25*, 1699–1715.

Belsky, J. (1993). Etiology of child maltreatment: A developmentalϵ cological analysis. *Psychological Bulletin, 114*, 413.

Belsky, J., & Pluess, M. (2009). Beyond diathesis stress: Differential susceptibility to environmental influences. *Psychological Bulletin, 135*(6), 885.

Belsky, J., Conger, R., & Capaldi, D. M. (2009). The intergenerational transmission of parenting: Introduction to the special section. *Developmental Psychology, 45*(5), 1201.

Belsky, J., Hancox, R. J., Sligo, J., & Poulton, R. (2012). Does being an older parent attenuate the intergenerational transmission of parenting? *Developmental Psychology, 48*, 1570–1574.

Bianchi, S. M., Sayer, L. C., Milkie, M. A., & Robinson, J. P. (2012). Housework: Who did, does or will do it, and how much does it matter? *Social Forces, 91*, 55–63.

Bitler, M., & Zavodny, M. (2002). Child Abuse and Abortion Availability. *The American Economic Review, 92*, 363–367.

Blurton Jones, N. (1986). Bushman birth spacing: A test for optimal interbirth intervals. *Ethology and Sociobiology, 7*(2), 91–105.

Boyer, D., & Fine, D. (1992). Sexual abuse as a factor in adolescent pregnancy and child maltreatment. *Family Planning Perspectives, 24*, 4–19.

Boggess, S., & Corcoran, M. (1999). Cycles of disadvantage? In S. Boggess, M. Corcoran, & S. Jenkins (Eds.), *Cycles of disadvantage?* Institute of Policy Studies: Wellington.

Brown, J., Cohen, P. J. G., Johnson, J. G., & Salzinger, S. (1998). A longitudinal analysis of risk factors for child maltreatment: Findings of a 17-year prospective study of officially recorded and self-reported child abuse and neglect. *Child Abuse and Neglect, 22*, 1065–1078.

Bronfenbrennner, U. (1979). *Ecology of human development: Experiments by nature and design.* New York, NY: Cornell University Press.

Burnette, C. E., Ferreira, R. J., & Buttell, F. (2015). Male parenting attitudes and batterer intervention: Assessing maltreatment risk. *Research on Social Work Practice.* doi:10.1177/1049731515579202.

Caspi, A., McClay, J., Moffitt, T. E., Mill, J., Martin, J., Craig, I. W., ... Poulton, R. (2002). Role of genotype in the cycle of violence in maltreated children. *Science, 297*, 851–854.

Chaffin, M., Kelleher, K., & Hollenberg, J. (1996). Onset of physical abuse and neglect: Psychiatric, substance abuse, and social risk factors from prospective community data. *Child Abuse and Neglect, 20*, 191–203.

Chassin, L., Pitts, S. C., DeLucia, C., & Todd, M. (1999). A longitudinal study of children of alcoholics: Predicting young adult substance use disorders, anxiety, and depression. *Journal of Abnormal Psychology, 108*(1), 106.

Chetty, R., Hendren, N., Kline, P., Saez, E., & Turner, N. (2014). Is the United States still a land opportunity? Recent trends in intergenerational mobility. *American Economic Review Papers and Proceedings, 104*.

Chodorow, N. J. (1999). *The reproduction of mothering: Psychoanalysis and the sociology of gender.* University of California Press.

Chronis-Tuscano, A., Raggi, V. L., Clarke, T. L., Rooney, M. E., Diaz, Y., & Pian, J. (2008). Maternal Attention-Deficit/Hyperactivity Disorder Symptoms and Parenting. *Journal of Abnormal Child Psychology, 36*, 1237–1250.

Cicchetti, D., Rogosch, F. A., Gunnar, M. R., & Toth, S. L. (2010). The differential impacts of early physical and sexual abuse and internalizing problems on daytime cortisol rhythm in school-aged children. *Child Development, 81*, 252–269.

Cicchetti, D., Rogosch, F. A., & Toth, S. L. (1998). Maternal depressive disorder and contextual risk: Contributions to the development of attachment insecurity and behavior problems in toddlerhood. *Development and psychopathology, 10*, 283–300.

Cicchetti, D., & Toth, S. L. (1995). A developmental psychopathology perspective on child abuse and neglect. *Journal of the American Academy of Child & Adolescent Psychiatry, 34*, 541–565.

Cicchetti, D., & Toth, S. L. (2005). Child maltreatment. *Annual Review of Clinical Psychology, 1*, 409–438.

Cohen, D., & Nisbett, R. E. (1994). Self-protection and the culture of honor: Explaining southern violence. *Personality and Social Psychology Bulletin, 20*, 551–567.

Coltrane, S., & Ishii-Kuntz, M. (1992). Men's housework: A life course perspective. *Journal of Marriage and the Family, 54*(1), 43–57

Cort, N. A., Toth, S. L., Cerulli, C., & Rogosch, F. (2011). Maternal intergenerational transmission of childhood multitype maltreatment. *Journal of Aggression, Maltreatment & Trauma, 20*, 20–39.

Corcoran, M., & Chaudry, A. (1997). The dynamics of childhood poverty. *The Future of Children, 7*(2), 40–54.

Cowell, R. A., Cicchetti, D., Rogosch, F. A., & Toth, S. L. (2015). Childhood maltreatment and its effect on neurocognitive functioning: Timing and chronicity matter. *Development and Psychopathology, 27*, 521–533.

Craddock, N., & Jones, I. (1999). Genetics of bipolar disorder. *Journal of Medical Genetics, 36*, 585–594.

Craig, L. (2007). Is there really a second shift, and if so, who does it? a time-diary investigation. *Feminist Review, 86*, 149–170.

Cummings, E. M., & Davies, P. T. (1994). Maternal depression and child development. *Journal of Child Psychology and Psychiatry, 35*, 73–112.

Currie, J., & Tekin, E. (2012). Understanding the cycle: Childhood maltreatment and future crime. *Journal of Human Resources, 7*, 1–41.

Dackis, M. N., Rogosch, F. A., Oshri, A., & Cicchetti, D. (2012). The role of limbic system irritability in linking history of childhood maltreatment and psychiatric outcomes in low-income, high-risk women: Moderation by FK506 binding protein 5 haplotype. *Development and psychopathology, 24*, 1237–1252.

Danese, A., Moffitt, T. E., Harrington, H., Milne, B. J., Polanczyk, G., Pariante, C. M., … Caspi, A. (2009). Adverse childhood experiences and adult risk factors for age-related disease. *Archives of Pediatrics and Adolescent Medicine, 163*, 1135–1143.

Daro, D. (2010). *Child abuse prevention: A job half done.* Chicago: Chapin Hall at the University of Chicago.

Davies, P. T., & Lindsay, L. L. (2004). Interparental conflict and adolescent adjustment: Why does gender moderate early adolescent vulnerability? *Journal of Family Psychology, 18*, 160.

Davies, P. T., & Windle, M. (1997). Gender-specific pathways between maternal depressive symptoms, family discord, and adolescent adjustment. *Developmental Psychology, 33*, 57–668.

Dawes, R. (1993). Prediction of the future versus an understanding of the past: A basic asymmetry. *The American Journal of Psychology, 106*, 1–24.

Dong, M., Anda, R. F., Felitti, V. J., Dube, S. R., Williamson, D. F., Thompson, T. J., … Giles, W. H. (2004). The interrelatedness of multiple forms of childhood abuse, neglect, and household dysfunction. *Child Abuse & Neglect, 28*, 771–784.

Dubowitz, H., Papas, M. S., Black, M. M., & Starr, R. H. (2002). Child Neglect: Outcomes in High-Risk Urban Preschoolers. *Pediatrics, 109*, 1100–1107.

Dubowitz, H., Pitts, S. C., & Black, M. M. (2004). The measurement of three major subtypes of neglect. *Child Maltreatment, 9*, 344–356.

Eckenrode, J., Laird, M., & Doris, J. (1993). School performance and disciplinary problems among abused and neglected children. *Developmental Psychology, 29*(1), 53.

Edwards, V., Holden, G. W., Felitti, V. J., & Anda, R. F. (2003). Relationship between multiple forms of childhood maltreatment: Implications for practice, policy and research. *American Journal of Psychiatry, 160*, 1453–1461.

Egeland, B., Jacobvitz, D., & Papatola, K. (1987). Intergenerational continuity of abuse. *Child Abuse and Neglect: Biosocial Dimensions, 82*, 255–276.

Ehrensaft, M. K., Cohen, P., Brown, J., Smailes, E., Chen, H., & Johnson, J. G. (2003). Intergenerational transmission of partner violence: A 20-year prospective study. *Journal of Consulting and Clinical Psychology, 71*, 741–753.

Fagnani, J. (2012). Recent reforms in childcare and family policies in France and Germany: What was at stake? *Children and Youth Services Review, 34*, 509–516.

Famularo, R., Kinscherff, R., & Fenton, T. (1992). Parental substance abuse and the nature of child maltreatment. *Child Abuse & Neglect, 16*, 475–483.

Fang, X., Brown, D. S., Florence, C. S., & Mercy, J. A. (2012). The economic burden of child maltreatment in the United States and implications for prevention. *Child Abuse & Neglect, 36*, 156–165.

Fantuzzo, J., Boruch, R., Beriama, A., Atkins, M., & Marcus, S. (1997). Domestic violence and children: Prevalence and risk in five major U.S. cities. *Journal of the American Academy of Child and Adolescent Psychiatry, 36*, 116–122.

Felitti, V. J., Anda, R. F., Nordenberg, D., Williamson, D. F., Spitz, A. M., Edwards, V., ... Marks, J. S. (1998). Relationship of childhood abuse and household dysfunction to many of the leading causes of death in adults: The Adverse Childhood Experiences (ACE) Study. *American Journal of Preventive Medicine, 14*, 245–258.

Fergusson, D. M., Boden, J. M., & Horwood, L. J. (2006). Examining the intergenerational transmission of violence in a New Zealand birth cohort. *Child abuse & neglect, 30*, 89–108.

Field, T. M., Widmayer, S. M., Stringer, S. E., & Ignatoff, E. (1980). Teenage, lower-class, Black mothers and their preterm infants: An Intervention and Developmental Follow-Up. *Child Development, 51*, 426–436.

Finkelhor, D. (2008). *Childhood victimization: Violence, crime and abuse in the lives of young People.* New York: Oxford University Press.

Finkelhor, D., & Jones, L. (2006). Why have child maltreatment and child victimization declined? *Journal of Social Issues, 62*, 685–716.

Garbarino, J. (1976). A preliminary study of some ecological correlates of child abuse: The impact of socioeconomic stress on mothers. *Child Development, 47*, 178–185.

Gelfand, D. M., & Teti, D. M. (1990). The effects of maternal depression on children. *Clinical Psychology Review, 10*, 329–353.

Geronimus, A. T., Korenman, S., & Hillemeier, M. M. (1994). Does young maternal age adversely affect child development? Evidence from cousin comparisons in the United States. *Population and Development Review, 20*, 585–609.

Gershoff, E. T. (2002). Corporal punishment by parents and associated child behaviors and experiences: A meta-analytic and theoretical review. *Psychological Bulletin, 128*, 539–579.

Giovannoni, J. (1989). Definitional issues in child maltreatment. In D. Cicchetti & Carlson, V. (Eds.) *Child Maltreatment: Theory and research on the causes and consequences of child abuse and neglect.* Cambridge: Cambridge University Press.

Goerge, R. M., & Bong, J. L. (1996). Abuse and neglect of the children. In R. Maynard (Ed.), *Kids having kids: Economic costs and social consequences of teen pregnancy.* Washington, DC: Urban Institute.

Goerge, R. M., & Lee, B. J. (1997). Child abuse and neglect. In R. Maynard (Ed.), *Kids having kids* (pp. 205–230). Washington, DC: Urban Institute Press.

Graham-Bermann, S. A., & Levendosky, A. A. (1998). Traumatic stress symptoms in children of battered women. *Journal of Interpersonal Violence, 13*(1), 111–128.

Graham-Bermann, S., & Seng, J. (2005). Violence exposure and traumatic stress symptoms as additional predictors of health problems in high-risk children. *Journal of Pediatrics, 146*, 349–354.

Grusky, D. B., & Hauser, R. M. (1984). Comparative social mobility revisited: Models of convergence and divergence in 16 countries. *American Sociological Review, 49*, 19–38.

Hackman, D. A., Farah, M. J., & Meaney, M. J. (2010). Socioeconomic status and the brain: Mechanistic insights from human and animal research. *Nature Reviews Neuroscience, 11*(9), 651–659.

Hall, K. S., Moreau, C., & Trussell, J. (2012). Determinants of and disparities in reproductive health service use among adolescent and young adult women in the United States, 2002–2008. *American Journal of Public Health, 102*, 359–367.

Hamby, S., Finkelhor, D., & Turner, H. (2010). The overlap of witnessing partner violence with Child maltreatment and other victimizations in a nationally representative survey of youth. *Child Abuse and Neglect, 34*, 734–741.

Hammen, C. (2005). Stress and depression. *Annual Review of Clinical Psychology, 1*, 293–319.

Hammen, C. (2012). Interpersonal stress and depression in women. *Journal of Affective Disorders, 74*, 49–57.

Hammen, C., Hazel, N. A., Brennan, P. A., & Najman, J. (2012). Intergenerational transmission and continuity of stress and depression: Depressed women and their offspring in 20 years of follow-up. *Psychological medicine, 42*, 931–942.

Hans, S. L. (1999). Demographic and psychosocial characteristics of substance-abusing pregnant women. *Clinics in Perinatology, 26*, 55–74.

Haveman, R., Wolfe, B., & Peterson, E. (2008). Consequences of teen childbearing for the life chances of children, 1968–88. *Kids having kids: Economic costs and social consequences of teen pregnancy* (pp. 324–341).

Heckman, J., & Carneiro, P. (2003). *Human capital policy* (No. w9495). National Bureau of Economic Research.

Henschel, S., de Bruin, M., & Möhler, E. (2014). Self-control and child abuse potential in mothers with an abuse history and their preschool children. *Journal of Child and Family Studies, 23*, 824–836.

Herman-Giddens, M. E., Brown, G., Verbiest, S., Carlson, P. J., Hooten, E. G., Howell, E., & Butts, J. D. (1999). Underascertainment of child abuse mortality in the United States. *JAMA, 282*(5), 463–467.

Herrenkohl, T., Sousa, c., Tajima, e., Herrenkohl, R. C., & Moylan, C. A. (2008). Intersection of child abuse and children's exposure to domestic violence. *Trauma, Violence and Abuse, 9*, 84–99.

Heyman, R. E., & Slep, A. M. (2002). Do child abuse and interparental violence lead to adulthood family violence? *Journal of Marriage and Family, 64*, 864–870.

Hochschild, A. (1992). *The second shift*. Berkeley: University of California Press.

Holden, G. W., & Ritchie, K. L. (1991). Linking extreme marital discord, child rearing, and child behavior problems: Evidence from battered women. *Child Development, 62*(2), 311–327.

Holtzworth-Munroe, A., Stuart, G.L., & Hutchinson, G. (1997) Violent versus non-violent husbands: DIfferences in attachment patterns, dependency and jealousy. *Journal of Family Psychology, 11(3)*, 314.

Horwitz, S. M., Klerman, L. V., Kuo, H. S., & Jekel, J. F. (1991). Intergenerational transmission of school-age parenthood. *Family Planning Perspectives, 23*, 168–177.

Hunter, R. S., & Kilstrom, N. (1979). Breaking the cycle in abusive families. *The American Journal of Psychiatry, 136*, 1320–1322.

Huth-Bocks, A., Levendosky, A. A., Theran, S. A., & Bogat, G. A. (2004). The impact of Domestic violence on mothers' prenatal representations of their infants. *Infant Mental Health Journal, 25*, 79–98.

Inhorn, M. C., Ceballo, R., & Nachtigall, R. (2009). Marginalized, invisible, and unwanted: American minority struggles with infertility and assisted conception. In L. Culley, N. Hudson, & F. Van Rooij (Eds.), *Marginalized reproduction: Ethnicity, infertility and reproductive technologies*, (Ch. 11, pp. 181–197). London: Earthscan Publishers.

Jaffee, S. R., Bowes, L., Ouellet-Morin, I., Fisher, H. L., Moffitt, T. E., Merrick, M. T., & Arseneault, L. (2013). Safe, stable, nurturing relationships break the intergenerational cycle of abuse: A prospective nationally representative cohort of children in the United Kingdom. *Journal of Adolescent Health, 53*(4), S4–S10.

Joosen, K. J., Mesman, J., Bakermans-Kranenburg, M. J., & van IJzendoorn, M. H. (2013). Maternal overreactive sympathetic nervous system responses to repeated infant crying predicts risk for impulsive harsh discipline of infants. *Child Maltreatment, 18*, 252–263.

Kahn, J. R., & Anderson, K. E. (1992). Intergenerational patterns of teenage fertility. *Demography, 29*(1), 39–57.

Kaufman, J., & Zigler, E. (1987). Do abused children become abusive parents? *American Journal of Orthopsychiatry, 57*(2), 186–198.

Keenan, H. T., Runyan, D. K., Marshall, S. W., Nocera, M. A., Merten, D. F., & Sinal, S. H. (2003). A population-based study of inflicted traumatic brain injury in young children. *JAMA, 290(5)*, 621–626.

Kelleher, K., Chaffin, M., Hollenberg, J., & Fischer, E. (1994). Alcohol and drug disorders among physically abusive and neglectful parents in a community-based sample. *American Journal of Public Health, 84*, 1586–1590.

Kempe, C. H., Silverman, F. N., Steele, B. F., Droegemueller, W., & Silver, H. K. (1962). Battered child syndrome. *JAMA, 181*, 17–27.

Kendler, K. S., Bulik, C. M., Silberg, J., Hettema, J. M., Myers, J., & Prescott, C. A. (2000) Childhood sexual abuse and adult psychiatric and substance use disorders in women: An epidemiological and Co-twin control analysis *Archives of General Psychiatry, 57*, 953–959.

Kim-Spoon, J., Cicchetti, D., & Rogosch, F. A. (2013). A longitudinal study of emotion regulation, emotion lability-negativity, and internalizing symptomatology in maltreated and nonmaltreated children. *Child Development, 84*(2), 512–527.

Knudsen, E. L., Heckman, J. J., Cameron, J. L., & Shonkoff, J. P. (2006). Economic, Neurobiological, and Behavioral Perspectives on Building America's Future Workforce. *Proceedings of the National Academy of Sciences, 103*, 10155–10162.

Kost, K., & Henshaw, S. (2012). *US teenage pregnancies, births and abortions, 2008: National trends by age, race and ethnicity*. New York: Guttmacher Institute.

Kotch, J. B., Browne, D. C., Ringwalt, C. L., Stewart, P. W., Ruina, E., Holt, K., et al. (1995). Risk of child abuse or neglect in a cohort of low-income children. *Child Abuse & Neglect, 19*, 1115–1130.

Kurz, D. (1989). Social science perspectives on wife abuse: Current debates and future directions. *Gender & Society, 3*, 489–505.

Laslett, A. M., Room, R., Dietze, P., & Ferris, J. (2012). Alcohol's involvement in recurrent child abuse and neglect cases. *Addiction, 107*, 1786–1793.

Lee, B. J., & Goerge, R. M. (1999). Poverty, early childbearing, and child maltreatment: A multinomial analysis. *Children and Youth Services Review, 21*, 755–780.

LeMoult, J., Chen, M. C., Foland-Ross, L. C., Burley, H. W., & Gotlib, I. H. (2015). Concordance of mother–daughter diurnal cortisol production: Understanding the intergenerational transmission of risk for depression. *Biological Psychology, 108*, 98–104.

Lester, B. M., Garcia-Coll, C. T., & Valcarcel, M. (1988). Perception of infant cries in adolescent and adult mothers. *Journal of Youth and Adolescence, 18*, 231–243.

Levendosky, A. A., & Graham-Bermann, S. A. (2000). Behavioral observations of parenting in battered women. *Journal of Family Psychology, 14*(1), 80.

Levendosky, A. A., Lannert, B., & Yalch, M. (2012). The effects of intimate partner violence on women and child survivors: An attachment perspective. *Psychodynamic Psychiatry, 40*(3), 397–433.

Levesque, R. J. (2001). Family violence and cultural life. In R. J. Levesque (Ed.), *Culture and family violence: Fostering change through human rights law. Law and public policy* (pp. 39–65). Washington, DC: American Psychological Association.

Ludwig, J., & Mayer, S. E. (2006). "Culture" and the Intergenerational Transmission of Poverty: The Prevention Paradox. *The Future of Children, 16*(2), 175–196.

Magdol, L., Moffitt, T. E., Caspi, A., & Silva, P. A. (1998). Developmental antecedents of partner abuse: A prospective-longitudinal study. *Journal of Abnormal Psychology, 107*, 375–390.

Magnusson, Å., Lundholm, C., Göransson, M., Copeland, W., Heilig, M., & Pedersen, N. L. (2012). Familial influence and childhood trauma in female alcoholism. *Psychological Medicine, 42*, 381–389.

Markowitz, S., & Grossman, M. (2000). The effects of beer taxes on physical child abuse. *Journal of Health Economics, 19*, 271–282.

Maughan, A., & Cicchetti, D. (2002). Impact of child maltreatment and inter-adult violence on children's emotion regulation abilities and socioemotional adjustment. *Child Development, 73*, 1525–1542.

Maynard, R. A. (1996). The study, the context and the findings in brief. In R. Maynard (Ed.), *Kids having kids: Economic costs and social consequences of teen Pregnancy*. Washington, DC: Urban Institute Press.

McCloskey, L. A. (2001). The" Medea complex" among men: The instrumental abuse of children to injure wives. *Violence and Victims, 16*, 19–38.

McCloskey, L. A. (2013). The intergenerational transfer of mother-daughter risk for gender-based abuse. *Psychodynamic Psychiatry, 41*, 303–328.

Mccloskey, L. A., & Bailey, J. A. (2000). The intergenerational transmission of risk for child sexual abuse. *Journal of Interpersonal Violence, 15*(10), 1019–1035.

McCloskey, L. A., Figueredo, A. J., & Koss, M. P. (1995). The effects of systemic family violence on children's mental health. *Child Development, 66*, 1239–1261.

McDonald, R., Jouriles, E. N., Ramisetty-Mikler, S., Caetano, R., & Green, C. E. (2006). Estimating the number of American children living in partner-violent families. *Journal of Family Psychology, 20*, 137.

McDonald, S., Wall, J., Forbes, K., Kingston, D., Kehler, H., Vekved, M., & Tough, S. (2012). Development of a prenatal psychosocial screening tool for post-partum depression and anxiety. *Paediatric and Perinatal Epidemiology, 26*, 316–327.

McLanahan, S. S. (1999). Father absence and the welfare of children. In E. M. Hetherington (Ed.), *Coping with divorce, single parenting and re-marriage*. New Jersey: Lawrence Erlbaum.

McLanahan, S. S., & Kelly, E. L. (2006). The feminization of poverty. In *Handbook of the sociology of gender* (pp. 127–145). Springer US.

Mihalic, S. W., & Elliott, D. (1997). A social learning theory model of marital violence. *Journal of Family Violence, 12*, 21–47.

Miller, B. A., Downs, W. R., Gondoli, D. M., & Keil, A. (1987). The role of childhood sexual abuse in the development of alcoholism in women. *Violence and Victims, 2*, 157–172.

Moffitt, T. E., Arseneault, L., Belsky, D., Dickson, C., Hancox, R. J., Harrington, H. L., ... Poulton, R. (2010). A gradient of childhood self-control predicts health, wealth, and public safety. *Proceedings of the National Academy of Sciences of the United States of America, 108*, 2693–2698

Neppl, T. K., Conger, R. D., Scaramella, L. V., & Ontai, L. L. (2009). Intergenerational continuity in parenting behavior: Mediating pathways and child effects. *Developmental Psychology, 45*(5), 1241–1249.

Noll, J. G., & Shenk, C. E. (2013). Teen birth rates in sexually abused and neglected females. *Pediatrics, 131*(4), e1181–e1187.

Nussbaum, M. (2003). Capabilities as fundamental entitlements: Sen and social justice. *Feminist Economics, 9*, 33–59.

O'hara, M. W., & Swain, A. M. (1996). Rates and risk of postpartum depression-a meta-analysis. *International Review of Psychiatry, 8*, 37–54.

Olds, D. L., Robinson, J., O'Brien, R., Luckey, D. W., Pettitt, L. M., Henderson, C. R., ... Talmi, A. (2002). Home visiting by paraprofessionals and by nurses: A randomized, controlled trial. *Pediatrics, 110*, 486–496.

Orshansky, M. (1965). Counting the poor: Another look at the poverty profile. *Social Security Bulletin, 28*, 3–29.

Paxson, C., & Waldfogel, J. (1999). Parental resources and child abuse and neglect. *American Economic Review, 28*, 239–244.

Pearce, D. (1978). The feminization of poverty: Women, work and welfare. *Urban and Social Change Review, 11*, 28–36.

Pears, K. C., & Capaldi, D. M. (2001). Intergenerational transmission of abuse: A two-generational prospective study of an at-risk sample. *Child Abuse & Neglect, 25*, 1439–1461.

Perry, B. D., Pollard, R. A., Blakley, T. L., Baker, W. L., & Vigilante, D. (1995). Childhood trauma, the neurobiology of adaptation, and use dependent development of the brain: How states become traits? *Infant mental health journal, 16*, 271–291.

Rogers, S. J., & White, L. K. (1998). Satisfaction with parenting: The role of marital happiness, family structure, and parents' gender. *Journal of Marriage and the Family, 60*, 293–308.

Romagnoli, A., & Wall, G. (2012). 'I know I'm a good mom': Young, low-income mothers' experiences with risk perception, intensive parenting ideology and parenting education programmes. *Health, Risk & Society, 14*(3), 273–289.

Roosa, M. W., Tein, J., Reinholtz, C., & Angelini, P. J. (1997). The relationship of childhood sexual abuse to teenage pregnancy. *Journal of Marriage and Family, 59*, 119–130.

Rothbart, M. K. (1995). Concept and method in contemporary temperament research. *Psychological Inquiry, 6*(4), 334–348.

Russo, N. F. (1976). The motherhood mandate. *Journal of Social Issues, 32*, 143–153.

Rutter, M. E. (1988). *Studies of psychosocial risk: The power of longitudinal data*. Cambridge: Cambridge University Press.

Sameroff, A. J., & Chandler, M. J. (1975). Reproductive risk and the continuum of caretaking causality. In F. D. Horowitz, M. Hetherington, S. Scarr-Salapatek, & G. Siegel (Eds.), *Review of child development research* (pp. 187–244). Chicago: University of Chicago.

Sameroff, A., Seifer, R., Zax, M., & Barocas, R. (1987). Early indicators of developmental risk: Rochester Longitudinal Study. *Schizophrenia Bulletin, 13*, 383.

Scheper-Hughes, N. (1992). *Death without weeping: The violence of everyday life in Brazil.* Berkeley, CA: University of California Press.

Sedlak, A. J., Mettenburg, J., Basena, M., Petta, I., McPherson, K., Greene, A., & Li, S. (2010). *Fourth national incidence study of child abuse and neglect (NIS-4): Report to Congress, executive summary.* Washington, DC: U.S. Department of Health and Human Services, Administration for Children and Families.

Shields, A., & Cicchetti, D. (1998). Reactive aggression among maltreated children: The contributions of attention and emotion dysregulation. *Journal of Clinical Child Psychology, 27*(4), 381–395.

Shonkoff, J. P., & Garner, A. S. (2012). The lifelong effects of early childhood adversity and toxic stress. *Pediatrics, 129*, e232–e246.

Simons, R. L., Whitbeck, L. B., Conger, R. D., & Wu, C. (1991). Intergenerational transmission of harsh parenting. *Developmental Psychology, 27*, 159–171.

Steinberg, L. D., Catalano, R., & Dooley, D. (1981). Economic antecedents of child abuse and neglect. *Child Development, 52*, 975–985.

Stevens, T. N., Ruggiero, K. J., Kilpatrick, D. G., Resnick, H. S., & Saunders, B. E. (2005). Variables differentiating singly and multiply victimized youth: Results from the national survey of adolescents and implications for secondary prevention. *Child Maltreatment, 10*, 211–223.

Stier, D., Leventhal, J., Berg, A., Johnson, L., & Mezger, J. (1993). Are children born to young mothers at increased risk of maltreatment? *Pediatrics, 91*, 642–648.

Stiffman, M. N., Schnitzer, P. G., Adam, P., Kruse, R. L., & Ewigman, B. G. (2002). Household composition and risk of fatal child maltreatment. *Pediatrics, 109*, 615–621.

Straus, M. A., & Mouradian, V. E. (1998). Impulsive corporal punishment by mothers and antisocial behavior and impulsiveness of children. *Behavioral Sciences and the Law, 16*, 353–374.

Sturge-Apple, M. L., Davies, P. T., Cicchetti, D., & Manning, L. G. (2012). Interparental violence, maternal emotional unavailability and children's cortisol functioning in family contexts. *Developmental Psychology, 48*(1), 237.

Styron, T., & Janoff-Bulman, R. (1997). Childhood attachment and abuse: Long-term effects on adult attachment, depression, and conflict resolution. *Child Abuse & Neglect, 21*, 1015–1023.

Sullivan, P. M., & Knutson, J. F. (2000). Maltreatment and disabilities: A population-based epidemiological study. *Child Abuse & Neglect, 24*, 1257–1273.

Tarullo, A. R., & Gunnar, M. R. (2006). Child maltreatment and the developing HPA axis. *Hormones and Behavior, 50*(4), 632–639.

Teti, D., & Gelfand, D. (1991). Behavioral competence among mothers of infants in the first year: The mediational role of maternal self-efficacy. *Child Development, 62*, 918–929.

Thompson, M. P., Kaslow, N. J., Kingree, J. B., Rashid, A., Puett, R., Jacobs, D., & Matthews, A. (2000). Partner violence, social support, and distress among inner-city African American women. *American Journal of Community Psychology, 28*, 127–143.

Toth, S. L., & Cicchetti, D. (1996). Patterns of relatedness, depressive symptomatology, and perceived competence in maltreated children. *Journal of Consulting and Clinical Psychology, 64*, 32.

Trocmé, N., Knoke, D., Fallon, B., & MacLaurin, B. (2008). Differentiating between substantiated, suspected, and unsubstantiated maltreatment in Canada. *Child Maltreatment.*

Walsh, C., MacMillan, H. L., & Jamieson, E. (2003). The relationship between parental substance abuse and child maltreatment: Findings from the Ontario Health Supplement. *Child Abuse & Neglect, 27*, 1409–1425.

Werner, E. E., & Smith, R. S. (1992). *Overcoming the odds: High risk children from birth to adulthood.* Cornell University Press.

Widom, C. S., Czaja, S. J., & DuMont, K. A. (2015). Intergenerational transmission of child abuse and neglect: Real or detection bias? *Social Science, 347*, 1480–1485.

Wolfe, D. A., & Jaffe, P. (1991). Child abuse and family violence as determinants of child psycho-pathology. *Canadian Journal of Behavioural Science, 23*, 282–299.

Yargawa, J., & Leonardi-Bee, J. (2015). Male involvement and maternal health outcomes: Systematic review and meta-analysis. *Journal of Epidemiology and Community Health*. doi:10.1136/jech-2014-204784.

Youngblade, L. M., & Belsky, J. (1989). Child maltreatment, infant-parent attachment security, and dysfunctional peer relationships in toddlerhood. *Topics in Early Childhood Special Education, 9*(2), 1–15.

Zinzow, H. M., Ruggiero, K. J., Resnick, H., Hanson, R., Smith, D., Saunders, B., & Kilpatrick, D. (2009). Prevalence and mental health correlates of witnessed parental and community violence in a national sample of adolescents. *Journal of Child Psychology and Psychiatry, 50*, 441–450.

Zolotof, A. J., Theodore, A. D., Runyan, D. K., Chang, J. J., & Laskey, A. L. (2011). Corporal punishment and physical abuse: Population-based trends for three-to-11-year-old children in the United States. *Child Abuse Review, 1*, 57–66.

Zuravin, S. J. (1988). Fertility Patterns: Their Relationship to Child Physical Abuse and Child Neglect. *Journal of Marriage and Family, 50*, 983–993.

Zuravin, S., McMillen, C., DePanfilis, D., & Risley-Curtiss, C. (1996). The intergenerational cycle of child maltreatment continuity versus discontinuity. *Journal of Interpersonal Violence, 11*, 315–334.

Environments Recreated: The Unique Struggles of Children Born to Abused Mothers

Jennie G. Noll, Jonathan M. Reader, and Heather Bensman

Overview

The intergenerational transmission of child maltreatment is a complicated and complex issue. Our field's dialog around transmission has historically been conceptualized in terms of the probability that those who were child abuse victims go on to abuse their own children. Some early research by Joan Kaufman and Ed Ziegler (1987) put forth estimates that roughly 30 % of victims would go on to become abusers themselves. However, these estimates were primarily based on physical abuse perpetration and the extent to which victims of physical abuse commit physical abuse of their own children. As such, this estimate is limited and does not take into account the transmission of other types of abuse, including sexual abuse, emotional abuse or child neglect. As such, true estimates are essentially unknown. This issue is further complicated by the fact that there are likely differing pathways for the transmission that are distinct to differing forms of abuse and neglect. For

J.G. Noll, Ph.D. (✉)
Department of Human Development and Family Studies, The Pennsylvania State University, State College, PA, USA

Network on Child Protection and Wellbeing, The Pennsylvania State University, University Park, PA, USA
e-mail: jgn3@psu.edu

J.M. Reader
Department of Human Development and Family Studies, The Pennsylvania State University, State College, PA, USA
e-mail: jmr5285@psu.edu

H. Bensman, Psy.D.
Division of Behavioral Medicine and Clinical Psychology, Cincinnati Children's Hospital Medical Center, Cincinnati, OH, USA
e-mail: Heather.Bensman@cchmc.org

© Springer International Publishing Switzerland 2017
D.M. Teti (ed.), *Parenting and Family Processes in Child Maltreatment and Intervention*, Child Maltreatment Solutions Network,
DOI 10.1007/978-3-319-40920-7_5

example, we might think about impoverished, neglectful environments persisting across the life course such that children born into the next generation experience physical neglect (Knutson, DeGarmo, & Reid, 2004). We might also think of violent and reactive punishment styles adopted as viable parenting strategies for victims of physical abuse (Milner, 1993; Milner & Chilamkurti, 1991). For victims of sexual abuse, we might think about cognitive distortions, confusion around sexual boundaries, and the inability to control sexual impulses and other compulsions that may describe the transmission process of sexual abuse for sexual abuse victims (Kwako, Noll, Putnam, & Trickett, 2010). We know that differing forms of abuse rarely occur in isolation. Even if we want to understand transmission in an empirical manner, we have maltreatment that is confounded with other types of abuse and adversity, rendering the issues exceedingly complicated.

In this chapter, we will put forth the premise that those who were abused in childhood do not necessarily become abusers, but fail to protect children, fail to prevent abuse or intervene to stop abuse, and in other ways recreate environments in which abuse by others is allowed to persist. In addition, we will assert that, via psychosocial and developmental sequelae attributable to their own abuse and neglect histories, victims can damage offspring in other equally profound ways. This conceptualization logically culminates in the conclusion that offspring born to parents who themselves endured abuse and neglect are at considerable risk—not only for involvement in protective services, but for a host of developmental and psychosocial maladies brought on by the sequelae of childhood abuse suffered by parents. This is important as we try to disentangle the issue of intergenerational transmission. We must carefully consider the complexities of this issue, and more carefully define the problems, in order to promote solutions that will ultimately curtail the problem and halt the cycle of violence.

Let's start with a case example. What follows is a true story from one of the mothers in our longitudinal cohort study. The names and specific circumstances have been altered to protect confidentiality and anonymity, but the tenor of story and the guttural realities of her struggle remain true. We will call her Jessica.

> On September 2, 1999, EMS responded to a frantic 911 call, referencing a bathtub drowning of a ten-month-old boy. Upon arrival, EMS found the heroin intoxicated single mother of three small children attempting to revive the already deceased infant. Months later in an inpatient substance rehabilitation unit, the clinically depressed, suicidal mother recounted the incident, admitting the use of illegal drugs and alcohol as means to cope with the severe depression and the painful reminders of her traumatic childhood. She was repeatedly raped by her father from age six or seven until age twelve. Now, with her remaining children removed from her custody by child protective services, this distraught mother reflects on how the harmful effects of her abuse experience are persisting and seem to crop up periodically throughout her life. "And now," she states, "the whole thing is spreading to my children. When will this nightmare end?"

Jessica's story is a painful illustration of how the damage to offspring is not simply brought on by their involvement in protective services, but via a multitude of additional sources of risk that parents bring to the environment *because* of their abuse histories. In Jessica's case, her crippling depression, substance dependencies and persisting PTSD would have taken their toll on her young children, even if her child had not died in that bathtub. Our argument is a simple one—children born to abuse victims face considerable obstacles that go beyond the transmission of child abuse and neglect per se, but extend into the environments that place children at risk for a multitude of problems. Those who are abused as children do not necessarily go on to abuse their own children, but in other ways re-create environments which are conducive to maltreatment.

Longitudinal, Intergenerational Study

We will use examples of intergenerational transmission from one of the few prospective, longitudinal studies of the impact of sexual abuse (Trickett, Noll, & Putnam, 2011) that is now in its thirtieth year. The Female Growth and Development Study (FGDS) began in 1987 and the investigators (Trickett et al., 2011) have retained 96 % of this sample of females with substantiated sexual abuse and matched comparisons (N = 173) in an accelerated longitudinal, cross-sequential design spanning 6 timepoints (T1–T6). A multi-level, biopsychosocial assessment was repeated three times in childhood/early adolescence (mean ages 11, 12 & 13), twice in late adolescence (mean ages 18 & 19), and once in early adulthood (mean age 24). Over 90 % of offspring were assessed at T6 (N = 123; mean age 4). Funding has recently been secured from NICHD to follow up with this cohort in the thirtieth year, when the original participants will be in their late 30's and early 40s. At that point, they will have an estimated 250 offspring ranging in age from newborn to 18 (Fig. 1).

Participants in this study represented a diverse range of race and socioeconomic status. The comparison families were well matched on a host of demographics, including age, income, and family constellation (e.g., single-parent households), and were recruited from the same zip codes. This longitudinal, cross-sequential design is powerful not only due to its prospective nature, but also because when we observe group differences later in development, or across generations, inferences can be relatively strong as compared to retrospective studies that do not span generations.

Offspring Born Premature

Let's start from the beginning. Why might we be concerned that abused mothers are at risk for giving birth prematurely? There are multiple reasons to be concerned about pregnancies in this high-risk group, not the least of which stems from what we know about the Hypothalamic Pituitary Adrenal (HPA) axis, or circulating cortisol activity. We have good evidence for hyperactivity of the HPA in abused females, both acutely after abuse disclosure and persisting through certain developmental periods (Trickett, Noll, Susman, Shenk, & Putnam, 2010).

We know that the HPA activity of the mother manifests in corticotrophin-releasing hormones (CRH) being secreted in the placenta. Hence, there is a positive feedback loop between the fetus' HPA system, through their adrenal activity, back

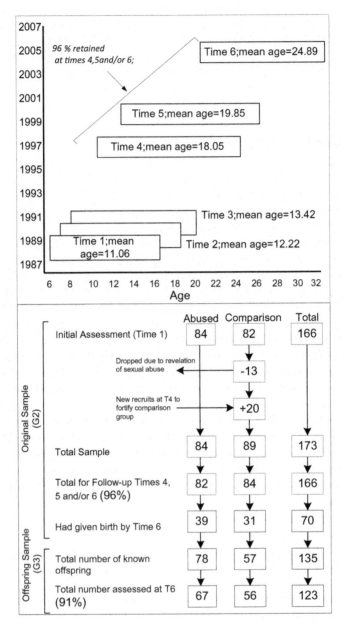

Fig. 1 Assessment flow and sample configuration for the Female Growth and Development longitudinal study of sexual abuse victims over time

to the mother through the placenta. In late gestation, the adrenal activity of the fetus then sends dehydroepiandrosterones (DHEAs) to the myometrium telling the maternal system that it is time for parturition. Starting at the beginning of the third trimester, extreme HPA activity through this loop signals artificially mature fetal lung development that is inconsistent with fetal age. Thus, the myometrium is activated prematurely, resulting in premature delivery.

Therefore, it is hypothesized that mothers abused in childhood are more susceptible to premature delivery than their non-abused counterparts. To address this hypothesis, we obtained labor and delivery records from hospitals where offspring were born and coded these records for prenatal complications and birth outcomes. Results indicated that the babies born to the abused group were more than twice as likely as those born to the control group to be born premature, at a rate of 19 %; roughly two and half times the national average. Circulating cortisol levels, as well as maternal prenatal alcohol use, were significant, and independent, predictors of premature delivery (Noll et al., 2007).

Prematurity has a profound impact on infant development, rendering newborns at considerable risk for cognitive and motor delays. Prematurity can also places babies at considerable risk for physical abuse, including shaken baby syndrome, as these infants often have difficult temperaments and are hard to console. Hence, even from birth, we have a powerful illustration of intergenerational transmission—not of the mother abusing her children, but of the mother's compromised HPA axis impacting neonatal health. Therefore, the starting point in life for these children is less than optimal.

Poor Cognitive Development and Attachment Insecurity

In terms of offspring cognitive development, we performed the Bayley Infant Development Scales (Bayley, 1969), Woodcock-Johnson Test of Cognitive Abilities-III (WJ-III; Woodcock, McGrew, & Mather, 2001) tests, and/or Peabody Picture Vocabulary Task-Revised (PPVT-R; Dunn & Dunn, 1981) tests, depending on the age of the offspring. Results indicated that children born to abused mothers scored approximately one full standard deviation below the population mean, and significantly lower than comparison offspring. Being born with a cognitive disadvantage is impactful in multiple domains of an individual's life, including school readiness and achievement (Duncan et al., 2007), antisocial behavior (Masten, 2001; Rogosch, Cicchetti, & Aber, 1995), and peer rejection (Rogosch et al., 1995). All of these factors may lead to increased risk for teen pregnancy, delinquent behavior, and the inability to maintain stable employment in adulthood (Campbell, Ramey, Pungello, Sparling, & Miller-Johnson, 2002). Thus, individuals who begin life with a cognitive disadvantage are at risk for a difficult trajectory throughout the life course. Further, cognitive disadvantage is related to insecure attachment (Jacobsen, Edelstein, & Hofmann, 1994), another risk factor for many poor adult outcomes.

We also performed dyadic attachment assessments with offspring utilizing Crittenden's Dynamic Model Coding System (2002), which distinguishes not only between secure and insecure attachment, but further classifies infants and children based on self-protective strategies used. We conducted the strange situation procedure (SSP) when offspring were infants and utilized a modified SSP when offspring were preschool-aged. Only 11 % of infants born to abused mothers were classified as secure, with an even distribution of avoidant, depressed, and anxious-reactive attachment across infants and children making up the remainder of the sample (Kwako et al., 2010). The abused group was also more notably represented in the "higher subscript" insecure categories, which are indicative of more compulsive and concerning attachment styles.

Attachment in infancy and childhood is related to later friendships, romantic relationships, and attachment with one's own children (Hazen & Shaver, 1994; van IJzendoorn, 1995). Thus, individuals who are at risk for developing an insecure attachment with their infant, such as those who have experienced maltreatment in their own childhood, may be setting up their children for a trajectory of subsequent relationship complexities. These may include psychological inflexibility, difficulties developing self-protective strategies, and problems forming healthy romantic relationships (Kwako et al., 2010).

Involvement in Child Protective Services and Death

Arguably, one of the most important aspects of intergenerational transmission is the extent to which offspring born to maltreated mothers are placed in the care of child protective services. An assessment of this involvement revealed that 17 % of offspring born to abused mothers were involved in child protective services in some way. This is compared to less than 1 % of comparison offspring involved in protective services. The majority of these cases were neglect, where mother was the "perpetrator," and due to her substance abuse problem, depression or other psychiatric conditions, and domestic violence situations, children were categorized as being neglected. In essence, mothers are creating environments in which their children are unable to thrive.

There were four cases of physical abuse, and one case of sexual abuse. Mothers were not the perpetrators in these cases. Forty percent of the children who were involved with child protective services were permanently removed from the home. There have also been four deaths in this offspring sample—two died from complications of prematurity, one died within the first year of life after being born heroin dependent, and the fourth was Jessica's boy who died in the bathtub. All of these deaths occurred within the abused group.

Cumulative Impact Across Generations

In order to understand how the offspring are faring, it is important to evaluate the health and adjustment of their mothers. As summarized in Trickett et al. (2011), compared to non-abused mothers, mothers who were sexually abused as children display post-traumatic stress disorder (PTSD) which persists into adulthood, more psychiatric diagnoses, higher levels of depression, and alcohol and drug use. They report higher rates of self-harm and suicide attempts, higher rates of obesity, more incidences of inter-partner and domestic violence, are more likely to have been raped, and are more likely to have been teen mothers. They are also not graduating from high school as frequently as non-abused counterparts and their overall cognitive performance is low. We know from developmental science that every single one of these main effects is a condition that exerts tangible risk to children.

To gain the most comprehensive picture of the risks that offspring born to sexually abused mothers endure, one needs to take into account what the mother brings to the environment, as well as what can be observed in the child's immediate and proximal experience. In addition, we can put all of these risks into developmental context in order to understand the relative impact that each has on the life-course of the child. To do this we performed a series of analyses deemed an "inter-generational life-line analysis" (Noll, Trickett, Harris, & Putnam, 2009). With this analytic technique, the risk factors that each member of the generation brings to the life of the child are mapped on to the child's life-line, such that we can understand visually how many risks that each child endures. For example, we can count all of the developmental risks that are observed during the life of the child, including being born premature, having a cognitive deficit, being insecurely attached and being involved in protective services. For that same child, we know something about his or her mother and can count the number of risks that mom brings to the life of her child, including experiencing domestic violence, having a psychiatric disorder, being obese, having a drug or alcohol dependency, dropping out of high school, etc. Finally, we were able to assess the grandmother of these offspring during the first few assessments of the FGDS study. We have information, for example, about whether or not grandmothers report being sexually abused as children. All of this information can be plotted along the life-line of the offspring and we can count up all of these risks and compare these totals across groups.

Results indicate that the average number of risks that offspring of abused mothers experience is 6.23, compared to 3.88 in the non-abused group ($p < .05$). Arguably, some risks are more profound than others and thus an informed weighting of risks can reflect the relative impact that each has on the development of children. To accomplish this weighting, we assumed that risks occurring during the life of the child should be weighted more heavily that those occurring prior to the birth of the child. For example, if a child was involved in protective services at age 3, this risk was weighted twice ($2\times$) compared to a risk that occurred before he or she was born. Following this logic, the weighted average for the abused group was 9.21, compared to 5.71 in the non-abused group ($p < .01$).

We can liken these analyses to the now-popular Adverse Childhood Experiences (ACES) studies that are showing how the number of adversities (analogous to "risks" in the case of life-line analyses) experienced renders individuals at increased risk for poor health outcomes. These studies have consistently found associations between the number of ACES (i.e., psychological, physical, and/or sexual abuse, household dysfunction, etc.) and adult outcomes. For example, individuals who have experienced an increased number of ACES are more susceptible to numerous risk factors in adulthood, such as depression (Chapman et al., 2004; Felitti et al., 1998), drug abuse (Dube et al., 2003), alcoholism (Felitti et al., 1998), risky sexual behaviors (Felitti et al., 1998), chronic health problems such as cancer and heart, lung, and liver diseases (Felitti et al., 1998), and were more likely to exhibit insecure attachment (Murphy et al., 2014). In a similar manner, these life-line analyses paint a comprehensive picture of the cumulative burden that children born to abused mothers carry through life. This burden is not simply understood by what can be observed when assessing children directly, but also by the developmental risk that mothers (and even grandmothers) transfer to children based on their own abusive pasts.

The Critical Link Between Teen Pregnancy and Intergenerational Transmission

Given that FGDS includes information regarding both the mother's history as well as her offspring's well-being, we are in a unique position to inform predictive models of the strongest predictors of children's involvement in protective services. In this way, prevention efforts can be more effectively tailored to families who are at the highest risk for intergenerational transmission. Analyses showed that the strongest predictor of whether children born to abused mothers ended up in protective services was the teen pregnancy status of the mother. In fact, 58 % of the sample's offspring who were in the care of protective services were born to a teenage mother who was sexually abused in childhood. This powerful deleterious combination of sexual abuse and teen pregnancy is not well understood in terms of the mechanisms involved in placing offspring at risk for child maltreatment.

To begin to address this question, a new study funded by NICHD was subsequently conducted (HD052533: PI:Noll). This new study assessed a cohort of 514 females aged 14–17 who were followed annually through the age of 19. Sexual activities and pregnancy histories were assessed in this sample, over half of whom were referred by protective services for having been maltreated. The study was aimed at understanding pathways to teen pregnancy and motherhood and how differing types of abuse and maltreatment exacerbate these risks. Outcome data confirm previous meta-analysis estimates (Noll, Shenk, & Putnam, 2008) that abused females become teen mothers at twice the rate of their non-abused peers. In fact, 20 % of this cohort of maltreated females became teen mothers, which is five times the current national average (Noll & Shenk, 2013).

Along with a plethora of quantitative data, we are currently conducting qualitative interviews with those subjects who became teen mothers during the course of the study. We are chiefly interested in how the experience of child maltreatment impacts parenting and how these women make sense of their own abuse in the context of the well-being of their own children. Several preliminary themes are emerging from these interviews. One prominent theme is a very strong and articulated desire to protect their children from any possible source of harm. This is a very visceral desire to spare their children from the suffering of an abusive childhood.

This desire is so strong that these women seem to have a very low tolerance for any type of suffering, to the extent that they will overindulge their children in order to avoid the negative emotions associated with deprivation and harm. For example, one mother told a story about giving her son a candy bar at the grocery store in order to spare her having to endure his crying, sobbing and ultimately, his unhappiness. This mother further articulated how this has resulted in her child becoming "spoiled," such that she has a hard time with setting limits and with discipline. "Everybody tells me my kid is spoiled," this mothers states, "and nobody wants to babysit him or spend time with us."

In this sense, we can see a process unfolding whereby, because of her abuse experience, a mother is hyper-vigilant about her own child's suffering. Being a young mother, she does not necessarily possess the parenting skills that will help her discern between authentic suffering and the emotional manipulations that young children often exhibit in order to win power struggles with parents. Further, young mothers are highly dependent on the support of others (including grandparents and extended family) to raise children and to handle the logistics of raising a child with limited resources. One can see a difficult scenario unfolding—neither the negative behavior patterns established by overly responsive or maladaptive parenting, nor a lack of social support for parenting bode well for this dyad. Ironically, this situation stems from a desire of a mother to protect her child from the kind of suffering that characterized her own childhood. In doing so, however, the potential to re-create an environment of vulnerability is heightened.

Clinical and Public Policy Implications

Given what we are learning from longitudinal, intergenerational studies of the impact of sexual abuse on the well-being of offspring and the myriad of risk factors that mothers who were abused as children bring to the lives of their own children, it will be essential that we identify clinical and preventive interventions that may serve to mitigate these risks and promote positive development. Such interventions should (1) target the short- and long-term sequelae that is present in the lives of victims, (2) maximize the health of the dyadic relationship between these women and their offspring, and (3) promote emotionally healthy, safe, and enriching environments for offspring. Trauma-informed treatment should ideally be extended across development or revisited at key points in life when developmentally salient issues arise, including the onset of sexual activity in adolescence, the transition to adulthood, at marriage, and at the birth of a baby.

Intervention to address symptoms of trauma, and to prevent the progression of symptoms into adulthood, can begin soon after disclosure of abuse. Trauma-focused cognitive behavioral therapy (TF-CBT) addresses many symptoms that may result from trauma, including cognitive distortions, affective difficulties, relationship difficulties, and trauma-specific symptoms (Cohen, Mannarino, & Deblinger, 2006). Treatment includes general CBT skills, as well as the development of a trauma narrative to provide exposure to trauma memories in a safe environment and the opportunity to engage in cognitive restructuring regarding maladaptive thoughts related to trauma. Notably, TF-CBT includes conjoint sessions with the caregiver, in order to improve family interactions; this serves the purpose of not only enhancing communication skills, but also bolstering family support.

Regarding treatment options for mothers with abuse histories who currently have children between the ages of 3 and 7, parent-child interaction therapy (PCIT) is a strongly supported intervention that espouses the goals of improving the parent-child relationship and the behavior management skills of the parent (Brinkmeyer & Eyberg, 2003). Originally designed to decrease disruptive child behaviors, it combines elements of attachment theory, social learning theory, and behavior modification. Parents receive instruction on the application of concrete strategies to enhance the parent-child relationship, increase positive behaviors, decrease problematic behaviors, reduce frustration, and improve the child's speech and language skills, thus addressing many of the difficulties experienced within these dyads. Research regarding the use of a standard 12-session PCIT intervention with high risk families has demonstrated positive outcomes, including decreased externalizing and internalizing behaviors in the child, decreased parental stress, increased positive parental verbalizations, and enhanced maternal sensitivity (Thomas & Zimmer-Gembeck, 2012). Multiple studies have demonstrated the efficacy of PCIT in decreasing recidivism in reports of physical abuse (Chaffin, Funderburk, Bard, Valle, & Gurwitch, 2011; Chaffin et al., 2004; Thomas & Zimmer-Gembeck, 2011), thereby lending support to the concept that this treatment prevents maltreatment and may interrupt the intergenerational transmission of abuse.

In terms of prevention, it should be recognized that some universal parenting programs fall short in terms of addressing the unique struggles that childhood abuse brings to parenthood and the parent/child relationship. For example, a home visiting program designed to enhance maternal sensitivity for depressed, first-time mothers was shown to be less effective for mothers who reported significant childhood trauma (Ammerman et al., 2012). This lack of efficacy may help explain why overall effect sizes for several evidence-based home visiting programs have not produced effect sizes commensurate with the level of public investment (Rubin, Curtis, & Matone, 2014). Perhaps these efforts could be enhanced if they included augmentations such as trauma-informed modules tailored for parents who experienced child abuse.

Finally, developmentally sensitive prevention efforts seem warranted. For example, David Wolfe is the inceptor of a curriculum designed to be delivered in the high school setting where relationship skills, reducing delinquency, and preventing teen pregnancy are major components. Wolfe and his colleagues (Crooks, Scott, Ellis, & Wolfe, 2011) conceptualized this program as a prevention tool for mitigating child maltreatment in the next generation. Although recognized as a downstream strategy, this program is thought to prevent child abuse by providing adolescents with the ability to recognize and form healthy relationships and avoid early parenthood—a very innovative way to think about child abuse prevention.

References

Ammerman, R. T., Shenk, C. E., Teeters, A. R., Noll, J. G., Putnam, F. W., & Van Ginkel, J. B. (2012). Impact of depression and childhood trauma in mothers receiving home visitation. *Journal of Child and Family Studies, 21*(4), 612–625. doi:10.1007/s10826-011-9513-9.

Bayley, N. (1969). *Bayley scales of infant development*. New York: Psychological Corporation.

Brinkmeyer, M. Y., & Eyberg, S. M. (2003). Parent-child interaction therapy for oppositional children. In A. E. Kazdin & J. R. Weisz (Eds.), *Evidence-based psychotherapies for children and adolescents* (pp. 204–223). New York: Guilford Press.

Campbell, F. A., Ramey, C. T., Pungello, E., Sparling, J., & Miller-Johnson, S. (2002). Early childhood education: Young adult outcomes from the Abecedarian Project. *Applied Developmental Science, 6*(1), 42–57. doi:10.1207/S1532480XADS0601_05.

Chaffin, M., Funderburk, B., Bard, D., Valle, L. A., & Gurwitch, R. (2011). A combined motivation and parent-child interaction therapy package reduces child welfare recidivism in a randomized dismantling field trial. *Journal of Consulting & Clinical Psychology, 79*(1), 84–95. doi:10.1037/a0021227.

Chaffin, M., Silovsky, J. F., Funderburk, B., Valle, L. A., Brestan, E. V., Balachova, T., … Bonner, B. L. (2004). Parent-child interaction therapy with physically abusive parents: Efficacy for reducing future abuse reports. *Journal of Consulting and Clinical Psychology, 72*(3), 500–510. doi:10.1037/0022-006X.72.3.500.

Chapman, D. P., Whitfield, C. L., Felitti, V. J., Dube, S. R., Edwards, V. J., & Andra, R. F. (2004). Adverse childhood experiences and the risk of depressive disorders in adulthood. *Journal of Affective Disorders, 82*(15), 217–225. doi:10.1016/j.jad.2003.12.013.

Cohen, J. A., Mannarino, A. P., & Deblinger, E. (2006). *Treating trauma and traumatic grief in children and adolescents*. New York: Guilford.

Crittenden, P. M. (2002). *A guide to expansions and modifications of the Infant Strange Situation*. Unpublished manuscript, available from the author.

Crooks, C. V., Scott, K., Ellis, W., & Wolfe, D. A. (2011). Impact of a universal school-based violence prevention program on violent delinquency: Distinctive benefits for youth with maltreatment histories. *Child Abuse & Neglect, 35*(6), 393–400. doi:10.1016/j.chiabu.2011.03.002.

Dube, S. R., Dong, M., Chapman, D. P., Giles, W. H., Anda, R. F., & Felitti, V. J. (2003). Childhood abuse, neglect, and household dysfunction and the risk of illicit drug use: The Adverse Childhood Experiences Study. *Pediatrics, 111*(3), 564–572. doi:10.1542/peds.111.3.564.

Duncan, G. J., Dowsett, C. J., Claessens, A., Magnuson, K., Huston, A. C., Klebanov, P., … Japel, C. (2007). School readiness and later achievement. *Developmental Psychology, 43*(6), 1428–1446. doi:10.1037/0012-1649.43.6.1428.supp.

Dunn, L. M., & Dunn, L. M. (1981). *Peabody picture vocabulary test-revised*. Circle Pines, MN: American Guidance Service.

Felitti, V. C., Anda, R. F., Nordenberg, D., Williamson, D. F., Spitz, A. M., Edwards, V., … Marks, J. S. (1998). Relationship of childhood abuse and household dysfunction to many of the leading causes of death in adults: The Adverse Childhood Experiences (ACE) Study. *American Journal of Preventive Medicine, 14*(4), 245–258. doi:10.1016/S0749-3797(98)00017-8.

Hazen, C., & Shaver, P. R. (1994). Attachment as an organizational framework for research on close relationships. *Psychological Inquiry, 5*(1), 1–22.

van IJzendoorn, M. (1995). Adult attachment representations, parental responsiveness, and infant attachment: A meta-analysis on the predictive validity of the adult attachment interview. *Psychological Bulletin, 117*(3), 387–403. doi:10.1037/0033-2909.117.3.387.

Jacobsen, T., Edelstein, W., & Hofmann, V. (1994). A longitudinal study of the relation between representations of attachment in childhood and cognitive functioning in childhood and adolescence. *Developmental Psychology, 30*(1), 112–124. doi:10.1037/0012-1649.30.1.112.

Kaufman, J., & Zigler, E. (1987). Do abused children become abusive parents? *American Journal of Orthopsychiatry, 57*(2), 186–192. doi:10.1111/j.1939-0025.1987.tb03528.x.

Knutson, J. F., DeGarmo, D. S., & Reid, J. B. (2004). Social disadvantage and neglectful parenting as precursors to the development of antisocial and aggressive child behavior: Testing a theoretical model. *Aggressive Behavior, 30*(3), 187–205. doi:10.1002/ab.20016.

Kwako, L. E., Noll, J. G., Putnam, F. W., & Trickett, P. K. (2010). Childhood sexual abuse and attachment: An intergenerational perspective. *Journal of Clinical Child Psychology and Psychiatry, 15*(3), 407–422. doi:10.1177/1359104510367590.

Masten, A. S. (2001). Ordinary magic: Resilience processes in development. *American Psychologist, 56*(3), 227–238. doi:10.1037/0003-066X.56.3.227.

Milner, J. S. (1993). Social information processing and physical child abuse. *Clinical Psychology Review, 13*(3), 275–294. doi:10.1016/0272-7358(93)90024-G.

Milner, J. S., & Chilamkurti, C. (1991). Physical child abuse: A review of the literature. *Journal of Interpersonal Violence, 6*(3), 345–366. doi:10.1177/088626091006003007.

Murphy, A., Steele, M., Dube, S. R., Bate, J., Bonuck, K., Meissner, P., … Steele, H. (2014). Adverse Childhood Experiences (ACEs) Questionnaire and Adult Attachment Interview (AAI): Implications for parent child relationships. *Child Abuse & Neglect, 38*(2), 224–233. doi:10.1016/j.chiabu.2013.09.004.

Noll, J. G., & Shenk, C. E. (2013). Teen birth rates in sexually abused and neglected females. *Pediatrics, 131*(4), 1181–1187. doi:10.1542/peds.2012-3072.

Noll, J. G., Schulkin, J., Trickett, P. K., Susman, E. J., Breech, L., & Putnam, F. W. (2007). Differential pathways to preterm delivery for sexually abused and comparison women. *Journal of Pediatric Psychology, 32*(10), 1238–1248. doi:10.1093/jpepsy/jsm046.

Noll, J. G., Shenk, C. E., & Putnam, F. W. (2008). Childhood sexual abuse and adolescent pregnancy: A meta-analytic update. *Journal of Pediatric Psychology, 34*(4), 366–378. doi:10.1093/jpepsy/jsn098.

Noll, J. G., Trickett, P. K., Harris, W. W., & Putnam, F. W. (2009). The cumulative burden borne by offspring whose mothers were sexually abused as children: Descriptive results from a multigenerational study. *Journal of Interpersonal Violence, 24*(3), 424–449. doi:10.1177/0886260508317194.

Rogosch, F. A., Cicchetti, D., & Aber, J. L. (1995). The role of child maltreatment in early deviations in cognitive and affective processing abilities and later peer relationship problems. *Development and Psychopathology, 7*(4), 591–609. doi:10.1017/S0954579400006738.

Rubin, D. M., Curtis, M. L., & Matone, M. (2014). Child abuse prevention and child home visitation: Making sure we get it right. *JAMA Pediatrics, 168*(1), 5–6. doi:10.1001/jamapediatrics.2013.3865.

Thomas, R., & Zimmer-Gembeck, M. J. (2011). Accumulating evidence for parent-child interaction therapy in the prevention of child maltreatment. *Child Development, 82*(1), 177–192. doi:10.1111/j.1467-8624.2010.01548.x.

Thomas, R., & Zimmer-Gembeck, M. J. (2012). Parent-child interaction therapy: An evidence-based treatment for child maltreatment. *Child Maltreatment, 17*(3), 253–266.

Trickett, P. K., Noll, J. G., & Putnam, F. W. (2011). The impact of sexual abuse on female development: Lessons from a multigenerational, longitudinal research study. *Development and Psychopathology, 23*(2), 453–476. doi:10.1017/S0954579411000174.

Trickett, P. K., Noll, J. G., Susman, E. J., Shenk, C. E., & Putnam, F. W. (2010). Attenuation of cortisol across development for victims of sexual abuse. *Development and Psychology, 22*(1), 165–175. doi:10.1017/S0954579409990332.

Woodcock, R. W., McGrew, K. S., & Mather, N. (2001). *Woodcock–Johnson III tests of cognitive abilities*. Itasca, IL: Riverside.

Part III
Intervening with Maltreated Children and Their Families

Evidence Based Intervention: Trauma-Focused Cognitive Behavioral Therapy for Children and Families

Judith A. Cohen and Anthony P. Mannarino

Introduction

A great deal of progress has been made in developing effective interventions for children who experience child abuse and other traumas. The most extensively evaluated child trauma treatment model is Trauma-Focused Cognitive Behavioral Therapy (TF-CBT). Initially developed for and tested with children or adolescents who experienced sexual abuse and their non-offending parents or primary caregivers (hereafter referred to as "children" and "parents", respectively), TF-CBT has now been tested in 20 randomized controlled trials for diverse trauma types, developmental levels, settings and cultures. Three core TF-CBT Principles are (1) proper duration and proportionality of the three TF-CBT treatment phases; (2) sequencing of the TF-CBT components, summarized by the acronym "PRACTICE"; (3) the use of gradual exposure throughout treatment; and (4) including parents or caregivers in treatment whenever possible. This chapter briefly describes the TF-CBT treatment model, reviews the current state of TF-CBT research, and provides information about TF-CBT therapist certification.

J.A. Cohen, M.D. (✉) • A.P. Mannarino, Ph.D.
Department of Psychiatry, Allegheny Health Network, Drexel University College of Medicine, Pittsburgh, PA, USA
e-mail: Judith.Cohen@ahn.org; anthony.mannarino@ahn.org

© Springer International Publishing Switzerland 2017
D.M. Teti (ed.), *Parenting and Family Processes in Child Maltreatment and Intervention*, Child Maltreatment Solutions Network,
DOI 10.1007/978-3-319-40920-7_6

The Trauma-Focused Cognitive Behavioral Therapy Model

General Description of TF-CBT

TF-CBT is a child and family-focused trauma treatment model that addresses problems associated with significantly traumatic events that children experience or witness. These traumas may include but are not limited to experiences such as sexual, physical and/or emotional abuse or neglect, domestic or community violence, bullying, serious accidents, natural or other disasters, fires, traumatic deaths, war, terrorism, medical traumas, or multiple or complex traumas. Complex trauma is not officially included in DSM-5 but as proposed in ICD-11, it includes the following features: (1) early repeated interpersonal trauma typically perpetrated by a caregiver (2) significant PTSD symptoms; and (3) significant dysregulation in multiple functional domains such as affect, negative self-perception, and interpersonal relationships.

TF-CBT does not treat traumatic experiences themselves, but children's trauma-related mental health problems. These may include PTSD symptoms (e.g., intrusion, avoidance, maladaptive cognitions or mood changes; or arousal) but children do not need to have a specified level of PTSD symptoms in order to receive TF-CBT. Due to traumatic avoidance, children may initially report relatively few of these symptoms, and if reassessed after a few treatment sessions, children may report substantially more. Other children may have difficulties in other areas and have relatively few PTSD symptoms. TF-CBT also addresses other trauma-related difficulties such as depressive, anxiety, behavioral, neurobiological, cognitive/perceptual, and relationship/attachment problems. Assessment is a crucial first step in determining whether trauma or another underlying problem is the primary problem for the child's presenting problems. Assessing traumatized children is complex and described in greater detail elsewhere (Kisiel, Conradi, Fehrenbach, Torgersen, & Briggs, 2014). TF-CBT components address re-regulation in each of the above domains, with goals of symptomatic improvement as well as returning children to healthier developmental trajectories and optimizing children's adaptive functioning.

Several psychological theories have been proposed to explain the development of post-traumatic difficulties. These include emotional processing theory, social cognitive theory, inhibitory learning, neurobiological disruption, attachment theory and others described in more detail elsewhere (Cohen, Mannarino, & Deblinger, 2006, 2012, 2016). These theories support the importance of (1) learning new skills and other more adaptive responses and practicing these repeatedly over time in order to replace previously learned maladaptive responses; (2) promoting habituation and reducing reinforcement of avoidance through titrated gradual exposure experiences; (3) simultaneously allowing the feared memories and emotions to be paired with therapeutic, corrective experiences that may produce new adaptive associations between trauma memories and feelings of safety and mastery; and (4) providing all of the above in the context of a supportive, trusting therapeutic relationship and with the support of a supportive non-offending parent or primary caregiver (hereafter referred to as "parent"), who is integrally included in the therapy process and through this process becomes more attuned and trustworthy to the child.

There are many reasons to include non-offending parents when treating traumatized children. Many parents (including foster parents) are frustrated by child behavior problems and need help recognizing the connections among trauma experiences, trauma reminders, and behavioral dysregulation (described below). This enables parents to become more compassionate and supportive, and enhances the parent-child relationship, as well as often improving sibling relationships and general family functioning. Non-offending parents often do not know the details of the child's trauma (e.g., child sexual abuse; community violence); foster parents may know little or nothing about the child's trauma experiences). Other parents may have co-experienced the trauma (e.g., during domestic violence) but have their own memories and cognitions about this experience which are different from their children's perspective. Parents and/or children generally have avoided openly addressing these experiences prior to therapy for various reasons (e.g., fear of upsetting the other, being blamed for the trauma or other family problems, retriggering past problems, etc.). TF-CBT helps parents cope with their own distress in the aftermath of trauma, while simultaneously enhancing their skills in responding to their children's trauma-related difficulties. In so doing, TF-CBT reduces parental distress and enhances parental support for their children, enabling parents to hear and support their children's perspective about their trauma experiences during conjoint sessions.

Children and their parents receive TF-CBT in parallel individual sessions as well as in conjoint child-parent or family sessions. Therapists spend about half of each session (25–30 min) with the child and half of each session with parents, with the same therapist seeing the child and parents in each family. Typically the same TF-CBT component is addressed during the parent session as during the child session, with the therapist providing information to the parent about how to implement and support the child in practicing that component at home. The TF-CBT conjoint sessions are spent primarily with the family together with a brief amount of time (5–10 min) spent individually with the child and the parents, respectively, at the start of the session in order to prepare for the conjoint session. For children in residential treatment facilities, when no parent is available or willing to participate in treatment, it is often beneficial to have a primary milieu worker (selected and agreed upon by the child and worker) participate in TF-CBT in lieu of a parent, i.e. that worker would participate in all TF-CBT sessions and receive the information typically provided to parents; if agreed upon and clinically appropriate this would include the child sharing the trauma narrative with this worker. Although the research suggests that including a parent or other primary caregiver in TF-CBT treatment leads to better outcomes, children receive TF-CBT alone with positive effects if it is not possible to include a parent or caretaker in treatment (Deblinger, Lippmann, & Steer, 1996).

TF-CBT is appropriate for children ages 3–18 years who have prominent trauma-related symptoms as described above. The model is applied in a developmentally-appropriate manner for children of different developmental levels and abilities as described in detail elsewhere (Cohen et al., 2012). Children in outpatient clinics, foster care, group homes, residential treatment facilities (RTF), day hospitals, inpatient programs, schools, medical settings (e.g., HIV treatment clinic), refugee settings and post-war settings (e.g., refugee camp or non-governmental organization), can receive TF-CBT.

TF-CBT Core Principles

TF-CBT is a phase- and components-based model, as depicted in Fig. 1. The TF-CBT phases are (1) Stabilization Skills Phase; (2) Trauma Narrative and Processing Phase; and (3) Integration/Consolidation Phase. The TF-CBT components are summarized by the acronym PRACTICE: Psychoeducation, Parenting Skills, Relaxation Skills, Affective Modulation Skills, Cognitive Coping Skills, Trauma Narration and Processing, In Vivo Mastery, Conjoint Child-Parent Sessions, and Enhancing Safety and Developmental Trajectory.

There are **four core principles** involved in providing TF-CBT with fidelity. The first is the *duration and proportionality of TF-CBT phases*. For typical traumas, treatment duration is generally 12–15 sessions, with the three phases receiving approximately equal numbers of sessions (4–5 sessions/phase). For complex trauma, duration of treatment may sometimes be longer (16–25 sessions) due to greater severity of dysregulation in multiple trauma domains although TF-CBT is still a time-limited treatment model in these situations (i.e. treatment is ~4–6 months, not 1–2 years). For complex trauma the proportionality may sometimes also modi-

Psychoeducation

Parenting Skills

Relaxation Skills   STABILIZATION SKILLS PHASE

Affect Modulation Skills

Cognitive Processing Skills

Trauma Narrative & Processing   TRAUMA NARRATIVE PHASE

In Vivo Mastery of Reminders

Conjoint Child-Parent Sessions   INTEGRATION/CONSOLIDATION PHASE

Enhancing Safety & Developmental Trajectory

Fig. 1 TF-CBT phases and components

fied with more emphasis on the initial Stabilization Skills which takes about half of the treatment (8–12 sessions), with the remaining two phases receiving about a quarter of the treatment, respectively (4–6 sessions). The second core principle is the correct *sequence of TF-CBT phases and components*. The TF-CBT phases must always be provided in sequential order (Stabilization Skills; Trauma Narrative and Processing; Integration/Consolidation Phases, respectively). Therapists should also generally provide all of the PRACTICE components in sequential order, because the model is progressive with each component building on previously mastered phases and components. However there are a few exceptions in which clinical judgment should be exercised when modifying the order of the PRACTICE components: (1) the In Vivo Mastery component is only provided for children with overgeneralized avoidance of innocuous situations that is interfering with adaptive functioning as described below; (2) the Enhancing Safety component should be provided first and in an ongoing manner throughout treatment for children who have ongoing trauma exposure, those who have complex trauma or those who have other significant safety concerns; and (3) some clinical judgment may be applied in adjusting the order of the early Stabilization Skills (for example, affective modulation may precede relaxation for some children, etc.).

The third core principle is the *use of Gradual Exposure throughout TF-CBT*. Gradual exposure is included in all of the TF-CBT treatment components. Gradual exposure involves incrementally increasing the intensity and/or duration with which exposure to trauma reminders is included in each sequential TF-CBT component. Gradual exposure may be achieved through talking, writing, creating arts or other activities that directly engage the child and parent in mastering avoidance of thoughts, feelings, reminders and memories of the child's traumatic experience(s). Specific examples of how to incorporate gradual exposure in each PRACTICE component are described elsewhere (Cohen et al., 2006).

The fourth core principle is *including parents or caregivers whenever possible*, as described above and throughout the descriptions of each component in the following sections. TF-CBT fidelity checklists are available to monitor therapists' adherence to the treatment model.

TF-CBT Treatment Components

The following section provides a brief description of each PRACTICE component. More information about how to implement the TF-CBT model is available at the free online training courses, TF-CBTWeb (www.musc.edu/tfcbt), CTG Web (for childhood traumatic grief, at www.musc.edu/ctg) and in the published TF-CBT treatment manuals (Cohen et al., 2006, 2012).

Psychoeducation: This component provides information to children and parents about the nature of the child's traumatic experience(s) such as how many other children experience this type of trauma, its causes, and common child and parent trauma reactions. Another important part of Psychoeducation is providing information about trauma reminders, and beginning to identify the child's personal trauma reminders. Trauma reminders are any cue (e.g, people, places, situations, body sensations, smells, sights, etc.) that remind children of their original traumatic experiences. Trauma reminders often set off a cascade of psychological and neurobiological responses leading to dysregulation in multiple domains. By educating children and parents about connections among children's trauma experiences, trauma reminders and trauma responses can help both children and parents make sense of children's trauma responses, helping them for the first time to understand why the child "loses control" in certain situations that they had never before connected to the trauma. Psychoeducation occurs throughout TF-CBT treatment.

Parenting Skills: As described above, parents participate in each PRACTICE component, receiving as much time in each component as their children. In addition, parents receive an additional specific Parenting Skills component in order to optimize their positive parenting of their children. This component includes recognizing the connection between children's trauma experiences and their current behavioral dysregulation, enhancing parental use of praise, positive and selective attention, and the use of appropriate behavioral interventions for trauma-related behavioral dysregulation children may be displaying. The therapist uses specific demonstrations of these skills, practices and role plays with parents how to implement these skills at home with children, and continues to check how they are working in subsequent sessions. The therapist also directly addresses parental distress related to children's trauma, and concrete ways to enhance parental support of children and optimize the overall child-parent relationship.

Relaxation Skills: Enjoyable, individualized relaxation interventions such as focused breathing, progressive muscle relaxation, exercise, singing, dance, yoga and other mind-body techniques , sports, blowing bubbles, drawing, reading, or others are developed as a personalized "tool kit" for children to use as strategies to reverse the physiological effects of trauma. Children develop an individualized relaxation plan which includes different activities for different settings. Parents then learn these skills and reinforce and support their children in implementing these skills, including when their children experience trauma reminders. Teachers or other adults may also be included to assist the child in implementing the plan in different settings. Children practice these skills during the week with parental support and encouragement, and the therapist continues to check how the plan is working with appropriate modifications until children are successfully self-soothing with increasing skill in diverse settings.

Affective Modulation Skills: The therapist helps children gain skills with affective expression through a variety of enjoyable games and other interactive activities. The therapist then introduces a variety of affective modulation strategies, which may include self-distraction techniques, problem solving, negotiating, social skills, role playing, seeking social support, thought interruption, positive imagery, assuring safety in the moment, and others that are described elsewhere (Cohen et al., 2006). During the parent sessions, parents learn the skills that their children are developing and how to support children's use and practice of these during the week, including in response to trauma reminders. Parents practice and role play how to assist children in expressing a variety of feelings, learn to understand, tolerate and encourage expression of a range of feelings in children (e.g. when children say "I hate you"), particularly in response to trauma reminders. The therapist also supports and encourages parents to express their personal feelings about their children's trauma experiences and to develop positive coping strategies for negative affective states in this regard.

Cognitive Processing Skills: Children and parents learn about the connections among thoughts, feelings and behaviors. During their individual sessions, therapists provide children and parents with examples from daily life (not traumatic experiences) in which their thoughts may not be accurate or helpful. For example, if a child's friend didn't call to invite him over as promised, his thought might be "No one likes me". The therapist asks, "How does this make you feel?" The child says, "Awful, sad". The therapist says, "What do you want to do when you feel that way?" The child says, "I don't want to go to school tomorrow." Then the therapist says, "Can you think of a different thought that you could tell yourself, instead of that no one likes you, that might explain why your friend didn't call you to come over? If the child can't come up with another explanation, the therapist might say, "What if someone in her family is sick and that's why she isn't allowed to have anyone over? How would you feel then? The child might say, "I guess I wouldn't feel so bad." The therapist asks, "What would you do if that's what you thought?" The child says, "I guess I'd ask her at school tomorrow if everything's okay". The therapist helps the child understand that there is no easy way to know what her friend was really thinking, but she can change what *she* is thinking. By using examples like this from ordinary life, children and parents learn to examine their negative thinking patterns can affect their feelings and behaviors. By practicing changing their thoughts ("Is my thought accurate? Is it helpful, does it make me feel better?), children and parents learn to feel and act more positively.

Trauma Narrative and Processing: During this component the therapist helps children create detailed narratives of their personal trauma experiences and cognitively process these experiences to make meaning of them in order to move forward in a more positive way. Narratives are often organized according to the temporal sequence of the child's life, often in chapter or timeline format, depending on clinical judgment and the types or severity of trauma the child experiences. For example, children with complex trauma are more likely to develop a "life narrative" organized around a central trauma theme, as described in detail elsewhere (Cohen, Mannarino, Kliethermes & Murray, 2012). Developing children's trauma narratives is described in greater detail elsewhere (Cohen et al., 2006). During subsequent sessions as children read over their trauma narratives, children include more details about what happened, as well as how they were feeling, what they were thinking, and their body sensations at the time the traumatic experiences occurred. This allows therapists to identify dysfunctional cognitions that children would not otherwise identify or share. Cognitive processing of the narrative includes addressing these inaccurate and unhelpful cognitions and replacing them with more optimal thoughts which can be added to the narrative.

As children develop their narratives, the therapist typically shares these with the parents during parallel parent sessions. This is often the first time parents have heard the details of their children's trauma experiences and/or the impact this has had on their children in the children's own words. As such it usually has a profound impact of parents, and it is important that the therapist use several sessions (as the narrative is being developed) to allow the parents to emotionally process the narrative in preparation for the conjoint sessions, during which children will directly share it with the parents.

In Vivo Mastery of Trauma Reminders: This component is only used if (1) the child has overgeneralized avoidance of trauma reminders; (2) the trauma reminders that are being avoided are now innocuous (i.e., no longer dangerous); and (3) the avoidance is causing significant impairment in the child's daily functioning (e.g., missing school, physical problems such as enuresis or sleep disturbance; problematic peer interactions, etc.). In distinction to the Trauma Narrative component, which provides imaginal exposure, this component involves actual in vivo ("in real life") exposure to the situations the child fears, and thus, is often particularly challenging for children and parents. Thus, there should be a sound reason to implement this component (e.g, the avoidance is clearly impairing the child's current functioning). For example, a child who was sexually abused in the bathroom who still avoids using bathrooms despite the perpetrator being in prison, and who is experiencing urinary retention, enuresis and frequent urinary tract infections as a result of the bathroom avoidance, would benefit from In Vivo Mastery. If the situation is not innocuous but is still dangerous, e.g., if the perpetrator were still in the home, this component would not be used; focus instead should be on enhancing safety, appropriate legal interventions, etc. If the child were avoiding a situation that was innocuous but was not impairing functioning (e.g., the child avoided walking by his old apartment where complex trauma occurred, but he had not need to walk in that neighborhood anymore), there would be no need to utilize In Vivo Mastery since returning to his old neighborhood would not serve a clear therapeutic purpose. The therapist, children, and parents collaborate to develop a graduated fear hierarchy ("ladder") and then work together (with school if appropriate, for example, for children who are avoiding attending school) to assist children in tolerating increasingly distressing reminders ("climbing the ladder" of increasingly difficult trauma cues). As children progressively accomplish each step on the In Vivo plan, they overcome the maladaptive fear and avoidance related to trauma reminders, learn and practice new, more adaptive coping responses, and gain progressively greater feelings of mastery; the parents and therapist provide praise and other rewards for each step as well. Children use skills acquired during the Stabilization Skills phase to process and tolerate fear, and parents use Parenting Skills (e.g. praise, selective attention) during this process. The therapist is particularly available during In Vivo work to provide support and to develop new coping strategies if this occurs.

Conjoint Child—Parent Sessions: As therapy is drawing to a close, the therapist gradually transfers the "agency" of change from the therapist to the parents. Conjoint sessions set the stage for this transition, in which children and parents will be talking directly to each other about trauma-related issues, initially with the therapist as a mediator but by the end of therapy, by themselves. During the first conjoint session, children typically share their trauma narrative directly with their parents and parents have been prepared to support and praise children in this process through hearing the narrative in sequential individual parent sessions. Other activities during conjoint sessions may include optimizing family communication about behavior problems and other difficult issues such as dating, sexuality, drug refusal, family rules, safety planning, etc. (e.g., dating, sex, drugs, appropriate peers, etc.). Safety planning is often done during family sessions, as described below

Enhancing Safety and Developmental Trajectory: The loss of safety and diversion of developmental resources are inherent parts of trauma experience; trauma-exposed children are at elevated risk for experiencing future traumatization. For these reasons enhancing concrete safety skills for both children and parents and addressing other issues that can enhance children's return to healthier developmental trajectories are critical for optimal outcomes. The therapist works carefully with children and parents to assess individual safety needs and abilities, and develop both personal and family safety plans. It is often important for the therapist to emphasize that the family safety plan applies to all members of the household, and to practice and role play with both child and parent how to implement this if violations occur. Prior to ending therapy, the therapist assesses and assures that remaining developmental and other mental health needs are addressed. Additional traumatic grief components are available as part of the TF-CBT model for children who have experienced traumatic grief; these are described in detail elsewhere (Cohen et al., 2006; www.musc.edu/ctg).

Empirical Studies Conducted with TF-CBT

As of September 2014, 15 randomized controlled treatment trials have been conducted using the TF-CBT treatment model. These studies are summarized in Table 1.

These provide significant evidence for the efficacy and effectiveness of TF-CBT in treating PTSD symptoms in children who have experienced sexual abuse and other traumatic events. TF-CBT has consistently been found to be superior to other comparison conditions for improving children's PTSD symptoms. This has been found across developmental levels, trauma types and settings, as well as different types of comparison treatments (e.g., supportive therapy, usual care, wait list control conditions). Many of these studies have also shown that TF-CBT reduces other symptoms including those often associated with complex trauma, such as affective problems (e.g. anxiety and depression), behavior problems, cognitive problems (e.g., shame; specific trauma-related attributions) and relationship/attachment problems (e.g. social competence; pro-social behaviors).

Table 1 Randomized controlled trials of TF-CBT

Study	Index trauma	Comparison	Major findings
Cohen and Mannarino (1996)	Sexually abused preschool children	TF-CBT vs. NST	TF-CBT significantly superior to NST in improving PTSD, internalizing and sexual behavior problems; differences sustained at 1-year follow-up
Cohen and Mannarino (1998a); Cohen, Mannarino, and Knudsen (2005)	Sexually abused children	TF-CBT vs. NST	TF-CBT significantly superior to NST in improving PTSD at 1 year follow-up
Deblinger et al. (1996)	Sexually abused children,	TF-CBT Child Only TF-CBT Parent Only TF-CBT Parent +Child UCC	TF-CBT provided to child (combined groups) significantly superior to UCC for improving PTSD; TF-CBT provided to parent (combined groups) significantly superior to UCC for improving child depression, behavior problems and parenting skills
King et al. (2000)	Sexually abused Australian children	TF-CBT-Child only TF-CBT-Family WL	TF-CBT significantly superior to WL for improving PTSD
Deblinger, Stauffer, and Steer (2001)	Sexually abused preschool children	TF-CBT Group vs. Supportive Therapy Group	TF-CBT significantly superior to ST for improving children's body safety skills and parental intrusive thoughts and trauma-related negative emotional reactions
Cohen, Deblinger, Mannarino, and Steer (2004)	Sexually abused children	TF-CBT vs. CCT	TF-CBT significantly superior to CCT for improving PTSD, depression, behavior and shame symptoms ; also for parental outcomes; results sustained at 1 year f/u
Cohen, Mannarino, Perel, and Staron (2007)	Sexually abused youth	TF-CBT+ Sertraline vs. TF-CBT + Pill Placebo	No significant group differences
Cohen et al. (2011)	Children exposed to domestic violence; treatment at community DV center	TF-CBT vs. CCT	TF-CBT significantly superior to CCT for improving PTSD and anxiety and for preventing serious adverse events

(continued)

Table 1 (continued)

Study	Index trauma	Comparison	Major findings
Deblinger, Mannarino, Cohen, Runyon, and Steer (2011)	Sexually abused children, TF-CBT dismantling study to examine effects of including (YES = Y) vs. excluding (NO = N) Trauma Narrative (TN) phase and length of treatment 8 vs. 16 sessions	8 sessions TF-CBT- N 8 session TF-CBT -Y 16 sessions TF-CBT- N 16 sessions TF-CBT- Y	8 sessions with TN was most effective and efficient at improving children's fear and anxiety and parents' abuse-specific distress. 16-sessions without TN led to significantly greater improvement in child externalizing behaviors and parenting skills
Jensen et al. (2013)	Trauma-exposed Norwegian children in community clinics	TF-CBT vs. TAU	TF-CBT significantly superior to TAU for improving PTSD, depression and general mental health symptoms
O'Callaghan et al. (2013)	Commercially sexually exploited, war-exposed Congolese girls	TF-CBT vs. WL	TF-CBT significantly superior to WL for improving PTSD, depression, anxiety, conduct problems and pro-social behavior
McMullen et al. (2014)	War-exposed Congolese boys	TF-CBT vs. WL	TF-CBT significantly superior to WL for improving PTSD, anxiety, depression, conduct symptoms and pro-social behavior
Diehle, Opmeer, Boer, Mannarino, and Lindauer Diehle et al. (2014)	Traumatized Dutch children	TF-CBT vs. EMDR	TF-CBT and EMDR equally effective and efficient in improving PTSD symptoms; TF-CBT significantly superior for improving children's depressive and hyperactivity symptoms
Murray et al. (2014)	HIV-affected Zambian children	TF-CBT vs. UCC	TF-CBT significantly superior to UCC for improving PTSD and adaptive impairment
Dorsey et al. (in press)	Traumatized children in foster care	Standard TF-CBT vs. TF-CBT+ Engagement Strategies	TF-CBT + Engagement significantly more likely to retain foster families in treatment through 4 sessions and prevent premature dropout

Key: *CCT* client centered therapy, *NST* non-directive supportive therapy, *ST* supportive therapy, *TAU* treatment as usual, *TF-CBT* trauma-focused cognitive behavioral therapy, *UCC* usual community care, *WL* wait list

Recent studies have expanded the generalizability of earlier TF-CBT research in several ways. First, several of these studies have been conducted by research teams operating independently of the TF-CBT developers, contributing to the scientific reliability of research findings that support the effectiveness of the treatment model.

Second, several of these studies have been conducted in community settings such as a community domestic violence center (Cohen, Mannarino, & Iyengar, 2011) or general community clinics (Dorsey et al., in press); and in different countries rather than the developers' or other researchers' clinics (e.g., Diehle, Opmeer, Boer, Mannarino, & Lindauer, 2014; Jensen et al., 2013), extending the applicability of the model to usual practice settings. These studies have confirmed that TF-CBT retains its effectiveness when provided by usual community therapists. Finally, recent studies in Africa, where trained mental health clinicians are scarce, have documented that TF-CBT is effective even when provided by lay counselors to children with severe and complex trauma (e.g., McMullen, O'Callaghan, Shannon, Black, & Eakin, 2014; Murray et al., 2014; O'Callaghan, McMullen, Shannon, Rafferty, & Black, 2013). These studies have lent additional evidence that TF-CBT effectively addresses children's trauma symptoms across developmental levels, settings, cultures, and trauma experiences.

In addition to these randomized controlled treatment trials, several quasi-randomized controlled studies have documented the effectiveness of TF-CBT for improving children's trauma symptoms after disasters such as the terrorist attacks of September 11, 2001 in New York City and Hurricane Katrina in New Orleans (CATS Consortium, 2010; Jaycox et al., 2010), for children who are suffering from traumatic grief related to homicides, suicides or other traumatic deaths (Cohen, Mannarino, & Knudsen, 2004; Cohen, Mannarino, & Staron, 2006), and for complexly traumatized children in foster care (Weiner, Schneider, & Lyons, 2009).

Several TF-CBT studies have examined the potential role of mediating factors in symptom reduction. For example, one study documented that in preschool children, parental emotional distress and parental support were significant predictors of children's symptoms (Cohen & Mannarino, 1998b). Another demonstrated that children's abuse-related attributions and perceptions as well as parental support predicted treatment outcome in older sexually abused children (Cohen & Mannarino, 2000). A third study revealed that multiple trauma history and higher levels of pretreatment depression served as a moderator and mediator, respectively of treatment outcome, but only for children receiving Client Centered Therapy (CCT), not for TF-CBT (Deblinger, Mannarino, Cohen, & Steer, 2006). This finding, in combination with the overall superiority of TF-CBT documented in the study, suggests that TF-CBT may be particularly preferential to CCT for children with multiple trauma histories or those with higher depressive symptoms at initial intake.

TF-CBT Therapist Certification

Licensed therapists who have at least a master's degree may become Certified TF-CBT Therapists. In order to become certified, therapists must complete the free online course, TF-CBTWeb, available at www.musc.edu/tfcbt. The TF-CBTWeb course offers ten free continuing education (CE) credits, and provides streaming video demonstrations of how to implement TF-CBT. After completing this course, therapists must attend a 2 day face-to-face TF-CBT training provided by a TF-CBT developer or approved national trainer, and participate in ongoing TF-CBT consultation calls during which the therapist presents TF-CBT treatment cases. The therapist must complete at least three TF-CBT cases with children (two of which include the child's parent or caregiver), using a standardized instrument to assess treatment progress. An alternative way of obtaining training and consultation is by participating in an approved TF-CBT learning collaborative, such as those sponsored by the National Child Traumatic Stress Network (www.nctsn. org). Upon completion of these requirements, therapists apply for certification on the TF-CBT National Therapist Certification website and pass an online knowledge-based test. Therapists are certified for 5 years. Certified therapists are listed (if desired) on the website for easy location by parents or insurers. TF-CBT implementation and research resources are made available to certified therapists on protected portions of the website. More information about this process is available at the TF-CBT National Therapist Certification website at https://.tfcbt.org.

Summary

TF-CBT is an evidence-based treatment for children and families impacted by child maltreatment and other traumas. Core TF-CBT principles include (1) proper duration and proportionality of the three TF-CBT treatment phases; (2) proper sequencing of the TF-CBT PRACTICE components; (3) use of gradual exposure throughout TF-CBT; and (4) inclusion of parents or caregivers whenever possible. TF-CBT has been evaluated in 15 randomized controlled treatment trials and several other effectiveness studies.

References

CATS Consortium (2010). Implementation of CBT for youth affected by the World Trade Center disaster: Matching need to treatment intensity and reducing trauma symptoms. *Journal of Traumatic Stress, 23*, 699–707.

Cohen, J. A., & Mannarino, A. P. (1996). A treatment study for sexually abused preschool children: Initial findings. *Journal of the American Academy of Child and Adolescent Psychiatry, 35*, 42–50.

Cohen, J. A., & Mannarino, A. P. (1998a). Factors that mediate treatment outcome of sexually abused preschooler: Six and twelve month follow-ups. *Journal of the American Academy of Child and Adolescent Psychiatry, 37*, 44–51.

Cohen, J. A., & Mannarino, A. P. (1998b). Interventions for sexually abused children: Initial treatment findings. *Child Maltreatment, 3*, 17–26.

Cohen, J. A., & Mannarino, A. P. (2000). Predictors of treatment outcome in sexually abused children. *Child Abuse and Neglect, 24*, 983–994.

Cohen, J. A., Deblinger, E., Mannarino, A. P., & Steer, R. (2004). A multisite, randomized controlled trial for children with sexual abuse-related PTSD symptoms. *Journal of the American Academy of Child and Adolescent Psychiatry, 43*, 393–402.

Cohen, J. A., Mannarino, A. P., & Deblinger, E. (2006). *Treating trauma and traumatic grief in children and adolescents*. New York: Guilford Press.

Cohen, J. A., Mannarino, A. P., & Deblinger, E. (Eds.) (2012). *Trauma-focused CBT for children and adolescents: Treatment applications*. New York: Guilford Press.

Cohen, J. A., Mannarino, A. P., & Iyengar, S. (2011). Community treatment of PTSD for children exposed to intimate partner violence: A randomized controlled trial. *Archives of Pediatrics & Adolescent Medicine, 165*, 16–21.

Cohen, J. A., Mannarino, A. P., Kliethermes, M., & Murray, L. A. (2012). Trauma-focused CBT for youth with complex trauma. *Child Abuse & Neglect, 36*, 528–541.

Cohen, J. A., Mannarino, A. P., & Knudsen, K. (2004). Treating childhood traumatic grief: A pilot study. *Journal of the American Academy Child & Adolescent Psychiatry, 43*, 1225–1233.

Cohen, J. A., Mannarino, A. P., & Knudsen, K. (2005). Treating sexually abused children: 1 year follow-up of a randomized controlled trial. *Child Abuse and Neglect, 29*, 135–146.

Cohen, J. A., Mannarino, A. P., Perel, J. M., & Staron, V. (2007). A pilot randomized controlled trial of combined trauma-focused CBT and Sertraline for childhood PTSD symptoms. *Journal of the American Academy Child & Adolescent Psychiatry, 46*, 811–819.

Cohen, J. A., Mannarino, A. P., & Staron, V. (2006). A pilot study of modified cognitive behavioral therapy for childhood traumatic grief. *Journal of the American Academy Child & Adolescent Psychiatry, 45*, 1465–1473.

Cohen, J. A., Mannarino, A. P., & Deblinger, E. (2016). *Treating trauma and traumatic grief in children and adolescents* (2nd ed.). New York: Guilford Press.

Deblinger, E., & Heflin, A. H. (1996). *Treating sexually abused children and their nonoffending parents: A cognitive behavioral approach*. Thousand Oaks, CA: Sage.

Deblinger, E., Lippmann, J., & Steer, R. (1996). Sexually abused children suffering posttraumatic stress symptoms: Initial treatment outcome findings. *Child Maltreatment, 1*, 310–321.

Deblinger, E., Mannarino, A. P., Cohen, J. A., Runyon, M., & Steer, R. (2011). Trauma-focused cognitive behavioral therapy for children: Impact of the trauma narrative and treatment length. *Depression & Anxiety, 28*, 67–75.

Deblinger, E., Mannarino, A. P., Cohen, J. A., & Steer, R. (2006). A follow-up study of a multi-site, randomized controlled trial for children with sexual abuse-related PTSD symptoms: Examining predictors of treatment response. *Journal of the American Academy of Child and Adolescent Psychiatry, 45*, 1474–1484.

Deblinger, E., Stauffer, L., & Steer, R. (2001). Comparative efficacies of supportive and cognitive behavioral group therapies for children who were sexually abused and their nonoffending mothers. *Child Maltreatment, 6*(4), 332–343.

Diehle, J., Opmeer, B. C., Boer, F., Mannarino, A. P., & Lindauer, R. J. L. (2014). Trauma-focused cognitive behavioral therapy of eye movement desensitization and reprocessing: What works in children with posttraumatic stress symptoms? A randomized controlled trial. *European Child Adolescent Psychiatry*. Retrieved from http://link.springer.com/article/10.1007/s00787-014-0572-5

Dorsey, S., Pullmann, M. D., Berliner, L., Koschmann, E., McKay, M., & Deblinger, E. (in press). Engaging foster parents in treatment: A randomized trial of supplementing Trauma-focused cognitive behavioral therapy with evidence-based engagement strategies. *Child Abuse & Neglect*.

Foa, E. B., Keane, T. M., Friedman, M. J., & Cohen, J. A. (Eds.), *Effective treatment for PTSD: Practice guidelines from the International Society for Traumatic Stress Studies* (2nd ed.). New York: Guilford Press.

Jaycox, L. H., Cohen, J. A., Mannarino, A. P., Langley, A., Walker, D. W., Geggenheimer, K., & Schoenlein, M. (2010). Children's mental health care following Hurricane Katrina: A field trial of trauma psychotherapies. *Journal of Traumatic Stress, 23*, 223–231.

Jensen, T., Holt, T., Ormhaug, S. M., Egeland, K., Granley, L., Hoaas, L. C., … Ollendick, T. H. (2013). *A randomized effectiveness study comparing trauma-focused cognitive behavioral therapy to therapy as usual for youth*. *Journal of Clinical Child & Adolescent Psychology*. Retrieved from http://dx.doi.org/10.1080/15374416.2013.822307.

King, N. J., Tonge, B. J., Mullen, P., Myerson, N., Heyne, D., Rollings, S., ... Ollendick, T. H. (2000). Treating sexually abused children with posttraumatic stress symptoms: A randomized clinical trial. *Journal of the American Academy of Child and Adolescent Psychiatry, 39*, 1347–1355.

Kisiel, C., Conradi, L., Fehrenbach, T., Torgersen, E., & Briggs, E. C. (2014). Assessing the effects of trauma in children and adolescents in practice settings. *Child Adolescent Clinics North America, 23*, 223–242.

McMullen, J., O'Callaghan, P., Shannon, C., Black, A., & Eakin, J. (2014). Group trauma-focused cognitive behavioural therapy with former child soldiers and other war-affected boys in the DR Congo: A randomized controlled trial. *Journal of Child Psychology & Psychiatry, 54*, 1231–1241.

Murray, L. K., Skavenski, S., Kane, J., Muntali, S., Kasoma, M., Baxter, P., ... Bolton, P. (2014). *A randomized controlled trial to determine the effectiveness of trauma-focused cognitive behavioral therapy (TF-CBT) among trauma-affected children in Lusaka*. Zambia: USAID Report.

National Crime Victims Research and Treatment Center. (2007). *TF-CBTWeb: First Year Report*. Retrieved from www.musc.edu/tfcbt/resources.

O'Callaghan, P., McMullen, J., Shannon, C., Rafferty, H., & Black, A. (2013). A randomized controlled trial of trauma-focused cognitive behavioral therapy for sexually exploited, war-affected Congolese girls. *Journal of the American Academy of Child & Adolescent Psychiatry, 52*, 359–369.

Weiner, D. A., Schneider, A., & Lyons, J. S. (2009). Evidence-based treatments for trauma among culturally diverse foster care youth: Treatment retention and outcomes. *Children & Youth Services Review, 31*, 1199–1205.

Parent-Child Interaction Therapy in Child Welfare

Carisa Wilsie, Christopher Campbell, Mark Chaffin, and Beverly Funderburk

Traditional and Evidence-Based Parenting Models in Child Welfare

In a large, nationally representative sample of child welfare cases, parenting programs were the single most common type of services offered to maltreating parents (NSCAW Research Group, 2005). This should come as no surprise, given that child maltreatment is inherently and primarily a parenting problem. Reliance on parenting programs by child welfare systems has a long history, but not necessarily a successful one. Traditional parent training models often relied on didactic presentation of abstract parenting principles, developing insight into presumed childhood underpinnings of current parenting behavior (e.g. the "abused-to-abuser cycle"), or unstructured group discussion. Results were disappointing (Cohn & Daro, 1987).

More recently, focus has shifted to adopting evidence-based behavioral skill-oriented parent training interventions that were originally designed as parent-mediated treatments for disruptive child behavior problems and then applying them as an intervention for maltreating parents in child welfare. This represents a substantial shift in purpose for these models—away from being a child treatment in which parent behavior is a mediating step, toward being a treatment whose benchmark outcome is parent behavior.

C. Wilsie, Ph.D. (✉) • M. Chaffin, Ph.D. • B. Funderburk, Ph.D.
Department of Pediatrics, Child Study Center, University of Oklahoma Health Sciences Center, 1100 N.E. 13th St, Oklahoma City, OK 73117, USA
e-mail: carisa-wilsie@ouhsc.edu; beverly-funderburk@ouhsc.edu

C. Campbell, Ph.D.
College of Education and Psychology, East Central University, Ada, OK, USA
e-mail: christopher-campbell@ouhsc.edu

© Springer International Publishing Switzerland 2017   107
D.M. Teti (ed.), *Parenting and Family Processes in Child Maltreatment and Intervention*, Child Maltreatment Solutions Network,
DOI 10.1007/978-3-319-40920-7_7

PCIT is not the only behavioral parenting model being adopted in child welfare. Other examples include The Incredible Years (Webster-Stratton, 2011) and Triple-P (Sanders, 2012) (California Evidence-Based Clearinghouse for Child Welfare, 2009; Centers for Disease Control and Prevention, National Center for Injury Prevention and Control, 2004). All share some basic skills and approaches in common. In contrast to traditional parenting models, which emphasize how parenting is conceptualized, understood, or talked about, these newer evidence-based models focus on parenting as it is behaviorally delivered. The newer models may target fewer parenting principles and skills, but target them with far greater detail, specificity, repetition, and intensity. Rather than teaching an abstract parenting concept, and then leaving it to parents to translate that concept into parenting behavior, these models teach the parenting skill directly, and in the case of PCIT, until the parent reaches an objective criterion for demonstrating skill competency.

Several meta-analyses of these newer behavioral parent training programs exist, including studies focused on the elements contained within specific parenting programs (e.g., Cedar & Levant, 1990; Thomas & Zimmer-Gembeck, 2007), orientations and approaches (e.g., Maughan, Christiansen, Jenson, Olympia, & Clark, 2005; Serketich & Dumas, 1996), delivery settings (e.g., Sweet & Appelbaum, 2004), and characteristics of participating families (e.g., Lundahl, Nimer, & Parsons, 2006; Lundahl, Risser, & Lovejoy, 2006; Reyno & McGrath, 2006). Overall, these meta-analyses describe a consistent and clinically meaningful positive effect across models for improving parenting behaviors and for reducing early behavior problems (e.g., Kaminski, Valle, Filene, & Boyle, 2008; Lundahl et al., 2006; Maughan et al., 2005; Reyno & McGrath, 2006).

None of the interventions listed above were originally designed for child welfare populations, nor created to reduce child maltreatment recidivism. These models were originally developed as parent-mediated treatments for children with disruptive behavior disorders, and their adoption as treatments intended to reduce parental maltreating behavior constitutes a significant departure from their original purpose. In a child welfare context, they are often used as *parent* treatments, not *child* treatments. Caregivers in child welfare are typically referred to parenting programs primarily to achieve *parent* behavior change, not *child* behavior change, and parenting programs are used regardless of whether children actually have behavior problems (e.g., Barth et al., 2005; Pinkston & Smith, 1998). Although the parenting skills taught in the child welfare adaptations of PCIT may be similar to those taught in standard PCIT (e.g. use of praise or time-out), the baseline parenting issues can be quite different between the populations. For example, when PCIT is used to treat child behavior problems, parenting may be inconsistent or reinforcement may be used ineffectively. But when PCIT is used to treat abusive parenting, the parenting may also be harsh, violent or detached. In the child welfare context, parenting can be complicated by poverty, parental depression, parental substance abuse, family violence, low motivation, or basic needs insufficiency to a greater extent than in standard behavior problem treatment. In other uses of PCIT within child welfare, such as for children in foster care, the goals and parenting issues may remain closer to their original design and intent, and the standard PCIT protocol may be better suited to case goals than the adapted protocol. Of course, parenting models may be used to deliver both types of outcomes simultaneously - reduced recidivism risk among parents and improved child wellbeing and reduced behavior problems among children. The fact that one intervention can serve either or both of these ends is a particular advantage.

Commonalities between etiological models for child behavior problems and child maltreatment may suggest a framework for understanding how a single intervention can deliver outcomes in both domains. The majority of parent-to-child violence occurs within the context of exaggerated child discipline or corporal punishment. Caregivers who physically harm their children often feel as though nothing short of harsh or violent discipline strategies will "work" with their children, whom they perceive (accurately or inaccurately) as having unmanageable behavior problems (Crouch & Behl, 2001). In fact, many physically abusive caregivers self-report their behavior as discipline rather than as child abuse.

Child behavior problems and parent-to-child violence may share a common and reciprocal developmental process described by Patterson's coercive cycle model (Patterson, 1976; Urquiza & McNeil, 1996). In this model, harsh discipline in response to real or perceived child defiance is reinforced by short-term child compliance, which in turn increases the caregiver's reliance on harsh discipline, potentially escalating to the point of seriously violent parent-to-child behaviors, particularly among at-risk caregivers (e.g., caregivers with depression, high distress, high anger, high emotional reactivity or low emotion regulation). In this cycle, negative interactions tend to escalate and positive exchanges tend to diminish. In the absence of positive interactions, a hostile parent-child relationship develops which can be categorized by negative caregiver attributions, unrealistic expectations, disengagement, inconsistent and harsh discipline, and failure to respond to the child's appropriate or prosocial behaviors. Notably, unresponsiveness to appropriate child behavior or child needs, deteriorated relationship quality, and withdrawn or weak parent-child attachments form the relational context for both child physical abuse and neglect (Stith et al., 2009). PCIT and related evidence-based behavioral parenting models directly target and interrupt coercive cycles, relationship deterioration, and disengaged aspects of parent-child interactions by creating or enhancing two sets of incompatible replacement behaviors— positive parent-child interaction skills, and a consistent step-by-step approach to non-violent discipline.

Parent-Child Interaction Therapy (PCIT)

Origin and influences. PCIT is one member of a family of parent-mediated models derived from Constance Hanf's (1969) two-stage model. Hanf and colleagues at the University of Oregon's School of Medicine broke with traditional child psychotherapy approaches of the day and began using parent-involved practices incorporating elements of developmental theory, social learning theory, behavioral principles, and interactional play techniques (Reitman & McMahon,

2012). Since its inception, variants of the Hanf model have been widely used and researched including, Helping the Noncompliant Child (McMahon & Forehand, 2003) and The Incredible Years (Webster-Stratton, 2005). Two-stage models correspond to a parenting orientation similar to Baumrind's authoritative parenting style (Baumrind, 1967), with the first phase emphasizing nurturance and warmth in the parent-child relationship and the second phase emphasizing consistent, developmentally appropriate limit-setting, and discipline.

PCIT structure and format. Following this template, PCIT is delivered in two phases which are called: (1) Child-Directed Interaction (CDI), and (2) Parent-Directed Interaction (PDI). Each phase begins with one didactic or teaching session where PCIT skills are introduced, explained, modeled, and role-played with the caregiver(s). Teaching sessions are followed by multiple live-coached dyadic sessions where skills are practiced and refined *in vivo*. Live, real-time, coached skill practice and feedback during parent-child interactions is perhaps the hallmark of PCIT, and a distinguishing feature of the model. During coaching sessions, therapists use prompting, modeling, reinforcement, and selective attention to shape each caregiver's acquisition and refinement of PCIT skills (Brinkmeyer & Eyberg, 2003). Standard PCIT coaching sessions are conducted with the therapist behind a one-way mirror, observing parent-child interactions. Variations of this delivery format, including home-based, in-room, and remote delivery formats have been used with some success. The average length of treatment intervention is a compact 14 sessions—one teaching session and approximately six coaching sessions per treatment phase (Callahan, Stevens, & Eyberg, 2010).

The goal of the CDI phase is to develop and strengthen the caregiver-child relationship and to use the relationship in positive ways to shape behavior. The relationship strengthening skills are described under an acronym known as "PRIDE," consisting of five elements: (**P**raise), which is used to recognize and encourage prosocial behaviors, particularly labeled praise (e.g. "you did a good job picking up the toys"); (**R**eflection), which is used to improve active listening and verbal communication; (**I**mitation) or modeling appropriate behaviors while enjoying time with children; (**D**escription) which is used to convey interest in positive behaviors; and (**E**njoyment) which sets an affective tone for the interaction (Eyberg & Funderburk, 2011). Differential social attention is another technique parents are coached to use. Differential attention involves attending to appropriate child behaviors (e.g., sharing, using manners, playing appropriately) and actively ignoring attention-seeking or inappropriate child behaviors (e.g., whining, playing roughly, temper tantrums) so long as they do not cause any safety concerns (Herschell & McNeil, 2005). Studies with child welfare involved parents demonstrate that these skills tend to be learned quickly, fairly uniformly, and result in rapid improvement in the observable parent-child interaction in session (Hakman, Chaffin, Funderburk, & Silovsky, 2009).

The overarching task for caregivers in the CDI phase is to follow the *child's lead*. During the CDI phase caregivers are coached to avoid behaviors that can take away the lead from their child, such as questioning, giving commands, criticism, sarcasm, and physically negative behavior or tones of voice. These negative interaction elements often are common among abusive parents prior to treatment. For example, prior to treatment, abusive parents may be equally as likely to respond to a positive child behavior with negative behavior as with praise (Hakman et al., 2009). During the CDI phase, parents would be expected both to eliminate the negative behavior and to increase their use of labeled praise in response to positive child behavior. A broad impact of this skill shift may be improving the quality, closeness and satisfaction of the parent-child relationship.

The second or Parent-Directed Interaction (PDI) phase is focused on additional behavior management techniques. The goals of PDI are to teach caregivers to give effective commands, set consistent and fair limits, follow through with commands in a predictable manner, and provide reasonable, age-appropriate consequences for misbehavior within the context of a positive parent-child relationship (Herschell & McNeil, 2005). During the PDI phase, caregivers learn a step-by-step time-out procedure for responding to noncompliance and severe misbehavior. With older school-age children, logical consequences (rather than time-out) are substituted. As the PDI phase progresses, increased emphasis is placed on practicing and generalizing PCIT skills outside of the clinic environment (e.g., home, shopping mall, grocery store) to facilitate real-world mastery (Callahan et al., 2010). For parents whose children are in foster care, practice and generalization opportunities may be limited, and findings suggest that a long delay between PCIT receipt and return of children to the home is associated with reduced treatment benefits (Chaffin et al., 2009). Even if children do not have serious behavior problems, learning these skills may benefit parents. All children require some discipline, and discipline is a context in which maltreatment commonly occurs. The protocol creates a structure for discipline—consequences are prescribed by the protocol, not driven by the anger of the moment. Consequences are instituted consistently and immediately, potentially cutting short escalation, reducing parenting stress, and softening negative attributions about the child. And the protocol has demonstrable effectiveness, meaning that over time it may be needed less often, which can contribute a sense of parental self-efficacy and satisfaction.

Standard PCIT—Efficacy for reducing child behavior problems. A long series of PCIT research findings have demonstrated the model's effectiveness in decreasing child disruptive behaviors (e.g., Eisenstadt, Eyberg, McNeil, Newcomb, & Funderburk, 1993; McNeil, Capage, Bahl, & Blanc, 1999), increasing child compliance with parental requests (e.g., Eyberg & Robinson, 1982), improving the parent-child relationship (e.g., Eyberg, Boggs, & Algina, 1995), and reducing parental stress (e.g., Schuhmann, Foote, Eyberg, Boggs, & Algina, 1998). Child behavior improvements have been found to generalize from the controlled clinic setting to the home environment (e.g., Schuhmann et al., 1998), as well as from the home to school classrooms, and from treated children in the family to untreated siblings (McNeil, Eyberg, Eisendstadt, Newcomb, & Funderburk, 1991). In a recent review of 17 PCIT outcome studies (a total of 368 children who participated in PCIT), statistically significant improvements of child behavior problems were found across all studies (Gallagher, 2003). In fact, Gallagher (2003) reported clinical significance in 82 % (14 of 17) of the studies, with *clinical significance* defined as changing behavior problems from the clinically significant range at pre-treatment to within the normal range at post-treatment.

Long-term maintenance of gain. Follow-up studies, evaluating the maintenance of treatment gains of PCIT, have demonstrated lasting benefits. For example, treatment gains in the home setting have maintained 1 and 2 years post-treatment (Eyberg et al., 2001). Funderburk et al. (1998) found that PCIT gains in a clinic setting generalized to the classroom (without direct classroom intervention), and these improvements were maintained up to 1 year post-treatment, and to a lesser extent at the 18-month follow-up. Boggs et al. (2004) found that families who completed PCIT maintained their gains (in both child and family functioning) 1–3 years post-treatment. Hood and Eyberg (2003) found that parent-child interactions continued to improve and mothers' confidence in controlling their child's behavior was maintained at 3–6 years post-treatment.

Efficacy across diverse populations. PCIT has been successfully adapted for services with a range of child populations. Examples include children with developmental delays (Bagner & Eyberg, 2007; McDiarmid & Bagner, 2005), separation anxiety disorder (Pincus, Choate, Eyberg, & Barlow, 2005), chronic illness (Bagner, Fernandez, & Eyberg, 2004), and children with histories of child maltreatment (Timmer, Urquiza, Zebell, & McGrath, 2005). Benefits also have been found across a range of caregiver populations, including nontraditional caregivers such as foster caregivers, adoptive parents, and kinship caregivers (e.g., McNeil, Herschell, Gurwitch, & Clemens-Mowrer, 2005; Timmer et al., 2006). More recently, successful outcomes have been reported across cultural backgrounds including implementations or adaptations for Mexican Americans (McCabe, Yeh, Garland, Lau, & Chavez, 2005), Puerto Ricans (Matos, Torres, Santiago, Jurado, & Rodriguez, 2006), Chinese (Leung, Tsang, Heung, & Yiu, 2009), Norwegians (Bjørseth & Wormdal, 2005), Dutch (Abrahamse et al., 2012), and Australians (Nixon, Sweeney, Erickson, & Touyz, 2003; Phillips, Morgan, Cawthorne, & Barnett, 2008). An American Indian cultural adaptation also has been developed (BigFoot & Funderburk, 2011).

Delivery approach. Dual phase parenting models share substantial content. What varies most among this family of models is delivery approach. The critical delivery element that distinguishes PCIT is individual in vivo skill *coaching*. Direct coaching has been called "both the heart and art" (McNeil & Hembree-Kigin, 2010, p. 8) of the PCIT program. Historically, parent training has relied on a variety of indirect approaches (e.g., didactics, modeling, rehearsal) in which caregivers are taught certain skills apart from their children, then instructed to implement those skills on their own and report problems in subsequent sessions. In PCIT, live *in vivo* coaching is done using a wireless earphone or "bug-in-the-ear" over which the therapist coaches the parent's behavior while the parent interacts with their child in order to shape and reinforce skill acquisition. This is most often accomplished by a therapist who is observing the parent-child interaction from behind a one-way mirror in a clinic that is specially equipped for PCIT, as diagrammed in Fig. 1. Direct coaching of parent-child interactions has

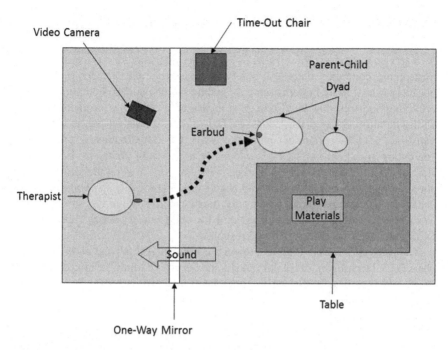

Fig. 1 Standard room configuration for PCIT

several advantages, including: (1) the ability to correct errors quickly, before caregivers consistently practice incorrect techniques; (2) the opportunity for the therapist to adapt as idiosyncratic problems arise; (3) increased parental confidence as new skills are encouraged and supported through coaching; (4) potentially faster learning resulting from immediate feedback; and (5) decreased reliance on self-reports which may not accurately reflect the context and/or parent/child behaviors (c.f., McNeil & Hembree-Kigin, 2010).

Parenting delivery approaches were examined in a meta-analysis by Kaminski et al. (2008) — programs where caregivers practiced new skills with their own child *in vivo* yielded significantly larger effect sizes, regardless of content differences. Among a range of content and delivery elements examined, direct skill practice with the parent's own child was one of the single most powerful predictors of larger effects. This is a particularly salient point when it comes to serving parents in the child welfare system, where large effects are presumably necessary. The benefits of live coached delivery do come with a price in terms of delivery or implementation challenges - live coached delivery is labor intensive, equipment intensive, may involve scheduling challenges, is vulnerable to failed appointments, and may involve logistic challenges due to the fact that both a parent and a child need to be present. Cost-effectiveness analyses suggest that the cost savings from reduced child welfare recidivism offset the added delivery costs (Lee, Aos, & Miller, 2008). Efficiency also benefits from the fact that PCIT is shorter than many traditional parenting programs.

How PCIT Fits Within Child Welfare Services Systems

As a service purchaser, child welfare systems are interested in services that achieve measurable concrete outcomes—safety, permanency, and wellbeing. Moreover, because child welfare systems serve the public interest and expend public monies, providing services that yield objective measurable outcomes promotes accountability (Chaffin & Friedrich, 2004). PCIT is a good match for public service systems such as child welfare in a number of ways. Child maltreatment is inherently a "parenting" problem and PCIT is inherently a parenting treatment. For example, Hakman et al. (2009) found that parents with a history of child physical abuse had about an equal chance of responding negatively or positively to *appropriate* child behavior; in contrast, these parents exhibited positive parenting strategies (i.e., describing or attending to the behaviors) for child *inappropriate* child behavior. PCIT addresses these inapt parental responses.

The peak ages for child maltreatment are in the preschool and early school-age years (U.S. Department of Health and Human Services, Administration on Children, Youth and Families, 2005), which corresponds well with standard PCIT inclusion criteria (although adaptations for children up to age 12 have been developed and tested). PCIT has rigorous evidence that it delivers benefits simultaneously in two of the three benchmark child welfare outcome domains—safety (i.e. reduced recidivism) and child wellbeing (i.e. reduced behavior problems). Because it is a compact intervention, it also may speed transitions to permanency, which is child welfare's third benchmark outcome domain. The model does not require collateral services or additional treatments in order to be effective—in fact, some evidence suggests that the model works sufficiently or even better when families are not inundated with multiple concurrent therapies (Chaffin et al., 2004; Kaminski et al., 2008). PCIT has been found effective among physically abusive parents and among chronic child welfare cases with long histories of both abuse and neglect, which are the most common maltreatment types in child welfare.

Child welfare also serves children in the foster care system, where child wellbeing is a benchmark outcome goal. Histories of trauma and entry into the foster care system alone increases the likelihood that children will develop mental health or behavior problems (Lawrence, Carlson, & Egeland, 2006), and as many as 50 percent or more of foster children may exhibit clinical problem levels (Clausen, Landsverk, Ganger, Chadwick, & Litrownik, 1998; Leslie, Hurlburt, Landsverk, Barth, & Slymen, 2004). Behavior problems in foster care are perhaps the single largest cause of disrupted foster care placements. Children with behavior problems are more likely to have foster care placement disruptions and foster care placement disruptions may create more behavior problems, potentially creating an escalating and pernicious cycle, not infrequently eventuating in a more restrictive psychiatric or residential placements (e.g., Cook, 1994; James et al., 2006; Newton, Litrownik, & Landsverk, 2000; Timmer et al., 2006). The work of Timmer, Urquiza, and others has focused on children in foster and kinship care settings. Findings suggest that PCIT can enhance the quality of the foster caregiver-child relationship and improve foster caregiver's parenting skills; which in turn can improve foster placement stability and child mental health outcomes (e.g., McNeil et al., 2005; Timmer et al., 2006). PCIT for foster parents may offer additional advantages—skills might generalize from current to future foster children, and reliance on psychotropic medication to control foster child behavior might be reduced. PCIT also has been included as a suggested part of a trauma informed foster care service portfolio (Klain & White, 2013).

Motivational adaptation for maltreating parents in child welfare. In standard PCIT for child behavior problems, caregivers are usually voluntary consumers who are self-motivated to seek services. Caregivers in child welfare are typically coerced into services and may or may not be motivated. This difference potentially poses an obstacle for PCIT because PCIT requires active practice and *in vivo* skill demonstration in session and active completion of homework and utilization of skills outside of session. Some types of parenting programs, such as didactic classes, can be passively consumed but PCIT cannot.

For this reason, the initial randomized trial with abusive parents included a pretreatment motivational intervention based on motivational interviewing principles before beginning PCIT. Elements of the motivational package included a testimonial from a treatment completer, examination of ability and readiness to change parenting practices, and exercises to develop the discrepancy between the current and the desired parenting relationship and family circumstances. The overall Motivation + PCIT package reduced downstream child welfare recidivism from 49 percent for a parenting class comparison condition to 19 percent for PCIT (Chaffin et al., 2004). A subsequent trial used a dismantling design to test the relative contribution of the motivational adaptation to overall recidivism reduction. Chaffin et al. (2009); Chaffin, Funderburk, Bard, Valle, and Gurwitch (2011)) found that the self-motivation component combined with PCIT yielded better program retention rates (85 percent vs. 61 percent cumulative program retention). In both the 2004 and 2010 randomized trials, child welfare recidivism reduction was found among highly comorbid and "deep-end" child welfare populations, including parents with an average of 4–6 prior child welfare entries. Effectiveness with complex and serious real-world cases, including in a trial done outside of a controlled laboratory setting and conducted by someone other than the model developer, are some of the strongest reasons why child welfare systems should consider adapted PCIT as a first-line treatment choice.

Non-motivational adaptations for maltreating parents. Maltreating parents may have problems with self-control, detachment, negative attributions, and anger. These issues necessitated minor adaptations to the standard PCIT model. In most respects, the adapted PCIT model developed for maltreating parents would be easily and immediately recognizable as PCIT by any standard PCIT practitioner. What remains virtually unchanged are the fundamental elements, techniques and structure of the model, including: (a) the overarching two-phase approach (CDI and PDI); (b) PRIDE skills; (c) basic time-out protocol; (d) command training; (e) generalization guidelines; (f) expected dose; (g) setting; (h) *in vivo* coaching techniques and technology; (i) theory base; (j) coding schemes; (k) measures; (l) CDI and PDI competency criteria; (m) homework assignments; and (n) treatment materials. Adaptations were made to some aspects of CDI coaching to make it more parent focused rather than child focused, such as selectively reinforcing parental self-control or sensitivity toward the child.

The time-out protocol for young children was modified in four ways. First, steps were added to boost parental self-control (e.g., coaching parents to stop, take a breath, monitor their stress level, and relax or count to ten before executing the time-out process). Second, only non-physical "back-ups" for time-out escape are taught. Third, the time out protocol is practiced first in role-plays with the therapist in order to verify that the parent can use time out appropriately and with good self-control. Finally, greater emphasis is placed on educating parents about developmentally normal child challenges and expectations. Adaptations may also be required for parents whose children are in foster care, and who have limited opportunities to practice skills or complete homework. These can include using role-plays, practicing CDI during scheduled visits, or practicing with other children in the home. We do not recommend starting PCIT in cases where the child in foster care is unlikely to ever return home, or if return may be delayed until well after PCIT is completed, because delays have been found to be associated with loss of treatment benefit (Chaffin et al., 2009).

Adaptations for parents of school-age children (up to approximately 12 years of age). One of the key differences between standard PCIT for early childhood behavior problems, and adapted PCIT for maltreating parents is *child age range*. Because children in the adapted protocol are in many ways secondary or collateral participants, the children do not necessarily have behavior problems, and the parents are the primary focus, a broader child age inclusion criterion seemed reasonable. Standard PCIT is geared for children under age 7 years, so adaptations were required for parents of older school-age children up to age 12 years. This extension did not appear to strongly impact parent outcomes—in both of the randomized trials with maltreating parents, age of the child did not moderate or significantly alter the recidivism reduction effect. Effectiveness of the adaptation for reducing older school-age behavior problems has not been specifically tested, but many of the adaptations parallel elements found in well-tested school age behavior problem models.

Again, the basic framework of PCIT remains intact (e.g., two-phase CDI and PDI structure, *in vivo* skill coaching, foundational behavioral theory base). In some cases, the adaptations for older children are simply matters of degree, such as continuing to emphasize labeled praise in response to positive child behavior, but coaching that praise to be less frequent and less effusive or demonstrative than it might be with a preschooler. In other cases, the adaptation involved substitutions, such as substituting logical consequences or loss of privileges for the time-out chair. Substitutions used parallel elements (i.e., an older child discipline element was substituted for a standard PCIT discipline element), and the substituted elements were drawn from techniques that cut across multiple behavioral parenting programs used with older children (e.g., in models such as Barkley's Defiant Child, or the Boy's Town Common Sense

Parenting). No hard chronological age line was established for migrating from usual PCIT to the older child adaptations, nor was there a requirement that the older child adaptation be adopted whole cloth. Rather, usual PCIT was treated as the default option and older child adaptation elements were selectively applied based on the clinician's assessment of developmental fit with the individual case. The following points describe the main adaptations made for parents of older school-age children:

- Older children are included more in explaining the goals of treatment ("to help parents and children get along better and reduce arguing"), obtaining assent, and included more in selecting what types of logical consequences and joint "special time" activities should be used.
- Older children are consulted about the most effective or preferred ways for parents to word some types of verbal skills, such as praise, reflections, and/or commands.
- More silence during CDI is permitted, along with less frequent and effusive praise. Drills with parents were used prior to sessions in order to create more practice opportunities for these skills given that the number of practice repetitions during *in vivo* coaching was reduced.
- Reflection was coached to rephrase or validate more complex child emotions.
- More age-appropriate CDI activities were selected, often with child input.
- Longer time is allowed between a command and expectation of compliance.
- The parent developed a menu of non-confrontational reasonable consequences and loss of privileges that can be used as discipline options (e.g., loss of a video game, loss of TV time for a day) either as a full or partial alternative to time-out or as a back-up to time-out. Care is taken to distinguish between "luxuries" that can be removed contingent on compliance (e.g., TV time), and activities that may be important to retain irrespective of compliance because they foster growth and positive behavior (e.g., participation in a prosocial school activity).
- Because older children have longer attention spans, consequences can be applied later in time rather than immediately. A cap is placed on the number of privileges that can be lost in a single discipline episode, in order to prevent unreasonable consequence escalation.
- Time-out can shifted from a time-out chair to being sent to a room.
- Physical back-ups to time out or consequences are eliminated.
- During the final 5–10 min of the session, while the therapist gives feedback and homework assignment to the parent, the child is allowed a choice of activities (e.g., hand-held video game, a choice of a preferred toy, time on the playground) if compliance during the session had been good. If the child was non-compliant in session, the parent could withhold increments of the child's free time.
- Given the generally better self-control of older children in session, and the fact that child behavior problems are not an inclusion criterion for the adapted model, many older children were rarely non-compliant in session, and therefore parents had limited in-session practice opportunities for discipline skills. In these cases,

therapists would use role-play in a parent-therapist session in which the therapist portrays a non-compliant child.

Less is sometimes more and the collateral treatment dilemma. Given that many parents in child welfare have multiple behavioral health problems, they may benefit from additional services (e.g., parental substance abuse treatment, parental depression treatment). However, recent perspectives on evidence-based case planning have questioned the extent to which "comprehensive" services are wise (Berliner, et al., 2014). Random assignment to tailored "comprehensive services" in addition to PCIT actually increased child welfare recidivism rates and lowered skill acquisition (Chaffin et al., 2004). This is not an unusual finding. For example, Kaminski et al. (2008) found in a review of 77 published parent training studies, that providing parents with services, in addition to the parent training program, was associated with smaller effects on parent behaviors and skills outcomes and cited that three other meta-analyses found the same result. In short, more service is not always better service. At this point, it is unclear which combinations of services are optimal. Keeping on focus, minimizing burden, and avoiding mixed or contradictory messages are all important considerations for any good case plan. It is likely that a few services beyond a parenting program like PCIT are helpful and perhaps even necessary in some cases, but there also comes a point at which additional services add little and begin to spoil any benefit. We lack any evidence-based algorithm for deciding how much is enough and how much is too much, although there are conceptual guidelines for developing a sufficient but efficient case plan (Berliner, et al., 2014).

Emerging Uses and Adaptations of PCIT in Child Maltreatment Cases

PCIT as an element of trauma informed care. Trauma related problems are common among maltreated children, so it is encouraging to note that some early pilot findings point to PCIT benefits in internalizing problem domains (e.g. depression, anxiety, PTSD symptoms), in addition to the well-tested and supported externalizing or behavior problem domain. Although it is premature to characterize PCIT as a "trauma treatment," emerging evidence suggests some benefits. Lenze, Pautsch and Luby (2011) adapted PCIT by adding an emotional-development module focused on internalizing and early small-scale controlled trial results are encouraging. Thomas and Zimmer-Gembeck (2012) have reported significant internalizing problem reductions in a randomized waitlist controlled trial of standard PCIT. Findings from uncontrolled trials of other adaptations have reported specific reductions in trauma related symptoms (Pearl et al., 2012) and anxiety symptoms (Puliafico, Comer, & Pincus, 2012). At this point, findings point toward benefits in the internalizing problem domain, but it remains unclear how robust these findings will be to replication in rigorous trials, or how durable they will prove with longer follow-up. It remains unclear whether adaptations to standard PCIT are necessary for outcomes in this domain. Recent work in evidence-based treatments (EBTs) implementation suggests that it may be both feasible and beneficial to "blend" modularized elements from established internalizing and externalizing EBTs based on assessment driven algorithms (Weisz et al., 2012).

PCIT implementation and scale-up. Implementing evidence-based models in field settings involves far more than simple "train-and-hope" methods such as workshops or dissemination of treatment manuals (Fixsen et al., 2005). Indeed, implementing EBTs may be more challenging than developing them. A full discussion of implementation practicalities and conceptual models is beyond our scope here, but suffice it to say that multiple systems, complexities and hurdles invariably are involved (Aarons, Hurlburt, & Horwitz, 2011), of which initial provider training may be the simplest to tackle. Few studies have examined how PCIT is taken up, or how it performs in scaled-up settings. In the absence of field-based effectiveness studies, there are no assurances that evidence-based models will retain the efficacy enjoyed in usually smaller and more tightly quality controlled research settings (Shirk, 2004). Adapted PCIT for child welfare parents has been tested in authentic but still small-scale field settings with some success, which is encouraging (Chaffin et al., 2009), but to our knowledge has not been tested at full system-wide scale-up.

PCIT does pose implementation challenges. For example, special equipment may be involved, such as one-way mirrors, remote coaching transmitters and receivers, and sound equipment. Non-traditional adaptations such as home-based PCIT have been explored, but most PCIT is still a clinic-based service and this by itself can pose a major obstacle to widespread population penetration, especially among the population segments served by child welfare systems (Kazdin & Blasé, 2011). Relative to parenting classes, PCIT is costly and labor intensive to deliver. And, like all EBTs, there are initial training requirements and ongoing provider competency development and quality control issues that must be addressed in order for the model to succeed in the field at scale.

PCIT began, and for many years was practiced, almost exclusively in a few university-based clinics. In 2009, PCIT International was incorporated as a governing body dedicated to maintaining the quality and fidelity of PCIT. Provider and trainer certification standards were established along with agency readiness guidelines. Traditionally, training in PCIT was conducted at a university-based doctoral psychology program via a mentoring model. A novice PCIT therapist learned the model first by observing an experienced expert therapist, then conducted sessions under co-therapy, and then under live supervision. This mentored training model, while perhaps ideal and still feasible for students in a doctoral program, is not feasible for large-scale implementation. It may not even be feasible for an established PCIT service agency considering the amount of trainer or coach time involved that might not be reimbursed under the unit-rate billing schemes on which many service agencies depend.

Distance training strategies have been developed to augment PCIT workshop training. Funderburk and colleagues compared supervision under a live video feed to the usual post-hoc telephone consultation in a controlled trial. In the live video feed condition, a remote consultant can see and hear both the therapist and the family participating in PCIT. Live video consultation resulted in cases reaching clinical improvement criteria faster and achieving lower behavior problem endpoints. The cost savings of fewer sessions was sufficient to offset the additional cost of live video consultation (Funderburk, et al., 2014).

Cross-cultural extensions. PCIT appears to be robust across diverse populations. Applications of the model with no adaptation or very minor adaptations have been successful in a variety of cultural contexts. PCIT is being disseminated in Puerto Rico, Australia, Norway, the Netherlands, South Korea, China, and Germany. A culturally adapted program, Project GANA, has been found effective (McCabe & Yeh, 2009). An American Indian cultural translation of PCIT, Honoring Children: Making Relatives, incorporates the language and concepts of traditional American Indian cultures into standard PCIT treatment (BigFoot & Funderburk, 2011). Deliverability across a range of cultures is important for state or county child welfare services systems because these systems are charged with serving diverse populations. In other contexts, such as tribal child welfare systems, it may be important to the community and the service system that evidence-based models consider local culture and are acceptable within their local community.

Conclusion and Future Directions

Parent training programs continue to represent the single most common type of services offered to maltreating parents. More recently, focus has shifted to adapting evidence-based behavioral skill-oriented parent training interventions for use with caregivers in child welfare. An adapted version of PCIT for use with maltreating parents has robustly delivered two types of benefits—reduced recidivism risk among abusive parents and improved wellbeing and behavior among children, making it particularly appealing for child welfare service systems. These benefits have been found in randomized trials conducted in real-world settings, and conducted by researchers other than the model developer. Lower child welfare recidivism has been found among real-world child welfare populations including complex and chronic cases. Future work with PCIT in child welfare may need to focus on how to improve the implementation, deliverability and scalability of the model within these types of service systems.

References

Aarons, G. A., Hurlburt, M., & Horwitz, S. M. (2011). Advancing a conceptual model of evidence-based practice implementation in public service sectors. *Administration and Policy in Mental Health and Mental Health Services Research, 38*(1), 4–23. doi:10.1007/s10488-010-0327-7.

Abrahamse, M. E., Junger, M., Chavannes, E. L., Coelman, F. J. G., Boer, F., & Lindauer, R. J. L. (2012). Parent-Child Interaction Therapy for preschool children with disruptive behaviour problems in the Netherlands. *Child and Adolescent Psychiatry and Mental Health, 6*, 1–9. doi:10.1186/1753-2000-6-24.

Bagner, D. M., & Eyberg, S. M. (2007). Parent-Child Interaction Therapy for disruptive behavior in children with mental retardation: A randomized control trial. *Journal of Clinical Child and Adolescent Psychology, 36*, 418–429. doi:10.1080/15374410701448448.

Bagner, D. M., Fernandez, M. A., & Eyberg, S. M. (2004). Parent-child interaction therapy and chronic illness: A case study. *Journal of Clinical Psychology in Medical Settings, 11*, 1–6.

Barth, R. P., Landsverk, J., Chamberlain, P., Reid, J. B., Rolls, J. A., Hurlburt, M. S., … Kohl, P. L. (2005). Parent-training programs in child welfare services: Planning for a more evidence-based approach to serving biological parents. *Research on Social Work Practice, 15*, 353–371. doi:10.1177/1049731505276321

Baumrind, D. (1967). Childcare practices antecedent three patterns of preschool behavior. *Genetic Psychology Monographs, 75*, 43–88.

BigFoot, D. S., & Funderburk, B. W. (2011). Honoring children, making relatives: The cultural translation of Parent-Child Interaction Therapy for American Indian and Alaska Native families. *Journal of Psychoactive Drugs, 43*, 309–318. doi:10.1080/02791072.2011.628924.

Bjørseth, Å., & Wormdal, A. K. (2005). Med terapeuten på øret [Parent child interaction therapy]. *Tidsskrift for Norsk Psykologforening, 42*, 693–699.

Boggs, S., Eyberg, S., Edwards, D., Rayfield, A., Jacobs, J., Bagner, D., & Hood, K. (2004). Outcomes of Parent Child Interaction Therapy: A comparison of treatment completers and study dropouts one to three years later. *Child & Family Behavior Therapy, 26*, 1–22.

Brinkmeyer, M. Y., & Eyberg, S. M. (2003). Parent-Child Interaction Therapy. In A. Kazdin & J. Weisz (Eds.), *Evidence-based psychotherapies for children and adolescents* (pp. 204–223). New York: Guilford Press.

California Evidence-Based Clearinghouse for Child Welfare. (2009). *Usage guide for the CEBC.* Retrieved from http://www.cachildwelfareclearinghouse.org.

Callahan, C. L., Stevens, M. L., & Eyberg, S. M. (2010). Parent-child interaction therapy. In C. E. Schaefer (Ed.), *Play therapy for preschool children* (pp. 199–221). Washington, DC: American Psychological Association.

Cedar, B., & Levant, R. F. (1990). A meta-analysis of the effects of parent effectiveness training. *American Journal of Family Therapy, 18*, 373–384.

Centers for Disease Control and Prevention, National Center for Injury Prevention and Control (2004). *Using evidence-based parenting programs to advance CDC efforts in child maltreatment prevention: Research brief.* Atlanta, GA: Author.

Chaffin, M., & Friedrich, W. (2004). Evidence-based practice in child abuse and neglect. *Children and Youth Services Review, 26*, 1097–1113.

Chaffin, M., Funderburk, B., Bard, D., Valle, L., & Gurwitch, R. (2011). A combined motivation and Parent-Child Interaction Therapy package reduces child welfare recidivism in a randomized dismantling field trial. *Journal of Consulting and Clinical Psychology, 79*, 84–95. doi:10.1037/a0021227.

Chaffin, M., Silovsky, J., Funderburk, B., Valle, L. A., Brestan, E. V., Balachova, T., … Bonner, B. L. (2004). Parent– child interaction therapy with physically abusive parents: Efficacy for reducing future abuse reports. *Journal of Consulting and Clinical Psychology, 72*, 500–510. doi:10.1037/0022-006X.72.3.500

Chaffin, M., Valle, L. A., Funderburk, B., Silovsky, J., Gurwitch, R., McCoy, C., … Kees, M. (2009). A motivational intervention can improve retention in PCIT for low-motivation child welfare clients. *Child Maltreatment, 14*, 356–368. doi:10.1177/1077559509332263.

Clausen, J. M., Landsverk, J., Ganger, W., Chadwick, D., & Litrownik, A. (1998). Mental health problems of children in foster care. *Journal of Child and Family Studies, 7*, 283–296.

Cohn, A., & Daro, D. (1987). Is treatment too late: What ten years of evaluative research tell us. *Child Abuse and Neglect, 1*, 433–442. doi:10.1016/0145-2134(87)90016-0.

Cook, R. J. (1994). Are we helping foster care youth prepare for the future? *Children and Youth Services Review, 16*, 213–229.

Crouch, J. L., & Behl, L. E. (2001). Relationships among parental beliefs in corporal punishment, reported stress, and physical child abuse potential. *Child Abuse & Neglect, 25*(3), 413–419. doi:10.1016/S0145-2134(00)00256-8.

Eisenstadt, T. H., Eyberg, S., McNeil, C. B., Newcomb, K., & Funderburk, B. (1993). Parent-child interaction therapy with behavior problem children: Relative effectiveness of two stages and overall treatment outcome. *Journal of Clinical Child Psychology, 22*, 42–51.

Eyberg, S. M., Boggs, S., & Algina, J. (1995). Parent-child interaction therapy: A psychosocial model for the treatment of young children with conduct problem behavior and their families. *Psychopharmacology Bulletin, 31*, 83–91.

Eyberg, S. M., & Funderburk, B. W. (2011). *Parent-child interaction therapy international protocol*. Retrieved from www.pcit.org.

Eyberg, S. M., Funderburk, B. W., Hembree-Kigin, T., McNeil, C. B., Querido, J., & Hood, K. K. (2001). Parent-child interaction therapy with behavior problem children: One- and two-year maintenance of treatment effects in the family. *Child & Family Behavior Therapy, 23*, 1–20.

Eyberg, S. M., & Robinson, E. A. (1982). Parent-child interaction training: Effects on family functioning. *Journal of Clinical Child Psychology, 11*, 130–137.

Fixsen, D. L., Naoom, S. F., Blase, K. A., & Friedman, R. M. (2005). *Implementation research: A synthesis of the literature*. Tampa, FL: University of South Florida, Louis de la Parte Florida Mental Health Institute, National Implementation Research Network.

Funderburk, B., Eyberg, S. M., Newcomb, K., McNeil, C. B., Hembree-Kigin, T., & Capage, L. (1998). Parent-Child Interaction Therapy with behavior problem children: Maintenance of treatment effects in the school setting. *Child and Family Behavior Therapy, 20*, 17–38.

Gallagher, N. (2003). Effects of parent-child interaction therapy on young children with disruptive behavior disorders. *Bridges: Practice-based Research Syntheses, 4*(1), 1–17. U. S. Department of Education, Research and Training Center on Early Childhood Development. Retrieved from http://www.evidencebasedpractices.org/bridges/bridges_vol1_no4.pdf.

Hakman, M., Chaffin, M., Funderburk, B., & Silovsky, J. F. (2009). Change trajectories for parent–child interaction sequences during Parent-Child Interaction Therapy for child physical abuse. *Child Abuse & Neglect, 33*, 461–470. doi:10.1016/j.chiabu.2008.08.003.

Hanf, C. A. (1969). *A two-stage program for modifying maternal controlling during mother-child (M-C) interaction*. Paper presented at the meeting of the Western Psychological Association, Vancouver, Canada.

Herschell, A. D., & McNeil, C. B. (2005). Parent-child interaction therapy for children experiencing externalizing behavior problems. In L. A. Reddy, T. M. Files-Hall, & C. E. Schaefer (Eds.), *Empirically based play interventions for children*. Washington, DC: American Psychological Association.

Hood, K. K., & Eyberg, S. M. (2003). Outcomes of parent-child interaction therapy: Mothers' reports on maintenance three to six years after treatment. *Journal of Clinical Child and Adolescent Psychology, 32*, 419–429.

James, S., Leslie, L. K., Hurlburt, M. S., Slymen, D. J., Landsverk, J., Davis, I., … Zhang, J. (2006). Children in out-of-home care: Entry into intensive or restrictive mental health and residential care placements. *Journal of Emotional and Behavioral Disorders, 14*(4), 196–208. doi:10.1177/10634266060140040301.

Kaminski, J. W., Valle, L. A., Filene, J. H., & Boyle, C. L. (2008). A meta-analytic review of components associated with parent training program effectiveness. *Journal of Abnormal Child Psychology, 36*, 567–589. doi:10.1007/s10802-007-9201-9.

Kazdin, A. E., & Blasé, S. L. (2011). Rebooting psychotherapy research and practice to reduce the burden of mental illness. *Perspectives on Psychological Science, 6*(1), 21–37. doi:10.1177/1745691610393527.

Klain, E. J., & White, A. R. (2013). *Implementing trauma-informed practices in child welfare.* Washington, DC: American Bar Association.

Lawrence, C., Carlson, E., & Egeland, B. (2006). The impact of foster care on development. *Development and Psychopathology, 18*, 57–76.

Lee, S., Aos, S., & Miller, M. (2008). *Evidence-based programs to prevent children entering and remaining in the child welfare system (Document 08–07-3901).* Olympia, WA: Washington State Institute for Public Policy.

Lenze, S. N., Pautsch, J., & Luby, J. (2011). Parent–child interaction therapy emotion development: A novel treatment for depression in preschool children. *Depression and Anxiety, 28*(2), 153–159. doi:10.1002/da.20770.

Leslie, L., Hurlburt, M. C., Landsverk, J., Barth, R., & Slymen, D. J. (2004). Outpatient mental health services for children in foster care: A national perspective. *Child Abuse and Neglect, 28*, 697–712. doi:10.1016/j.chiabu.2004.01.004.

Leung, C., Tsang, S., Heung, K., & Yiu, I. (2009). Effectiveness of Parent-Child Interaction Therapy (PCIT) among Chinese families. *Research on Social Work Practice, 19*, 304–313. doi:10.1177/1049731508321713.

Lundahl, B. W., Nimer, J., & Parsons, B. (2006). Preventing child abuse: A meta-analysis of parent training programs. *Research on Social Work Practice, 16*, 251–262.

Lundahl, B. W., Risser, H. J., & Lovejoy, M. C. (2006). A meta-analysis of parent training: Moderators and follow-up effects. *Clinical Psychology Review, 26*, 86–104.

Matos, M., Torres, R., Santiago, R., Jurado, M., & Rodriguez, I. (2006). Adaptation of Parent-Child Interaction Therapy for Puerto Rican families: A preliminary study. *Family Process, 45*, 205–222.

Maughan, D. R., Christiansen, E., Jenson, W. R., Olympia, D., & Clark, E. (2005). Behavioral parent training as a treatment for externalizing behaviors and disruptive behavior disorders: A meta-analysis. *School Psychology Review, 34*, 267–286.

McCabe, K., & Yeh, M. (2009). Parent–child interaction therapy for Mexican Americans: A randomized clinical trial. *Journal of Clinical Child and Adolescent Psychology, 38*(5), 753–9. doi:10.1080/15374410903103544.

McCabe, K. M., Yeh, M., Garland, A. F., Lau, A. S., & Chavez, G. (2005). The GANA Program: A tailoring approach for adapting Parent Child Interaction Therapy for Mexican Americans. *Education and Treatment of Children, 28*, 111–129.

McDiarmid, M. D., & Bagner, D. M. (2005). Parent-Child Interaction Therapy for children with disruptive behavior and developmental disabilities. *Education and Treatment of Children, 28*, 130–141.

McMahon, R. J., & Forehand, R. L. (2003). *Helping the noncompliant child: Family-based treatment for oppositional behavior* (2nd ed.). New York: Guilford.

McNeil, C. B., Capage, L. C., Bahl, A., & Blanc, H. (1999). Importance of early intervention for disruptive behavior problems: Comparison of treatment and waitlist-control groups. *Early Education & Development, 10*, 445–454.

McNeil, C. B., Eyberg, S. M., Eisendstadt, T. H., Newcomb, K., & Funderburk, B. W. (1991). Parent-Child Interaction Therapy with behavior problem children: Generalization of treatment effects to the school setting. *Journal of Clinical Child Psychology, 20*, 140–151.

McNeil, C. B., & Hembree-Kigin, T. L. (2010). *Parent-child interaction therapy* (2nd ed.). New York: Springer.

McNeil, C. B., Herschell, A. D., Gurwitch, R. H., & Clemens-Mowrer, L. C. (2005). Training foster parents in parent-child interaction therapy. *Education and Treatment of Children, 28*, 182–196.

Newton, R. R., Litrownik, A. J., & Landsverk, J. A. (2000). Children and youth in foster care: Disentangling the relationship between problem behaviors and number of placements. *Child Abuse & Neglect, 24*, 1363–1374.

Nixon, R. D. V., Sweeney, L., Erickson, D. B., & Touyz, S. W. (2003). Parent-Child Interaction Therapy: A comparison of standard and abbreviated treatments for oppositional defiant preschoolers. *Journal of Consulting and Clinical Psychology, 71*, 251–260.

NSCAW Research Group (2005). *National survey of child and adolescent well-being (NSCAW) CPS sample component wave 1 data analysis report, April 2005.* Washington, DC: U.S. Department of Health and Human Services, Administration for Children, Youth and Families.

Patterson, G. R. (1976). The aggressive child: Victim and architect of a coercive system. In E. Mash, L. A. Hamerlynch, & L. C. Handy (Eds.), *Behavior modification and families. I. Theory and research. II. Applications and developments* (pp. 265–316). New York: Brunner/Mazel.

Pearl, E., Thieken, L., Olafson, E., Boat, B., Connelly, L., Barnes, J., & Putnam, F. (2012). Effectiveness of community dissemination of parent–child interaction therapy. *Psychological Trauma: Theory, Research, Practice, and Policy, 4*(2), 204–213. doi:10.1037/a0022948.

Phillips, J., Morgan, S., Cawthorne, K., & Barnett, B. (2008). Pilot evaluation of parent-child interaction therapy delivered in an Australian community early childhood clinic setting. *Australian and New Zealand Journal of Psychiatry, 42*, 712–719.

Pincus, D. B., Choate, M. L., Eyberg, S. M., & Barlow, D. H. (2005). Treatment of young children with separation anxiety disorder using parent-child interaction therapy. *Cognitive and Behavioral Practice, 12*, 126–135.

Pinkston, E. M., & Smith, M. D. (1998). Contributions of parent training to child welfare: Early history and current thoughts. In J. R. Lutzker (Ed.), *Handbook of child abuse research and treatment* (pp. 377–399). New York: Plenum Press.

Puliafico, A. C., Comer, J. S., & Pincus, D. B. (2012). Adapting parent–child interaction therapy to treat anxiety disorders in young children. *Child and Adolescent Psychiatric Clinics of North America, 21*, 607–619. doi:10.1016/j.chc.2012.05.005.

Reitman, D., & McMahon, R. J. (2012). Constance "Connie" Hanf (1917–2002): The mentor and the model. *Cognitive and Behavioral Practice, 20*, 106–116. doi:10.1016/j.cbpra.2012.02.005.

Reyno, S. M., & McGrath, P. J. (2006). Predictors of parent training efficacy for child externalizing behavior problems: A meta-analytic review. *Journal of Child Psychology and Psychiatry, 47*, 99–111.

Sanders, M. R. (2012). Development, evaluation, and multinational dissemination of the Triple P-Positive Parenting Program. *Annual Review of Clinical Psychology, 8*, 345–379.

Schuhmann, E. M., Foote, R. C., Eyberg, S. M., Boggs, S. R., & Algina, J. (1998). Efficacy of parent-child interaction therapy: Interim report of a randomized trial with short-term maintenance. *Journal of Clinical Child Psychology, 27*, 34–45.

Serketich, W. J., & Dumas, J. E. (1996). The effectiveness of behavioral parent training to modify antisocial behavior in children: A meta-analysis. *Behavior Therapy, 27*, 171–186.

Shirk, S. R. (2004). Dissemination of youth ESTs: Ready for prime time? *Clinical Psychology: Science and Practice, 11*, 308–312. doi:10.1093/clipsy.bph086.

Stith, S. M., Liu, T., Davies, L. C., Boykin, E. L., Alder, M. C., Harris, J. M., … Dees, J. E. (2009). Risk factors in child maltreatment: A meta-analytic review of the literature. *Aggression and Violent Behavior, 14*, 13–29. doi:10.1016/j.avb.2006.03.006

Sweet, M. A., & Appelbaum, M. I. (2004). Is home visiting an effective strategy? A meta-analytic review of home visiting programs for families with young children. *Child Development, 75*, 1435–1456.

Thomas, R., & Zimmer-Gembeck, M. J. (2007). Behavioral outcomes of Parent–Child Interaction Therapy and Triple P-Positive Parenting Program: A review and meta-analysis. *Journal of Abnormal Child Psychology, 35*, 475–495.

Thomas, R., & Zimmer-Gembeck, M. J. (2012). Parent–child interaction therapy: An evidence-based treatment for child maltreatment. *Child Maltreatment, 17*(3), 253–66. doi:10.1177/1077559512459555.

Timmer, S. G., Urquiza, A. J., Herschell, A. D., McGrath, J. M., Zebell, N. M., Porter, A. L., & Vargas, E. C. (2006). Parent–Child Interaction Therapy: Application of an empirically supported treatment to maltreated children in foster care. *Child Welfare, 85*, 919–939.

Timmer, S. G., Urquiza, A. J., Zebell, N. M., & McGrath, J. M. (2005). Parent–Child Interaction Therapy: Application to maltreating parent-child dyads. *Child Abuse & Neglect, 29*, 825–842.

U.S. Department of Health and Human Services, Administration on Children, Youth and Families (2005). *Child Maltreatment 2003* (p. 2005). Washington, DC: U.S. Government Printing Office.

Urquiza, A. J., & McNeil, C. B. (1996). Parent– child interaction therapy: An intensive dyadic intervention for physically abusive families. *Child Maltreatment, 1*, 134–144. doi:10.1177/107 7559596001002005.

Webster-Stratton, C. (2005). The Incredible Years parents, teachers, and children training series: Early intervention and prevention programs for young children. In P. S. Jensen & E. D. Hibbs (Eds.), *Psychosocial treatments for child and adolescent disorders: Empirically based approaches* (pp. 507–556). Washington, DC: American Psychological Association.

Webster-Stratton, C. (2011). *The incredible years parents, teachers, and children's training series: Program content, methods, research and dissemination 1980–2011*. Seattle, WA: Incredible Years, Inc.

Weisz, J. R., Chorpita, B. F., Palinkas, L. A., Schoenwald, S. K., Miranda, J., Bearman, S. K., … Gibbons, R. D. (2012). Testing standard and modular designs for psychotherapy treating depression, anxiety, and conduct problems in youth: A randomized effectiveness trial. *Archives of General Psychiatry, 69*(3), 274–282.

Preventing the Intergenerational Transmission of Child Maltreatment Through Relational Interventions

Danielle J. Guild, Michelle E. Alto, and Sheree L. Toth

The formation of attachment relationships involves a critical pattern of human interaction that occurs in infancy to ensure survival, regulate closeness to others, and increase a sense of security (Bowlby, 1982). It is an evolutionarily adaptive emotional tie and reciprocal process by which emotional connection develops. While all infants are biologically predisposed to develop attachments, the quality of these attachments varies as a function of the context in which they are formed (Ainsworth, 1979). Attachment also is affected by intergenerational influences, whereby maladaptive attachment patterns are likely to be transmitted from parent to child (Cort, Toth, Cerulli, & Rogosch, 2011; Steele, Steele, & Fonagy, 1996).

Research has identified four major attachment classifications: secure, insecure-ambivalent, insecure-avoidant, and disorganized (Ainsworth, Blehar, Waters, & Wall, 1978; Main & Solomon, 1990). Securely attached children have developed an adaptive and organized method for utilizing their parent as a secure base from which to explore the environment and return to for comfort when distressed. By contrast, insecure-ambivalent children demonstrate a pattern of preoccupation with the caregiver relationship, but have difficulty deriving comfort from it as a result of the unpredictably responsive caregiving they have received. Insecure-avoidant children generally avoid interaction with and proximity to their caregiver because they have repeatedly had the experience of their needs going unmet. Finally, children with disorganized attachment do not exhibit any particular pattern of behavior, and tend to respond to their caregiver in unpredictable and unusual ways. Such children often have caregivers who are erratic, inconsistent, and possibly abusive in their

D.J. Guild, M.A. (✉) • M.E. Alto, B.A. • S.L. Toth, Ph.D.
Mt. Hope Family Center, University of Rochester,
187 Edinburgh Street, Rochester, NY 14608, USA
e-mail: danielle.guild@rochester.edu; michelle.alto@rochester.edu;
sheree.toth@rochester.edu

© Springer International Publishing Switzerland 2017
D.M. Teti (ed.), *Parenting and Family Processes in Child Maltreatment
and Intervention*, Child Maltreatment Solutions Network,
DOI 10.1007/978-3-319-40920-7_8

127

interactions with their child. Insecure attachment, and disorganized attachment in particular, is linked to a myriad of problems in later childhood and adulthood, whereas secure attachments are related to positive development (Belsky & Nezworski, 1988). In order to best support the emergence of secure attachments and their positive trajectories, it is important to understand how different environmental contexts influence their development.

Childhood maltreatment is an example of how adverse early experiences influence the development and quality of attachments. Maltreatment has been found to be one of the strongest predictors of disorganized attachment (Van IJzendoorn, Schuengel, & Bakermans–Kranenburg, 1999), with rates as high as 90 % being observed in maltreated infants (Cicchetti, Toth, & Lynch, 1995). Because attachment relationships developed in infancy provide the framework for one's future perspectives with respect to the self and self in relation to others (Sroufe & Fleeson, 1986), these insecure attachments put young children at risk for less adaptive social functioning. Unfortunately, in the absence of intervention insecure attachments in maltreated children tend to be stable, whereas secure attachments become unstable over time (Cicchetti & Barnett, 1991).

Aside from the risk maltreatment poses for the development of children's attachments, it also puts children at risk for disturbances in other areas of development, including: emotion recognition, expression, and regulation; self-development; symbolic development; moral development; peer relationships and social information processing; and school adaptation (c.f. Cicchetti & Valentino, 2006). In addition, maltreatment may exert negative neurobiological effects, including changes in brain volume and development (De Bellis et al., 1999), arousal systems (Cicchetti & Rogosch, 2001; Cicchetti, Rogosch, Gunnar, & Toth, 2010), and neurochemistry (Watts-English, Fortson, Gibler, Hooper, & De Bellis, 2006). Given that maltreatment affects a myriad of developmental systems, its sequelae tend to be cascading in nature, such that disruption at a particular stage in development affects the scaffolding necessary for future growth and leads to maladaptive outcomes at later stages, thereby creating a cycle which continues into adulthood.

Intergenerational Transmission of Maltreatment.

Maltreatment often follows an intergenerational trend, whereby parents who have their own history of childhood maltreatment are more likely to demonstrate poor parenting practices or to maltreat their own children (Cort et al., 2011). It is these parents who were maltreated in their own childhood who are in need of the most support in order to prevent the pattern of maltreatment from continuing. Research has shown that unresolved challenges from a parent's past (e.g. maltreatment) can also exert negative effects on the evolving parent-child relationship (Fraiberg, Adelson, & Shapiro, 1975). Given the significant association between maltreatment and attachment, considerable empirical evidence supports the provision of interventions based on attachment theory (Lieberman & Zeanah, 1999). A number of attachment-focused interventions have been developed to capitalize on the window of opportunity this developmental domain presents. For example, attachment and biobehavioral catch-up (ABC; Dozier, Lindhiem, & Ackerman, 2005), Steps Toward Effective/Enjoyable Parenting (STEEP; Erickson, Korfmacher, & Egeland, 1992), Circle of Security (Marvin, Cooper, Hoffman, & Powell, 2002), and Child-Parent Psychotherapy (CPP; Lieberman, 2004; Lieberman & Van Horn, 2005, 2008) are all empirically supported interventions informed by attachment theory. Intervening in the parent-child relationship and supporting the development of secure attachment provides a vital opportunity to reduce the risk of future maltreatment and promote positive social development in these young children. Because the sequelae of maltreatment are present at multiple developmental levels, it is important to employ a comprehensive perspective embodied by a developmental psychopathology framework when considering how to provide and evaluate prevention interventions.

A Developmental Psychopathology Perspective

A central tenet of developmental psychopathology involves bridging the gap between research and practice for the purpose of promoting positive development and preventing or mitigating pathological outcomes (Cicchetti, 1990; Masten, 2006; Toth, Petrenko, Gravener Davis, & Handley, 2016). This conceptual framework has provided a scaffolding from which to build an understanding of the causes and long-term consequences of child maltreatment (Cicchetti & Valentino, 2006; Toth & Cicchetti, 2013), thereby facilitating the identification of developmental periods during which positive therapeutic outcomes for maltreated children and their families may be maximized (Toth & Cicchetti, 1999). Adopting a lifespan perspective, the discipline of developmental psychopathology emphasizes the mutual interaction between normal and abnormal functioning, while also accounting for the interplay among biological, psychological, and social-contextual factors throughout development.

Researchers within the field of developmental psychopathology have designed, implemented, and evaluated developmentally-informed interventions through the examination of risk factors associated with psychopathology, elucidation of the mediating and moderating processes that protect against maladaptation, and the incorporation of principles of normative development (Cicchetti & Toth, 2006; Erickson & Egeland, 2004; Toth, Pianta, & Erickson, 2011). Developmental psychopathologists conceptualize preventive intervention research as experiments in rerouting the course of development towards more adaptive outcomes (Cicchetti & Toth, 2009). Appropriate intervention during stage-salient periods is therefore critical for maltreated children because of the increased likelihood that subsequent developmental processes will progress along normative pathways (Sroufe & Rutter, 1984).

Prevention and Intervention

Relational interventions are of particular importance in the treatment of maltreated children and their caregivers as traditional parent skills training may be insufficient in generalizing to the numerous risk factors faced by maltreating families (Stronach, Toth, Rogosch, & Cicchetti, 2013). For example, parents with their own histories of childhood trauma may learn effective parenting skills, but then struggle to implement them in the home environment because the underlying cause of their relational difficulties has not been addressed. By contrast, attachment-based interventions are relational in nature and focus specifically on improving the child-caregiver relationship with the goal of promoting greater attachment security and guiding children toward more adaptive developmental trajectories. Given the existence of multiple randomized-controlled trials on various relationally based interventions (for a more in-depth review, see Toth, Gravener Davis, Guild, & Cicchetti, 2013), this chapter focuses on clinical and translational research conducted at Mt. Hope Family Center in Rochester, NY.

One of the most widely studied relational interventions for child maltreatment has been Child-Parent Psychotherapy (CPP). It was conceived out of Fraiberg et al.'s (1975) "psychotherapy in the kitchen" model, a psychoanalytically-based intervention intended to help parents with their own histories of abuse and neglect to recognize how the traumatic experiences from their past were negatively influencing their interactions with their own children. Therapists working within this model aimed to build a close relationship with the parent in order to elucidate past trauma and facilitate more attuned and empathic caregiving. Lieberman and Van Horn (2005, 2008) later expanded upon the intervention to create CPP, a dyadic therapy that strives to improve the parent-child relationship and foster secure attachment.

CPP may be administered by clinicians with various degrees of training, and is typically taught in settings that provide psychology predoctoral internships and postdoctoral fellowships, master's level social work placements, and/or residency rotations in adult, child, and adolescent psychiatry. More import than the actual professional degree, completion of requisite training accompanied by supervision from an approved trainer is essential to gaining the skill level necessary to implement CPP. The intervention is appropriate for children ages 0–5 and their caregiver(s). Treatment is typically implemented in weekly hour-long sessions that last for approximately 10–12 months. However, the duration of treatment may be briefer depending on the severity and chronicity of the child's and parent's mental health problems, as well as the specific clinical needs of the family. The delivery of CPP is meant to be flexible, such that it may be conducted in the home or in an office setting provided that there are developmentally appropriate toys to facilitate joint play and interaction between child and caregiver. CPP is unique in that it does not focus solely on the parent or child, but rather on the dyad as an entity. Therapists implementing the intervention work to foster positive interactions between parent and child and use spontaneous play and/or conflict as opportunities to gently explore areas for growth in the relationship. In this way, therapists are able to facilitate increased parental sensitivity, emotional attunement, and responsivity to the child's needs.

Through their interactions with the child, therapists model appropriate parental behavior, and when necessary, provide a voice for the child, gradually enabling parents to better understand and attend to their child's verbal and non-verbal communication. Simultaneously, therapists strive to build a trusting and supportive relationship with the parent(s) for the purpose of creating a corrective emotional experience in which their needs, wishes, and fears, particularly those relating to their past experiences with their own caregivers, are acknowledged and addressed. In this way, parents are able to develop healthier internal representations of the self in relation to other. CPP provides a supportive environment that fosters improved parental sensitivity, attunement, and responsiveness to the child's needs; enhances the parent's ability to promote their child's autonomy, while successfully balancing their own needs in relation to those of the child; and addresses any distorted perceptions or inappropriate behavior that parents may have towards the child that stem from maladaptive representational models from the parent's history.

CPP has successfully been implemented across a variety of cultures, ethnicities, and socioeconomic strata. Research by Cicchetti, Rogosch, and Toth (2006) demonstrated that CPP is effective at reorganizing early attachment patterns from insecure to secure. The authors randomized 1-year-old infants from maltreating families and their mothers to one of three conditions—CPP, a psychoeducational parenting intervention (PPI), or a community standard (CS) comparison group. A fourth group of infants from nonmaltreating families and their mothers constituted a nonmaltreated comparison (NC) group. Families in the CS and nonmaltreated control conditions were free to seek available services in the community. Compared to CPP, the PPI intervention was more didactic in nature and aimed to provide parent skills training and psychoeducation relevant to child development, while also reducing maternal stress, and fostering social support. Both interventions were administered weekly for approximately 1 year.

All participants were from low-income urban neighborhoods, and the majority were of minority race/ethnicity. Infant attachment security was measured via the Strange Situation paradigm (Ainsworth et al., 1978). At baseline, infants (M_{age} = 13.31 months, SD = 0.81) from maltreating families evidenced significantly higher rates of insecure attachment than infants from the nonmaltreated group. However, at post-intervention, when children were 26 months, those in the CPP and PPI groups showed significant increases in secure attachment, whereas children in the CS and NC groups did not evidence such changes. These results suggested that both CPP and PPI can be effective interventions in the short-term. The authors also examined potential mediators of intervention efficacy. It was hypothesized that for participants in the CPP condition improvements in attachment security would be mediated by increased maternal sensitivity and improvements in maternal representations of her own mother. For the PPI intervention, it was hypothesized that change in parenting attitudes, decreases in child-rearing related stress, and increased social support would lead to improvements in attachment security. Unexpectedly, however, none of these constructs were found to be significant mediators of intervention outcome, indicating the necessity of further research for elucidating mechanisms of change.

The same mother-child dyads were also followed 1-year post-intervention to examine the sustained efficacy of CPP compared to PPI (Stronach et al., 2013). These findings revealed that children in the CPP condition evidenced higher rates of secure attachment and lower rates of disorganized attachment than children in both the PPI and CS conditions. Furthermore, there were no significant differences in the rate of disorganized attachment between children in the CPP and nonmaltreated comparison groups. Taken together, the data suggest that while a psychoeducational parenting intervention may be equally as efficacious as CPP in the short-term, only CPP was successful in maintaining attachment security over time.

Another follow-up of Cicchetti et al.'s (2006) original sample indicated that CPP and PPI may normalize the development of cortisol regulation among maltreated infants. As previously discussed, children exposed to maltreatment encounter numerous stressful experiences which exert harmful impacts on their developing neurobiological systems (Heim, Shugart, Craighead, & Nemeroff, 2010; McCrory, De Brito, & Viding, 2012). In particular, the regulation of cortisol, a glucocorticoid involved in the body's stress response system, is often disrupted (Strüber, Strüber, & Roth, 2014; Tarullo & Gunnar, 2006). Cicchetti et al. (2011) examined daily cortisol rhythms in infants across the CPP, PPI, CS, and NC conditions at baseline (13 months), mid-intervention (19 months), post-intervention (26 months), and 1-year post-intervention follow-up (38 months). For statistical purposes the two intervention conditions, CPP and PPI, were combined into a single maltreated intervention (MI) group.

At baseline, findings revealed no differences between groups in morning cortisol regulation. However, beginning at mid-intervention, divergence among groups had already emerged. While morning cortisol in the MI and NC conditions remained stable and indistinguishable over time, the CS group evidenced significantly lower levels of morning cortisol, which continued to decline through the 1-year post-intervention follow-up. Morning cortisol levels of maltreated infants who received intervention were therefore normalized, while maltreated infants in the community standard condition showed progressive cortisol dysregulation as they entered toddlerhood. Further research will be necessary to distinguish potential differences in cortisol regulation among children who receive CPP compared to those who participate in alternative interventions for maltreatment, such as PPI.

A fourth study with the same participants explored the effects of child maltreatment and polymorphisms of the serotonin transporter linked promotor region (5-HTTLPR) and dopamine receptor D4 (DRD4) genes on infant attachment and intervention efficacy (Cicchetti, Rogosch, & Toth, 2011). 5-HTTLPR and DRD4 are genes that have previously been demonstrated to relate to attachment styles among nonmaltreated infants (for a review see Papageorgiou & Ronald, 2013). As with the aforementioned study, Cicchetti and colleagues (2011) combined participants in the CPP and PPI conditions into a single maltreated intervention group for the purpose of statistical analyses. Interestingly, the authors found that genetic variation significantly affected attachment in nonmaltreated, but *not* maltreated infants. It was posited that the high rates of disorganized attachment among maltreated infants may overpower the genetic contribution of 5-HTTLPR and DRD4 to attachment style. Finally, results also indicated that early intervention for maltreated infants was effective irrespective of genetic variation, suggesting that beneficial outcomes are likely to generalize to children of varying phenotypes.

In light of the evidence that attachment plasticity is possible, even in children with divergent genetic polymorphisms, these studies suggest that many of the harmful sequelae of child maltreatment need not be permanent. As an attachment-based relational intervention, CPP is effective in promoting secure attachment that remains stable over time. Furthermore, the evidence base suggests that early intervention can alter neurobiological development, such that young maltreated children receiving CPP or PPI show a normalization of cortisol regulation over time.

Translational Research

Once interventions have been proven efficacious it becomes critical that research is translated to broader settings, such that implementation occurs within the larger clinical world. Unfortunately, evidence-based modalities tend to take considerable time to reach the community and continue to remain scarce in non-university settings (Masten, 2011). Bridging the gap between research and practice, which is of central importance within the discipline of developmental psychopathology, therefore becomes essential in future scientific endeavors. It is only through translational research that evidence-based interventions will be able to benefit the broader population.

The Monroe County Department of Human Services and the United Way of Greater Rochester have funded an initiative to aid the Rochester, NY community in making progress towards translating efficacy findings. As a result, traumatized children have gained greater access to evidence-based prevention programs. Building Healthy Children (BHC) is one such program being implemented at the Mt. Hope Family Center. BHC targets young mothers who have had a child before the age of 21 and are living in poverty. Mother-child dyads are referred through Pediatrics Departments at local hospitals. There are numerous risk factors within this population, with some of the most prominent being: domestic violence, maternal depression, criminal activity, indicated CPS reports as children, and sexual abuse histories.

BHC provides a tiered service pyramid that offers evidence-based interventions according to each family's level of need (Paradis, Sandler, Manly, & Valentine, 2013). Families enrolled in the program begin with a home visit by a pediatric social worker and a paraprofessional outreach worker, during which time the needs of mother and child are assessed and community service referrals are made. Soon after enrollment, caregivers who do not exhibit symptoms of maternal depression or difficulties in the parent-child relationship are assigned to a Parents as Teachers (PAT; *Parents as Teachers*, n.d.) educator. PAT is a didactic intervention that provides caregivers with parenting support by teaching principles of child development and addressing psychosocial issues. It is delivered through weekly visitations to the family's home and continues until the child turns three or the intervention goals are fully met. For families with a higher level of need, CPP is provided. Finally, mothers with depressive symptoms may also receive Interpersonal Psychotherapy (IPT; Weissman, Markowitz, & Klerman, 2000).

Promising preliminary results from BHC have shown that mothers who completed the program exhibited decreased levels of depression, parental rigidity, child abuse potential, difficulty in social relationships, and perceived loneliness. In addition, families in BHC are evidencing increased rates of infant immunizations and well-baby visits, and perceived social support from family members. These findings highlight the benefits of relational and attachment-based interventions for high-risk families, and support the importance of translational research in the community.

Policy Implications and Future Directions

As our research shows, evidence-based interventions are available and their provision can foster positive socioemotional and neurobiological outcomes in maltreated infants. However, if these interventions are to be successfully disseminated into the wider community, researchers must consider the implications of their research for social policy. In doing so, preventive interventions will be more easily integrated into public policy initiatives and made more accessible to the general population. Therefore, it is important for future research on preventive interventions to consider policy utility in their designs.

In addition, given the deleterious effects of maltreatment across levels of development, future research could benefit from the utilization of a developmental psychopathology perspective that stresses the importance of multi-level investigations that account for both neurobiological and psychological systems (Toth & Cicchetti, 2013). Further, additional research is warranted with respect to the largely neglected period between adolescence and adulthood given that this critical time has the potential to moderate the effects of early adversity on subsequent psychopathology and mental health (Sroufe, 1997). The sequelae of maltreatment and treatment outcomes in socioeconomically advantaged families are also largely neglected areas that merit additional attention. Finally, dissemination of evidence-based models and effectiveness studies must be increased in order to close the gap between research and implementation, and ensure that at-risk children can be successfully protected from maltreatment.

In summary, significant progress has been made with respect to providing and evaluating relationally based interventions to minimize the likelihood of perpetuating the intergenerational transmission of maltreatment. Although challenges remain, efforts also are increasingly being devoted to translating the findings of efficacy studies into broader community settings. Such efforts hold great promise for benefitting vulnerable children and families.

Acknowledgements Work reported herein was supported by grants from NIMH (MH067792 and MH54643) and funding from the United Way of Greater Rochester and the Monroe County Department of Human Services. We thank our colleagues, Dante Cicchetti, Fred Rogosch, and Jody Todd Manly, as well as the numerous therapists, research assistants and graduate students who were involved with the conduct and evaluation of these interventions. We also thank the families who have participated in these interventions.

References

Ainsworth, M. D. (1979). Infant-mother attachment. *American Psychologist, 34*(10), 932–937.

Ainsworth, M. D. S., Blehar, M. C., Waters, E., & Wall, S. (1978). *Patterns of attachment: A psychological study of the strange situation.* Hillsdale, NJ: Erlbaum.

Belsky, J. E., & Nezworski, T. E. (1988). *Clinical implications of attachment.* Hillsdale, NJ: Lawrence Erlbaum.

Bowlby, J. (1982). *Attachment and loss* (Vol. 1). New York: Basic Books. Original work published on 1969.

Cicchetti, D. (1990). Developmental psychopathology and the prevention of serious mental disorders: Overdue detente and illustrations through the affective disorders. In P. Muehrer (Ed.), *Conceptual research models for prevention of mental disorders* (pp. 215–254). Rockville, MD: National Institute of Mental Health.

Cicchetti, D., & Barnett, D. (1991). Attachment organization in maltreated preschoolers. *Development and Psychopathology, 3,* 391–411.

Cicchetti, D., & Rogosch, F. A. (2001). Diverse patterns of neuroendocrine activity in maltreated children. *Development and Psychopathology, 13*(3), 677–693.

Cicchetti, D., & Toth, S. L. (2006). A developmental psychopathology perspective on preventive interventions with high risk children and families. In A. Renninger & I. Sigel (Eds.), *Handbook of child psychology* (6th ed.). New York: Wiley.

Cicchetti, D., & Toth, S. L. (2009). The past achievements and future promises of developmental psychopathology: The coming of age of a discipline. *Journal of Child Psychology and Psychiatry, 50*(1–2), 16–25.

Cicchetti, D., & Valentino, K. (2006). An ecological-transactional perspective on child maltreatment: Failure of the average expectable environment and its influence on child development. *Developmental Psychopathology, 3,* 129–201.

Cicchetti, D., Rogosch, F. A., & Toth, S. L. (2011). The effects of child maltreatment and polymorphisms of the serotonin transporter and dopamine D4 receptor genes on infant attachment and intervention efficacy. *Development and Psychopathology, 23*(2), 357–372.

Cicchetti, D., Rogosch, F. A., Toth, S. L., & Sturge-Apple, M. L. (2011). Normalizing the development of cortisol regulation in maltreated infants through preventive interventions. *Development and Psychopathology, 23,* 789–800.

Cicchetti, D., Rogosch, F. A., Gunnar, M. R., & Toth, S. L. (2010). The differential impacts of early physical and sexual abuse and internalizing problems on daytime cortisol rhythm in school-aged children. *Child Development, 81*(1), 252–269.

Cicchetti, D., Rogosch, F. A., & Toth, S. L. (2006). Fostering secure attachment in maltreating families through preventive interventions. *Development and Psychopathology, 18,* 623–650.

Cicchetti, D., Toth, S. L., & Lynch, M. (1995). Bowlby's dream comes full circle: The application of attachment theory to risk and psychopathology. In T. Ollendick & R. Prinz (Eds.), *Advances in clinical child psychology* (Vol. 17, pp. 1–75). New York: Plenum Press.

Cort, N. A., Toth, S. L., Cerulli, C., & Rogosch, F. (2011). Maternal intergenerational transmission of childhood multitype maltreatment. *Journal of Aggression, Maltreatment & Trauma, 20*(1), 19–38.

De Bellis, M. D., Baum, A. S., Birmaher, B., Keshavan, M. S., Eccard, C. H., Boring, A. M., … Ryan, N. D. (1999). Developmental traumatology part I: Biological stress systems. *Biological Psychiatry, 45*(10), 1259–1270.

Dozier, M., Lindhiem, O., & Ackerman, J. P. (2005). Attachment and biobehavioral catch-up: An intervention targeting empirically identified needs of foster infants. In L. J. Berlin, Y. Ziv, L. Amaya-Jackson, & M. T. Greenberg (Eds.), *Enhancing early attachments: Theory, research, intervention, and policy. Duke series in child development and public policy* (pp. 178–194). New York: Guilford Press.

Erickson, M. F., & Egeland, B. (2004). Linking theory and research to practice: The Minnesota Longitudinal Study of Parents and Children and the STEEP™ program. *Clinical Psychologist, 8*(1), 5–9.

Erickson, M. F., Korfmacher, J., & Egeland, B. R. (1992). Attachments past and present: Implications for therapeutic intervention with mother-infant dyads. *Development and Psychopathology, 4*(4), 495–507.

Fraiberg, S., Adelson, E., & Shapiro, V. (1975). Ghosts in the nursery: A psychoanalytic approach to impaired infant-mother relationships. *Journal of the American Academy of Child Psychiatry, 14*, 387–421.

Heim, C., Shugart, M., Craighead, W. E., & Nemeroff, C. B. (2010). Neurobiological and psychiatric consequences of child abuse and neglect. *Developmental Psychobiology, 52*(7), 671–690.

Lieberman, A. F. (2004). Child-parent psychotherapy: A relationship-based approach to the treatment of mental health disorders in infancy and early childhood. In A. J. Sameroff & S. C. McDonough (Eds.), *Treating parent-infant relationship problems: Strategies for intervention* (pp. 97–122). New York: Guilford Press.

Lieberman, A. F., & Van Horn, P. (2005). *Don't hit my mommy: A manual for child parent psychotherapy with young witnesses of family violence.* Washington, DC: Zero to Three Press.

Lieberman, A. F., & Van Horn, P. (2008). *Psychotherapy with infants and young children: Repairing the effects of stress and trauma on early attachment.* New York: Guilford Press.

Lieberman, A. F., & Zeanah, C. H. (1999). Contributions of attachment theory to infant–parent psychotherapy and other interventions with infants and young children. In J. Cassidy & P. R. Shaver (Eds.), *Handbook of attachment: Theory, research, and clinical applications* (pp. 555–574). New York: Guilford Press.

Main, M., & Solomon, J. (1990). Procedures for identifying infants as disorganized/disoriented during the Ainsworth Strange Situation. In M. T. Greenberg, D. Cicchetti, & M. E. Cummings (Eds.), *Attachment in the preschool years: Theory, research, and intervention* (pp. 121–160). Chicago: University of Chicago Press.

Marvin, R., Cooper, G., Hoffman, K., & Powell, B. (2002). The circle of security project: Attachment-based intervention with caregiver-pre-school child dyads. *Attachment & Human Development, 4*(1), 107–124.

Masten, A. S. (2006). Developmental psychopathology: Pathways to the future. *International Journal of Behavioral Development, 30*, 47–54.

Masten, A. S. (2011). Resilience in children threatened by extreme adversity: Frameworks for research, practice, and translational synergy. *Developmental Psychopathology, 23*(493), 506.

McCrory, E., De Brito, S. A., & Viding, E. (2012). The link between child abuse and psychopathology: A review of neurobiological and genetic research. *Journal of the Royal Society of Medicine, 105*(4), 151–156.

Papageorgiou, K. A., & Ronald, A. (2013). "He who sees things grow from the beginning will have the finest view of them" a systematic review of genetic studies on psychological traits in infancy. *Neuroscience and Biobehavioral Reviews, 37*(8), 1500–1517.

Paradis, H. A., Sandler, M., Manly, J. T., & Valentine, L. (2013). Building Healthy Children: Evidence-based home visitation integrated with pediatric medical homes. *Pediatrics, 132*, S174–S179.

Parents as Teachers. (n.d.). Retrieved from www.parentsasteachers.org/

Sroufe, L. (1997). Psychopathology as an outcome of development. *Development and Psychopathology, 9*(2), 251–268.

Sroufe, L. A., & Fleeson, J. (1986). Attachment and the construction of relationships. In W. Hartup & Z. Rubin (Eds.), *Relationships within Families* (pp. 27–47). Oxford: Clarendon Press.

Sroufe, L. A., & Rutter, M. (1984). The domain of developmental psychopathology. *Child Development, 55*(1), 17–29.

Steele, H., Steele, M., & Fonagy, P. (1996). Associations among attachment classifications of mothers, fathers, and their infants. *Child Development, 67*(2), 541–555.

Stronach, E. P., Toth, S. L., Rogosch, F., & Cicchetti, D. (2013). Preventive interventions and sustained attachment security in maltreated children. *Development and Psychopathology, 25*(4), 919–930.

Strüber, N., Strüber, D., & Roth, G. (2014). Impact of early adversity on glucocorticoid regulation and later mental disorders. *Neuroscience and Biobehavioral Reviews, 38*, 17–37.

Tarullo, A. R., & Gunnar, M. R. (2006). Child maltreatment and the developing HPA axis. *Hormones & Behavior, 50*, 632–639.

Toth, S. L., & Cicchetti, D. (1999). Developmental psychopathology and child psychotherapy. In S. Russ & T. Ollendick (Eds.), *Handbook of psychotherapies with children* (pp. 15–44). New York: Kluwer Academic/Plenum.

Toth, S. L., & Cicchetti, D. (2013). A developmental psychopathology perspective on child maltreatment. *Child Maltreatment, 18*(3), 135–139.

Toth, S. L., Gravener Davis, J. A., Guild, D. J., & Cicchetti, D. (2013). Relational interventions for child maltreatment: Past, present, and future perspectives. *Development and Psychopathology, 25*, 1601–1617.

Toth, S. L., Petrenko, C. L. M., Gravener Davis, J., & Handley, E. D. (2016). 16 advances in prevention science: A developmental psychopathology perspective. In D. Cicchetti, (Ed.), *Developmental psychopathology* (Vol. 4, 3rd ed.). New York: Wiley.

Toth, S. L., Pianta, R. C., & Erickson, M. F. (2011). From research to practice: Developmental contributions to the field of prevention science. In D. Cicchetti & G. I. Roisman (Eds.), *Minnesota symposia on child psychology, volume 36: The origins and organization of adaptation and maladaptation* (pp. 323–378). Hoboken: Wiley.

Van IJzendoorn, M. H., Schuengel, C., & Bakermans–Kranenburg, M. J. (1999). Disorganized attachment in early childhood: Meta-analysis of precursors, concomitants, and sequelae. *Development and Psychopathology, 11*(2), 225–250.

Watts-English, T., Fortson, B. L., Gibler, N., Hooper, S. R., & De Bellis, M. D. (2006). The psychobiology of maltreatment in childhood. *Journal of Social Issues, 62*(4), 717–736.

Weissman, M. M., Markowitz, J. C., & Klerman, G. L. (2000). *Comprehensive guide to interpersonal psychotherapy*. New York: Basic Books.

Part IV
Preventing Child Maltreatment: Current Efforts, Future Directions

Getting the Most Juice for the Squeeze: Where SafeCare® and Other Evidence-Based Programs Need to Evolve to Better Protect Children

Katelyn Guastaferro and John R. Lutzker

A single case of child maltreatment is, of course, unacceptable. However, it is esti-mated that one in eight children experience a reported instance of child maltreat-ment by their 18th birthday (Wildeman et al., 2014). In 2013, in the United States there were 678,932 substantiated cases of child maltreatment (U.S. Department of Health and Human Services [DHHS], 2015). That said, there is what can surely be considered good news when taken in context because in the 23 years from 1990 to 2012 physical abuse of children declined by 54 % and the decline for sexual abuse declined 62 % (Finkelhor, Jones, Shattuck, & Saito, 2013). However, during that 23-year span neglect had only a 14 % decline. Beginning in the early 1990s, improvements were made to child welfare practices, policies, and program initia-tives (Diaz & Petersen, 2014). However, Finkelhor and his colleagues (Finkelhor, Shattuck, Turner, & Hamby, 2014) have speculated that there is no one explanation for these declines, but are likely from a variety of reasons such as public awareness, advocacy, legal and policy efforts, increased penetration of evidence-based prac-tices (EBP), and even prescription selective serotonin uptake inhibitors for many parents (Lutzker, Guastaferro, & Whitaker, 2014).

The serious problem with the smaller decline in neglect is that neglect is the mode reason for referral and substantiation for maltreatment in all U.S. states; nationally, the incidence rate is nearly 80 % percent (DHHS, 2015). It is cliché to say that neglect is the neglected type of child maltreatment, but it does appear to be

K. Guastaferro, M.P.H., Ph.D. (✉)
The Methodology Center, The Pennsylvannia State University, University Park, PA 16802, Atlanta, GA 30302, USA
e-mail: Kguastaferro1@gsu.edu

J.R. Lutzker, Ph.D.
Mark Chaffin Center for Healthy Development, School of Public Health, Georgia State University, Atlanta, GA 30302, USA
e-mail: jlutzker@gsu.edu

© Springer International Publishing Switzerland 2017
D.M. Teti (ed.), *Parenting and Family Processes in Child Maltreatment and Intervention*, Child Maltreatment Solutions Network,
DOI 10.1007/978-3-319-40920-7_9

the case. Why? It is again cliché to say that caseworkers in child protective service systems are overworked and underpaid, but that is the case. Further, understandably, the press locks onto dramatic cases of abuse and usually death of children. Thus, limited resources tend to go toward abuse cases over neglect. And, with increased penetration of EBP, service agencies and families in child maltreatment prevention, most of the behavioral parenting EBP focus on behavior management and not skill deficits related to neglect. The less behavioral EBP have more of a focus on neglect issues, such as the conditions of the home and medical issues, but those elements are more subtlety embedded within their curricula than the SafeCare curriculum.

In this chapter we will describe the movement towards the exclusive use of EBP in the prevention of child maltreatment, focusing on home-based parent-support approach (i.e., home visiting). Then, we will describe SafeCare®, an EBP that has shown effectiveness for with parents referred for neglect. In doing so, we will provide a brief history of SafeCare and its widespread scale-up. Next, we will review some of the necessary elements of implementation and dissemination of evidence-based programs and some important cautions for providers seeking to choose such programs. Finally, we will suggest that there is more to be done to provide the best possible practices for families at-risk or substantiated for child maltreatment.

Evidence-Based Practices

In recent years, the field of child abuse and neglect prevention has shifted toward a public health model. That is, the shift has been towards primary prevention (reducing risk before maltreatment occurs) rather than secondary prevention (reducing risk and recidivism after suspected or confirmed maltreatment) (Klevens & Whitaker, 2007). In addition, funds from the Federal Maternal Infant and Early Childhood Home Visiting (MIECHV) program, administered out of the Health Resources and Services Administration (HRSA), is largely allocated through state health departments. To ensure these primary prevention practices delivered to parents are in-line with the highest quality of evidence available, there has been a move towards the implementation and funding of strictly EBP; that is, "practices done within known parameters and with accountability to the consumers and funders of those practices" (Fixsen, Naoom, Blasé, Friedman, & Wallace, 2005, p. 26). This transition follows the recognition that social services commonly used were based out of local traditions and not necessarily based on scientific research (Chaffin & Friedrich, 2004; Self-Brown, Whitaker, Berliner, & Kolko, 2012). An EBP has undergone a number of efficacy and effectiveness trials, the most rigorous of which is the randomized controlled trial. Practices without such a rigorous body of evidence (e.g., only quasi-experimental designs) may be determined to be evidence-informed.

Though some definitions have been offered, it is difficult for funders, the public, and raters to determine exactly what constitutes an EBP in child maltreatment prevention. Despite the ambiguities, in early 2015, MIECHV received an allocation of $386 million to continue to provide voluntary and evidence-based programs to par-

Table 1 HomVEE review procedure

1	Conduct a broad search of the literature
2	Screen publications for relevance
3	Prioritize models for review
4	Rate the quality of impact of programs that used eligible research designs
5	Assess evidence of effectiveness
6	Review implementation information
7	Address conflicts of interest

ents of young children. This is in addition to the $1.5 billion allocated through the 2010 Affordable Care Act.

The programs supported by MICHEV were reviewed in the Home Visiting of Effectiveness (HomVEE) by contractors from Mathematica Policy Research who are guided by an interagency work group overseen by the Department of Health and Human Services. The HomVEE review process, initiated in 2009 and is ongoing, follows seven steps (Table 1) in rating EBP (Avellar et al., 2014).

In addition to federally funded reviews of programs, there are a number of organizations that offer ratings of EBP in child welfare, such as the California Evidence-based Clearinghouse for Child Welfare (CEBC) (www.cebc4cw.org) and Blueprints for Healthy Youth Development (www.blueprintsprograms.com). The CEBC is the only peer-reviewed rating system and the site offers a number topic areas: Anger management, Domestic Violence, and Substance Abuse; Behavior Management including Parent Training, Core Child Welfare Services including Placement and Reunification; Engagement and Parent Partnering Programs; Mental Health; Prevention and Early Intervention; and, Support Services for Youth in the Child Welfare System. It is also more expansive than most in that it details age ranges and many other characteristics of families served by each rated program. Blueprints is a provider-accessible repository of evidence-based youth programs focused on the prevention of violence, delinquency, and substance use as well as the promotion of educational achievement and mental and physical health. Programs are reviewed by Blueprints staff and Advisory Board in contrast to the peer-review approach of the CEBC.

Policy-makers at all levels, public and private, will make increased use of rating systems to make funding or adoption decisions. But, how valid are these systems? They are at best narrowly useful there is still the need for agencies to decide on adoptions of EBP based on their own needs, the kinds of families they serve, how well the EBP may match the organization's culture, and how good any EBP implementation practices are. Many organizations use more than one EBP. We do not believe there is any research showing whether or not such a practice enhances, diminishes or is neutral in outcomes for families. It is largely not known on what basis programs are chosen and why some are dropped; however, it is quite possible that provider or family testimonials and consumer marketing materials are a factor in these decisions.

The push toward the exclusive use of EBP by funders and government agencies was met initially with skepticism and resistance (Chaffin & Friedrich, 2004;

Self-Brown et al., 2012). A common argument from providers centered upon their perception of the 'evidence', the effect, of the non-EBP that their agency may long have been delivering to families. For the provider it may be perceived as working, because clinicians observe differences in the families' skills, behaviors and/or attitudes, but more importantly, the practice did not exacerbate the issue or risk. Other practitioners, whom Chaffin and Friedrich (2004) labeled as middle ground practitioners, make the choice to implement a given intervention based on their personal experience and their personal interpretation of the literature base. This approach is flawed in its subjectivity and the influence of the current social or political climate (Chaffin & Friedrich, 2004).

The scientific testing of an EBP through randomized controlled trials ensures internal validity (the researcher can evaluate that the intervention is responsible for the change in behavior) and external validity (the researcher evaluates the generalization of the intervention to the general/larger population). Together, these forms of validity create a rigorous scientific knowledge base from which providers, funders, and clients alike can have some degree of assuredness that the program they are providing, funding, or receiving will actually, and safely, make a positive change. It is not the case that only trials who have met and exceeded the criterion for scientific support should be exclusively implemented. Stated differently, a randomized trial is not the exclusive standard when it comes to an evidence base (Chaffin & Friedrich, 2004). A program that is well tested, but has not undergone a randomized controlled trial, can indeed be evidence-based or evidence-informed. At the most basic level, EBP means that the approach is supported and validated by a mixture of research trials such as randomized trials or quasi-experimental designs (Chaffin & Friedrich, 2004).

In a time where budgets are constrained and caseworkers have extensive caseloads, but where the need is not by any means lessened, implementing an EBP is all the more critical. Without an effective intervention approach backed by rigorous scientific evaluation, there is no way to operate an efficient and effective child welfare system (Barth et al., 2005). Stated differently, EBP provide some assurance that the services delivered are safe and effective and the chance of a family's repeat or prolonged involvement with child protective services is reduced (Chaffin & Friedrich, 2004).

Evidence-Based Practices and Child Well-Being

There are many similarities among EBP. Of the most effective ones, the similarities include: manualized or standardized to varying degrees, role-playing between home visitors and parents in varying degrees, high fidelity of implementation (though defined differently among most programs), focus on aspects of child development, delivered at appropriate developmental levels, positive parenting, delivered in-home, and some requirement of parental mastery performance criteria before the parent is taught another new skill set. Many of the EBP that focus particularly on behavior management come from very similar 'roots' in social learning, behavior therapy, cognitive therapy, and applied behavior analysis. These programs are: Trauma-Focused Cognitive Behavior Therapy (TF-CBT), Parent-Child Interaction therapy (PCIT), Cognitive Processing Therapy, Prolonged Exposure Therapy, SafeCare, Incredible Years, Parent Management Training, Cognitive Behavioral Therapy for Children with Sexual Problems, Functional Family Therapy, Dialectical Behavior Therapy, Multi-dimensional Treatment Foster Care, Multisystemic Therapy, and Triple P—Positive Parenting Program. As with other EBP, each of these programs are for parents of children from differing age groups; some are for victims, others for parents, some to prevent behavioral challenges, others particularly for trauma. Some are brief interventions, others are longer. Some are implemented within child welfare systems with parents already in the system. Some focus primarily on high-risk parents not in the child welfare system.

Other EBP tend to be longer in duration, focus more on prevention, have curricula that tend to be somewhat less structured, and are mostly focused on prevention and delivered through a variety of systems and organizations. Some of the largest of these programs are: Nurse Family Partnership (NFP), Home Instruction for Parents of Preschool Youngsters (HIPPY), Parents as Teachers, and Early Head Start. The similarities and differences among EBP scope and implementation makes collaborative work across EBP a challenge.

Home Visiting

In the field of child abuse and neglect prevention, home visitation is one of the leading approaches used by numerous EBP. Home visiting is an umbrella term for a method of delivery of child welfare services. As early as 1993, the value of home visiting was recognized nationally: "no other single intervention has the promise for preventing child abuse that home visitation has" (US Advisory Board on Child Abuse and Neglect, as quoted by Chaffin, Bonner, & Hill, 2001). The needs of at-risk families with young children are addressed in home visiting programs because of the removal of accessibility barriers (Peacock, Konrad, Watson, Nickel, & Muhajarine, 2013). Delivery of the intervention in-home eliminates the need for parents to arrange transportation, child care, or time off work (Peacock et al., 2013; Sweet & Appelbaum, 2004), but also increases the potential for skill generalization, personalized sessions, retention in the program, and reduced rates of recidivism (MacMillan et al., 2005). Delivery in the individual home allows for personalized and tailored approaches (Peacock et al., 2013). The literature also suggests that delivering services in the home may be more cost-effective to child welfare agencies over time (Barth et al., 2005).

Generally, providers focus on teaching the parent to interact with the child rather than interacting with the child directly. Barth et al. (2005) explain four core components of parent training: assessment, teaching new skills, practicing the skills, and feedback. These components are aligned with social learning theory and are considered the gold standard (Sanders, Kirby, Tellegen, & Day, 2014). The focus of assessment and training is on the parent directly (Sweet & Appelbaum,

2004); if the parent improves observable skills it inherently benefits the child, there is no need to train the child. Home visiting programs vary on the type of families served, the duration and frequency of sessions, qualifications of the providers, ages of children in the home, and the types of behaviors targeted (Sweet & Appelbaum, 2004). Kaminski, Valle, Filene, and Boyle (2008) used meta-analytic techniques to determine program components consistent with large effect sizes in parent-training programs. These were: increasing communication and positive parent-child interaction, teaching parents the importance of consistency and requiring the parent to practice skills with the child directly during training sessions. That is to say, however, that EBP not using these components are not capable of producing positive outcomes. Continued effectiveness trials, that is research conducted in applied settings, are essential.

A review of home visiting EBP, writ large, is challenging given the extensive implementation variations discussed above, but also with regard to the diverse populations comprising the evaluations (Lundahl, Risser, & Lovejoy, 2006). However, as a whole it is the case that home visiting is an effective strategy for helping parents and children (Diaz & Petersen, 2014; Peacock et al., 2013; Selph, Bougatsos, Blazina, & Nelson, 2013; Sweet & Appelbaum, 2004). The change in parental attitudes and behavior that occurs in home visiting parent training models benefits the children (Sweet & Appelbaum, 2004). However, the more general effect of home visiting is often most apparent in the follow-up; that is, families who receive models using a home visiting approach have lower recidivism rates (Selph et al., 2013). In a systematic review of paraprofessional home visiting programs, Peacock et al. (2013) found that among high-risk families, effectiveness of the home visiting program is greatest when the intervention is delivered in high dosage, mothers are approached prenatally, and the program focuses on a single issue rather than remedying multiple problems. The extant literature also suggests the benefit of primary prevention; that is, home visiting prevention programs delivered to at-risk families not involved with child protective services (Chaffin et al., 2001; MacMillan et al., 2005).

We know that home visiting parenting programs are effective in improving family outcomes; for example, home visiting recipient mothers were more likely to go back to school or seek some form of education than comparison groups (Sweet & Appelbaum, 2004). Less is known about how these programs are viewed at the parent level. Kane, Wood, and Barlow (2007) conducted a systematic review of qualitative research with the intent to examine the parents' experience and perceptions of parenting programs. They reported that prior to intervention, parents described feelings of powerlessness and a lack of knowledge related to child behavior, but the intervention aided in the acquisition of skills and knowledge, feelings of support, and ability to cope (Kane et al., 2007).

SafeCare is but one of a relative multitude of evidence-based practices used in the prevention of child maltreatment. However, SafeCare is unique in its focus and effect on neglect specifically, the most pervasive form of maltreatment reported in the U.S. today.

SafeCare®

SafeCare is designed for parents at-risk for maltreatment and who have at least one child between birth and 5-years old. It is used as a primary prevention tool for families who are at-risk for maltreatment, but is also used as secondary or tertiary prevention in families already involved in the social service system. The curriculum is delivered by a variety of agencies and organizations including, but not limited to: child protective services, universities, community-based organizations, and prevention agencies (Guastaferro, Lutzker, Graham, Shanley, & Whitaker, 2012). Refined over several iterations since its inception in 1979 and validated three times by content experts, SafeCare trains parents in three core skill areas: parent-child/parent-infant interaction, home safety, and child health (Guastaferro et al., 2012; Lutzker & Chaffin, 2012). The three modules are delivered in situ (in the home) where it is believed generalization is most likely to occur over the course of approximately 18 session of 60–90 min.

Program Content

The parent-child/parent-infant interaction modules are determined by child age: parents of infants who are not yet ambulatory and who do not respond to simple verbal commands (usually under 12-months old) receive the parent-infant interaction (PII) module whereas parents of toddlers and children up to age five receive the parent-child interaction (PCI) module. As a child's needs and behaviors vary by these age distinctions, the goals of the interaction modules also vary. The PII module focuses on increasing positive, affective expressions from parent to infant and to improve the child's attachment to the parent. Skills focus on what is called the *LoTTS of Bonding Behaviors* which emphasize the importance of looking, talking, touching and smiling in every daily or play activity while holding, rocking, and imitating should occur only when the activity allows. In contrast, the PCI module, delivered to parents with ambulatory children, trains parents in Planned Activity Training (Bigelow & Lutzker, 2000) as a method for preventing challenging behaviors. For example, if children are told bath time will start in 5 min, they will be more prepared for the change in activity and, thus, the potential for challenging behaviors (e.g., temper tantrum) are minimized. Both PII and PCI modules review developmental milestones and provide suggestions for age appropriate play activities.

Home safety has seldom been incorporated into child abuse and neglect home visiting programs in a structured manner. The physical home environment can be an indicator of neglect, but can also pose threats to a child's safety and health. The SafeCare home safety module addresses the physical environment of the home, including hazards and filth. The module teaches the parent to identify and remove ten categories of hazards from the home: poisons, choking, suffocation, drowning, fire/electrical, fall/activity restriction, sharp objects, firearms, crush, and organic/

allergen (Guastaferro et al., 2012). Home visitors meticulously conduct observations with the parent in three rooms in the home, including opening closets and drawers, to make the environment as safe as possible for the child(ren) by making hazards inaccessible or unreachable. Parents must consent to the process and though it may on the surface seem invasive, after completing the module parents, and home visitors alike, express enthusiasm for what the module teaches them.

The child health module was developed to answer young parent's questions and needs related to their children's health (Delgado & Lutzker, 1988), addressing the potential for medical neglect in families at-risk for maltreatment. The module teaches parents how to assess symptoms, the severity of illness, and where to seek appropriate care (Guastaferro et al., 2012). Through a step-by-step approach, parents are trained to use health reference materials when identifying symptoms and to use a checklist in determining whether to care for the child at home, make a medical appointment, or to go to an emergency department. The need for this kind of training is evident: in a national survey of emergency departments in 2011, there were 87.3 visits per 100 persons per year for children under 1 year and 60.5 visits per 100 persons per year for children 1–4 (Centers for Disease Control and Prevention, 2011). In addition, the child health module briefly covers topics of shaken baby syndrome, car seat safety, and nutrition.

Each SafeCare module has been validated three times by content experts over the years. The PII and PCI modules have been validated by experts in early childhood education, child development and child behavior management. The safety module was initially validated by safety experts and subsequently by child protective service caseworkers who rated photos pf the physical home environment as acceptable or not. The health module was validated by family practice and pediatric residents.

Effectiveness and Program Outcomes

Throughout the history of SafeCare the modules have been individually and collectively studied. As the curriculum is rooted in the principles of applied behavior analysis, a number of single-case design studies have been conducted to examine specific behavior change with families in each module. Studies have been described in detail elsewhere (see Guastaferro et al., 2012), however, Table 2 provides references for studies of each module (full citations provided in reference section).

A prior version of SafeCare, called Project 12-Ways, included additional modules such as marital counseling and budgeting in addition to training in parenting, home safety, and child health. These modules were also tested with a number of single-case research designs and evaluations as depicted in the right most column of Table 2. These designs of these studies demonstrated the internal validity of the intervention; that is, the data indicated that observed changes in behavior were caused by intervention as opposed to external factors. However, in the dissemination and scale-up of SafeCare, these modules were dropped from the curriculum as we will discuss below.

Table 2 Single-case design studies conducted throughout the development of SafeCare

PCI	PII	Home safety	Child health	Additional interventions
Dachman, Halasz, Bickett, and Lutzker (1984)	Lutzker, Lutzker, Braunling-McMorrow, and Eddleman (1987)	Tertinger, Greene, and Lutzker (1984)	Delgado and Lutzker (1988)	Rosenfeld-Schlicter, Sarber, Bueno, Greene, and Lutzker (1983)
Lutzker, Megson, Webb, and Dachman (1985)	Gaskin, Lutzker, Crimmins, and Robinson (2012)	Barone, Greene, and Lutzker (1986)	Cordon, Lutzker, Bigelow, and Doctor (1998)	Campbell, O'Brien, Bickett, and Lutzker (1983)
McGimsey, Lutzker, and Greene (1994)	Morales, Lutzker, Shanley, and Guastaferro (2015)	Watson-Perzcel, Lutzker, Greene, and McGimpsey (1988)	Bigelow and Lutzker (2000)	Sarber, Halasz, Messmer, Bickett, and Lutzker (1983)
McGimsey, Greene, and Lutzker (1995)		Cordon et al. (1998)	Strong et al. (2014)	Lutzker, Campbell, and Watson-Perczel (1984)
Bigelow and Lutzker (1998)		Mandel, Bigelow, and Lutzker (1998)		Stilwell, Lutzker, and Greene (1988)
Cordon et al. (1998)		Metchikian, Mink, Bigelow, Lutzker, and Doctor (1999)		
Guastaferro, Lutzker, Jabaley, Shanley, and Crimmins (2013)		Jabaley, Lutzker, Whitaker, and Self-Brown (2011)		

The single-case design studies for the PCI and PII modules have tested the efficacy of those curricula in teaching the skills to at-risk parents (Guastaferro et al., 2013; Lutzker et al., 1985, 1987). More recent studies have tested the program with different populations: Morales et al. (2015), tested the PII module delivered in Spanish to Latino mothers who had experienced domestic violence. Gaskin et al. (2012), evaluated the enhancement of a digital picture frame in the PII module to teach the skills to a mother with intellectual and developmental disabilities by utilizing the principle of self-modeling, whereby the mother was staged and photographed correctly performing behaviors and the photographs were subsequently used in practice of those behaviors and to promote behavior change (Dowrick, 1999, 2012).

Similarly, the designs for home safety started with the practicality of teaching skills to parents (Tertinger et al., 1984) and subsequently tested with technological enhancements. Barone et al. (1986) included an audio-slide show package to illustrate how to remove hazards. Mandel et al. (1998) similarly used a video component.

Jabaley et al. (2011) introduced an iPhone™ to evaluate whether face-to-face time of the home visitor in the home could be reduced. Parents were taught to video record rooms and send the videos to the home visitor who would then count the number of hazards in the home and provide feedback without being in the home. Among the three families enrolled, hazards in their homes were reduced in three rooms by 74, 93, and 97 %, respectively.

Fewer single-case design studies have been conducted with the health module. Delgado and Lutzker (1988) demonstrated that parents were able to follow outlined steps for determining how to best care for their child based on symptoms. Bigelow and Lutzker (2000) streamlined the delivery of the health module, such that only steps that were performed incorrectly, compared to all steps in the 1988 study, were modeled and role-played during training sessions. Collectively, these two studies demonstrated written materials alone did not improve successful demonstration of trained behaviors, but with practice and feedback, the number of correct behaviors observed was 100 %. Strong et al. (2014) examined the health module with mothers in a residential home for substance use treatment. Mothers excelled in identifying when to take the child to the emergency room, though mastering the skills to identify when the child could be cared for at home or when a medical professional should be called necessitated additional training. Given the inclination for this population to take their children to the emergency room for all medical needs, this finding is actually not that surprising and emphasizes the importance of training parents to identify symptoms and decide the best course of treatment for their sick or injured children.

The SafeCare curriculum was translated and provided in Spanish. Cordon et al. (1998) evaluated the Spanish protocols for the PII, child health, and home safety with one Latina mother. In multiple-baseline studies of the individual modules, the Latina mother's data mirrored prior studies: behaviors improved from preintervention to postintervention and the improvement was maintained over time. The mother highly rated all aspects of the social validation: content and outcome of the training, the usefulness of the training strategies, and the counselor (Cordon et al., 1998). Delivery of the PII module in Spanish was evaluated by Morales et al. (2015) and produced similar high ratings.

In addition to the single-case design studies, several larger scale quasi-experimental studies helped establish the evidence base of the effectiveness of SafeCare. A comparison of recidivism in families who received SafeCare to families in standard family preservation services (comparison) revealed that SafeCare families had statistically significant lower reports of maltreatment than the comparison group (Gershater-Molko, Lutzker, & Wesch, 2002). At 36-months postinervention, 85 % of the SafeCare families had no child maltreatment reports compared to only 54 % of the comparison families (Wilcoxon = 11.41, p < .001). SafeCare was more successful in preventing repeat reports of child maltreatment in this sample and the dissemination of the model ensued. In the statewide randomized trial of nearly 2200 families comparing SafeCare to enhanced services as usual in Oklahoma, Chaffin Bard, Silovsky, and Beasley (2012) found a decrease in re-reports by 26 % for families who received the SafeCare curriculum specifically compared to families who received home-based services as usual over 7 years postintervention. It is believed that this represents the largest-ever study with the longest follow-up with families substantiated for child maltreatment.

The National SafeCare Training and Research Center (NSTRC) and colleagues external to NSTRC, as a result of the trials discussed above, have focused research on understanding the elements of the program from which participants' success can be attributed. In an investigation of cultural competency, client satisfaction and engagement, families who received the SafeCare curriculum completed more treatment goals and had higher ratings on cultural competence and satisfaction than services as usual (Damashek, Bard, & Hecht, 2012). A subanalysis of the Oklahoma trial examined the utility of SafeCare among an American Indian subpopulation (Chaffin, Bard, Bigfoot, & Maher, 2012). Recidivism reduction among this subpopulation mirrored what was observed in the overall population; that is, American Indian families who received SafeCare were less likely to have repeat encounters with child protective services. Additionally, SafeCare had higher consumer ratings and cultural sensitivity ratings among the American Indian population than home based services as usual.

Program Implementation

Program implementation, by definition, requires a set of activities to put a program into practice (Fixsen et al., 2005). In 2008, funding from the Doris Duke Charitable Foundation established the National SafeCare Training and Research Center (NSTRC) housed within the Mark Chaffin Center for Healthy Development in the School of Public Health at Georgia State University. NSTRC is the hub of SafeCare implementation, as the purpose of the center is to train home visitors, coaches, and trainers to deliver SafeCare nationally and internationally in addition to conducting and supporting research on implementation efforts. Presently, there are implementation efforts in 23 U.S. states, 6 of which are statewide rollouts, and SafeCare is delivered in 6 other countries across several sites (Belarus, United Kingdom, Spain, Australia, Israel, and Canada). Research trials within NSTRC and external to NSTRC are ongoing.

The SafeCare curriculum embodies a train-the-trainer paradigm; NSTRC trains agencies to deliver and sustain SafeCare overtime. Three levels of training are provided by NSTRC: home visitor, coach, and trainer. Training specialists from NSTRC travel to agencies and train providers to be home visitors. Training of the providers follows the same paradigm as training the parents: explain, model, practice, and feedback. Home Visitor training occurs over the course of 4 days, one module per day, in addition to an overview of effective communication strategies and structured problem-solving. At the end of each module, trainees complete a content quiz on which they must achieve a minimum of 80 %. Additionally, the trainees engage in role-modeling sessions which are evaluated by their trainers. The training process continues in early intervention through intensive coaching, or fidelity monitoring. The Home Visitor audio records a predetermined number of sessions which are reviewed by the NSTRC training specialist. Once fidelity is achieved in addition to the criteria satisfied during training, the Home Visitor is certified by NSTRC. The level of coaching is reduced as the Home Visitor continues to implement SafeCare.

At an organization or agency, one Home Visitor (or more depending on size) is identified or selected to serve as the coach for their organization. NSTRC training specialists provide an additional day of training for coaches who are then supported as they begin to coach home visitors at their sites. In this arrangement, the NSTRC training specialist is actively monitoring both the Home Visitor and the coach. With time, the level of coaching provided to the coach is reduced as well. The final level of the train-the-trainer model is the training of trainers. A coach and a trainer may, but are not always, one in the same person. As with other levels, an NSTRC training specialist provides extra training and closely monitors fidelity through observation. Once certified as a trainer, this individual has the capacity to accommodate staff turnover at sites, but also is used by NSTRC to extend the model's reach. This multi-tiered approach to training adds to the strength of the SafeCare approach in implementation, dissemination, and sustainability.

Dissemination and Implementation of EBP

The dissemination of an intervention is more than creating a training manual or providers attending a workshop (Chaffin & Friedrich, 2004); the goal of any implementation effort is to have providers use and deliver the program effectively (Fixsen, Blase, Naoom, & Wallace, 2009). Implementation science is in its relative infancy in the field of child maltreatment prevention (Self-Brown et al., 2012). Much of it actually imitates what the business world has done. In a singular source, we find the monograph, *Implementation research: A synthesis of the literature* (Fixsen et al., 2005) disseminated by the National Implementation Research Network (NIRN) to be a helpful and reliable tool that serves as a veritable manual for planning and conducting implementations. NIRN identify six stages critical to the implementation process: (1) exploration/adoption, (2) program installation, (3) initial implementation, (4) full operation, (5) innovation, and (6) sustainability (Fixsen et al., 2005, 2009; Self-Brown et al., 2012). A special issue of *Child Maltreatment* in 2012 dedicated to research on implementing evidence-based practices in the prevention of child maltreatment framed research efforts in each of the NIRN implementation phases (Self-Brown et al., 2012); though, as is true in the larger literature base, the majority of research is conducted in the initial implementation phase.

NIRN suggests, in addition, seven core implementation elements, also called implementation drivers, which guide the high-fidelity delivery of any intervention (Fixsen et al., 2005, 2009): recruitment and selection of staff, preservice training, consultation/coaching, staff performance evaluation, decision support/data systems, facilitative administrative support, and large-scale systems intervention. These elements have a cyclical relationship and one driver leads to the next.

Selecting the appropriate staff to deliver the intervention requires a consideration of what provider educational level or background is needed. Fixsen et al. (2009) note that the move toward EBP has raised concerns about the availability of a suitable workforce in the event a more advanced education background (inherently more expensive) is required for the delivery of the EBP. Providing preservice training to providers may mediate any discrepancies with past experience or knowledge deficits and, most importantly, provides the opportunity for practice and feedback of newly taught skills. Continued coaching and consultation allows for oversight and monitoring of the providers' implementation skills. It is acknowledged in this phase that training provides basic skills, but the real learning of how to utilize those skills occurs in the field. Related, frequent staff performance assessment provides the opportunity to enhance coaching and provides feedback to the purveyors regarding the implementation process. The provider assessment also directly impacts the benefit to the recipients of a program. Data from every phase of implementation drive decision-making that improve overall implementation. To be effective, an intervention must build in the infrastructure and respond to the data, a process completed in facilitative administration. Collectively, these elements drive systems intervention and, in so doing, provide for the funding, infrastructure support, and resources to support the intervention with external support (e.g., stakeholders, funding, or policies).

There are endless nuances involved in implementation. An EBP may be broadly implemented, but each new agency is organized differently and thus may require minor adaptations by the purveyors in implementing the program. There are regional subcultures in the U.S. as well as other countries. For these, too, adaptations may be needed. International implementations require considerable attention. Oscar Wilde is purported to have said, speaking of English-speaking countries across the world, "we are separated by a common language." Lutzker experienced this is a speaking tour in Australia when he more than once used American idioms that had very embarrassing different meanings in Australia! The SafeCare implementation in the United Kingdom required a number of word changes in the curriculum, such as replacing the word diapers with nappies. Many writers and researchers find that there a words and idioms that do not translate well from one language to another. Even some well-respected standardized assessments have items that create an entirely different meaning or contexts when translated.

Barriers to Implementation and Dissemination of EBP

Any EBP is ultimately only as good as its ability to be embraced by providers and families and to be delivered effectively with fidelity to large numbers of families. An EBP that has undergone rigorous evaluation, but is not disseminated and implemented effectively begs the question as to the validity of calling it an EBP. Stated differently, children and families cannot benefit from services they do not receive. No matter the strength of the model, however, there are inherent issues in implementation and dissemination. Chaffin and Friedrich (2004) identified several key barriers in the uptake of an EBP including funding and program goals: limited awareness of EBP models, concerns about funding, lack of interest or willingness to participate in modifying practice, emphasis on program outcomes rather than participant outcomes, and the gap between research and practice.

Today, perhaps the more pressing implementation and dissemination issue for agencies who have decided to use an EBP is the decision of what EBP should be selected in the first place. Though there are an increasing number of website ratings of EBP for child welfare, there are no ratings or evaluations as to how well these EBP implement their programs. Previously, the use of EBP was limited because few providers were aware of the variety of programs that existed (Chaffin & Friedrich, 2004). Today, a search of the prevention and early intervention topic area of the CEBC yields more than 40 programs from which an agency may select.

Additional implementation barriers occur on the individual provider level. Although an EBP may be effective, it requires the buy-in of the providers. That is, the attitude of providers is one of the key components in the implementation process. To assess a provider's perception of evidence-based practices, Aarons (2004) developed the Evidence-Based Practice Attitude Scale (EBPAS). The scale measures provider's attitudes towards EBP in four categories: appeal, adoption, openness, and perceived divergence of the EBP from an agency's typical intervention. Aarons (2004) demonstrated, among a sample of 322 public sector clinical service workers, that attitudes towards EBP could be assessed and used in predicting implementation successes and barriers. However, of interest, is the variation of answers observed among provider educational level, years of experience, and organization type (level of bureaucracy). The EBPAS and general attitude toward implementing an EBP, at both agency and provider levels, should be considered in the dissemination and implementation process.

SafeCare Research on Dissemination

SafeCare effectively employs the core implementation elements specified by NIRN (Fixsen et al., 2005). Through questionnaires and consultation prior to implementation, NSTRC assesses the organizational readiness and capacity of the agency to be trained. This step is crucial as it maximizes the capacity of the organization. The curriculum is designed to be delivered by a provider of any educational level; most home visitors are bachelor's level. Trainees (home visitors, coaches, and trainers) receive intensive training prior to delivering the curriculum and are coached at a high frequency immediately following training which is reduced with time. Staff evaluation occurs at the sites where NSTRC has trained providers, however, the certification process overseen by NSTRC is a component of the evaluation. Development of an online portal for real-time data collection is well underway and will soon be available to providers. This will allow for a comprehensive evaluation of implementation efforts on multiple levels: trainers, providers, and families. Increasingly, SafeCare is participating in systems intervention processes with other parent-training EBPs. In particular, two current projects speak to system intervention: An ongoing cluster randomized trial is examining the effect of braiding SafeCare with Parents as Teachers on parent and child outcomes. This multi-site trial created a braided curriculum called Parents as Teachers and SafeCare at Home, or PATSCH. In addition, NSTRC was awarded a research grant to create a non-model specific engagement framework and to test with small pilot projects. Unique about this engagement research is the non-model specific nature of the research in an attempt to explore a cross-model problem: parent engagement with EBP. These examples of collaborative research have a strong implication for potential systems interventions.

Despite the presence and use of these implementation drivers, SafeCare, not unlike any home visiting program, is effected by a host of implementation barriers. As stated previously, early in dissemination the number of SafeCare modules delivered was reduced from 12 (Project 12-Ways) to 3 as an effort most effectively and efficiently disseminate the model. However, the most commonly and prolifically cited implementation barrier includes engagement, often measured by program rates of attrition and retention. A study of engagement conducted by Damashek, Doughty, Ware, and Silovsky (2011) sought to reduce high program attrition. Families were randomized to receive services as usual or SafeCare+, a version of SafeCare which includes motivational interviewing. Families who received the SafeCare+ program were 8.5 times more likely to complete services compared to families in services as usual (Damashek et al., 2011). Comparing SafeCare+ to services as usual in a strictly rural population produced similar results (Silovsky et al., 2011). Families enrolled in SafeCare+ remained in services for an average of 35-h compared to only 8 h in services as usual.

Engagement is also of concern at the provider level. Whitaker et al. (2012) described implementation issues in a statewide rollout of SafeCare within a child welfare system. Though the trainees in this sample successfully completed training and appeared to be enthusiastic about and engaged in the model, once in the field they conducted very few SafeCare sessions. The authors describe this as an implementation issue of "high quality, low quantity" (Whitaker et al., 2012, p. 99). However, in comparison, in the statewide trial of SafeCare in Oklahoma (Chaffin et al., 2012), Aarons, Fettes, Flores, Sommerfeld, and Palinkas (2012) conducted a mixed-methods evaluation of providers' fidelity and turnover rates. The 2 × 2 design compared four groups: SafeCare coached, SafeCare uncoached, services as usual coached, and services as usual uncoached. Providers who were coached had a higher probability of staying with an agency for more than 12 months compared to uncoached providers, the highest observed probability in the SafeCare coached group. Additionally, there was a 2.6 times greater likelihood of staff turnover in all conditions relative to the SafeCare coached group (Aarons et al., 2012). Further, among a different group of providers, Aarons, Fettes, Flores, and Sommerfeld (2009) concluded that providers of SafeCare had lower levels of burnout, staff turnover, and emotional exhaustion when compared to services as usual. In large part, this is attributable to the structured coaching and fidelity processes inherent to SafeCare implementation. Thus, implementation of an EBP with structured coaching improved staff retention and satisfaction. This is an example of research and outcome that has important implications that are not specific to a given model.

Future Directions

The use of and support for EBP in the field of child maltreatment prevention will continue to grow. As with program implementation, in the widespread use of EBP purveyors and providers must respond to and reflect on the stages of implementation. That is, as a field, we must be critical of the implementation of EBP, regardless of the program, and adjust or tailor approaches to better achieve implementation goals. Fixsen, Blase, Metz, and Van Dyke (2013) offer the following equation when contemplating the effective implementation of EBP:

$$\textit{Effective Interventions} \times \textit{Effective Implementation} = \textit{Improved Outcomes}$$

By definition, an EBP generally has some degree of scientific evidence that supports its effectiveness, but only when it is implemented effectively using the core implementation elements, can improved outcomes be expected.

Barth et al. (2005) suggest that valuable program characteristics: "brevity, low cost per family, not requiring advanced degrees for trainers, applicability to families with children at home and those endeavoring to achieve reunification of their out-of-home children, and concepts that are easy to communicate" (p. 361). There is a concern that the use of EBP requires providers to have an advanced degree (Fixsen et al., 2009), thus developers must not only consider who it is that can deliver their intervention, but also if they can reduce the educational burden on providers. Using Bachelor's level providers, reduces the implementation cost. Additionally, a reexamination of the educational qualifications of providers potentially provides a larger work force body from which providers may be recruited and selected.

The implementation process is dynamic. Therefore, collectively EBP must consider innovations that can enhance the effect of the intervention. Including technological enhancements, such as an iPhone (Jabaley et al., 2011) or a digital picture frame (Gaskin et al., 2012) is but one way in which innovation should be considered. The content of the interventions, and its relationship and effect on the parent and child needs, must be considered as well. Lutzker and colleagues, in Lutzker, McGimsey, McRae, & Campbell, 1983, reviewed peer-reviewed and popular literature to suggest that what these sources had to offer, in fact, did not satisfy much of the concerns of parents and the needs of parent-child interactions. The authors offer a call of action to prevent complacency, a call that should be continually revisited in the implementation of EBP.

Is the Juice Worth the Squeeze?

The prevalence of child maltreatment has steeply declined in the past 20+ years. How much of that decline can we attribute that to EBP? Clearly, some at this point as penetration of EBP has expanded. But, that said, there are a host of other explanations for why the trend has continued, discussed earlier. Will increased penetration produce a steeper decline? Only time (and funding) will tell. Even MIECHV is very limited in penetration at this point. Approximately $2 million per state does not go very far in EBP penetration, though use of child welfare funds by states has likely added to the MIECHV impact. Triple P (Prinz, Sanders, Shapiro, Whitaker, & Lutzker, 2009) offers a universal approach that would theoretically have greater penetration, though it has not been the case in the U.S. as much as countries that otherwise have more developed universal health systems and thus a culture supporting such efforts. With the exception of the follow-up to the NFP Elmira study (Olds et al., 2014), we know little about the long-term impact of parenting EBP on child maltreatment, and other child development and academic/social success. What more could EBP do to help ensure long-term success of families? And, are there resources to support the necessary adaptations to existing EBP or new ones to address these sustainability issues? Some thoughts are delineated below.

Protective Factors

The literature is clear with youth violence prevention, and to some degree dating violence prevention (Dahlberg & Simon, 2006) that engagement is a preventive factor. Youth who participate in athletics and other extracurricular activities in middle school and high school are at lower risk for perpetrating violence. Similarly, in terms of what we might call "family development," are behavior management skills for parents, along with health, safety, and other training offered by EBP sufficient to promote family development, good decision-making by parents and their children, and academic and social success? It is relatively easy to teach the skills offered by most EBP, but can enrichment be taught? And, while some enrichment can be offered across socioeconomic status such as increasing language between parents and their children and reading and storytelling, other enrichment activities such as camp, museums, attending athletic events and concerts, and so forth may be very restricted for families trapped in poverty. Even taking a walk together may be a challenge for a family living in a dangerous neighborhood. In any case, would it be possible to add to EBP curricula enrichment activities that all parents can use? Also, can we learn more about protective factors in families living in abject situations who succeed as parents with healthy successful children?

Praise

There is a 50-year-old literature showing the beneficial effects of praise on improving child behavior management. In natural environments there is an inverse relationship between age and praise (White, 1975). That is, the older the child, the less praise is offered by teachers. And, praise carries less weight (value) the older the child. For the parent of a preschool child to say, "I like how you are using your fork to eat your potatoes," will likely serve as a reinforcer to maintain fork use. For a parent to use that kind of descriptive praise to a 12-year-old will likely have little value as a reinforcer, thus parents need to be equipped with other more age-appropriate behavior management skills. It is of concern that over use of praise for all children may cheapen its value. Proposed here is that children may need to hear and "feel" real pride from their parents. That is, rather than hearing too often, "I am proud of you" for this skill or that, they need parents to look them in the eyes and tell them how proud they are for major accomplishments and to hear their parents "bragging on them" to friends and family members.

Language

The seminal work of Hart and Risley (1995, 2003) demonstrated the critical importance of vocabulary developed through parent-child vocalizing. The more parents talk to their children, the more words children hear the better the vocabulary and social and academic outcomes for the children. Projects such as *Providence Talks* (http://www.providencetalks.org/about/) in which parents are taught to talk more to their children by reading books may produce improved outcomes for children. Only more research will determine this. But, the advantage of programs that foster more language between parents and their children is that the talking more to children is cost-free for the parents. That said, it takes funding to support such programs, but technology and public service spots could go a long way in promoting parents' use of talking as a tool to improve child development. It might also naturally produce a generalized bonding phenomenon in that talking to children in positive ways naturally brings parents closer to them.

Beyond What EBP Offer

A perusal of popular press advice books for parents suggests that parents are interested in much more than behavior management advice regarding their children, especially in the child middle years and beyond. Parents appear to want information/advice on how to deal with sex education, drugs, dating, religious and spiritual issues, sibling relationships, and dealing with divorce or death. With the exception of some attention to some of these matters by Triple P, EBP largely ignore them despite their apparent importance to parents. Is it in the realm of extant EBP to explore curricula on these matters for parents? There is next to no evidence base for outcomes from current advice books. Are EBP better equipped to design and test materials to deal with these subjects? Is the current "juice" offered by EBP a little watery in the bigger picture?

If EBP are to remain vital sooner than later, increased collaboration will be essential. As we have noted, there are no panaceas and how could there be? For example, no one antibiotic serves all. EBP are diverse (not unlike antibiotics), serving different populations with different curricula. Can we conduct more research, such as PATSCH, that examines the braiding or blending of EBP to best serve families? Can we create algorithms that help providers determine what program is best for a given family, or let families choose? HRSA and other federal agencies are pushing for more collaboration among EBP and it is happening, though there seems to be more talk than action. If we do, our "juice" will be richer and more satisfying.

Summary

In this chapter we have documented the practicalities and pitfalls of the movement towards EBP in the field of child maltreatment prevention with a particular focus on the implementation of EBP. We identified commonalities in EBP approaches, specifically among those that utilize a home visiting approach. Using SafeCare as an example, we have described the development and dissemination of an EBP focusing in particular on the implementation considerations as identified by NIRN. Despite the declines in rates of maltreatment, EBP must increase their penetration through effective and continuously adaptive implementation efforts.

Commonalities and differences of EBP target, content, and dissemination aside, we question whether we as a field are doing enough, getting the most juice from the squeeze. In order to continue the reduction of instances of maltreatment, EBP must engage a feedback loop from providers and clients and encourage adaptations to best meet the needs of client families. Our field is a dynamic one and only through constant monitoring of needs can we most effectively and consistently continue to see the decline in rates of maltreatment.

References

Aarons, G. A. (2004). Mental health provider attitudes toward adoption of evidence-based practice: The Evidence-Based Practice Attitude Scale (EBPAS). *Mental Health Services Research, 6*(2), 61–74.

Aarons, G. A., Fettes, D. L., Flores, L. E., & Sommerfeld, D. H. (2009). Evidence-based practice implementation and staff emotional exhaustion in children's services. *Behaviour Research and Therapy, 47*, 954–960.

Aarons, G. A., Fettes, D. L., Flores, L. E., Sommerfeld, D. H., & Palinkas, L. A. (2012). Mixed methods for implementation research: Application to evidence-based practice implementation and staff turnover in community-based organizations providing child welfare services. *Child Maltreatment, 17*(1), 67–79.

Avellar, S., Paulsell, D., Sama-Miller, E., Del Grosso, P., Akers, L., & Kleinman, R. (2014). *Home visiting evidence of effectiveness review: Executive summary*. Washington, DC: Office of

Planning, Research and Evaluation, Administration for Children and Families, U.S. Department of Health and Human Services.

Barone, V. J., Greene, B. F., & Lutzker, J. R. (1986). Home safety with families being treated for child abuse and neglect. *Behavior Modification, 10*, 93–114.

Barth, R., Landsverk, J., Chamberlain, P., Reid, J. B., Rolls, J. A., Hurlburt, M. S., … Kohl, P. L. (2005). Parent-training programs in child welfare services: Planning for a more evidence-based approach to serving biological parents. *Research on Social Work Practice, 15*(5), 353–371.

Bigelow, K. M., & Lutzker, J. R. (1998). Using video to teach planned activities to parents reported for child abuse. *Child and Family Behavior Therapy, 20*(4), 1–14.

Bigelow, K. M., & Lutzker, J. R. (2000). Training parents reported for or at risk for child abuse and neglect to identify and treat their children's illnesses. *Journal of Family Violence, 15*, 311–330.

Campbell, R. V., O'Brien, S., Bickett, A., & Lutzker, J. R. (1983). In-home parent-training, treatment of migraine headaches, and marital counseling as an ecobehavioral approach to prevent child abuse. *Journal of Behavior Therapy and Experimental Psychiatry, 14*, 147–154.

Centers for Disease Control and Prevention. (2011). *National Hospital Ambulatory Medical Care Survey: 2011 Emergency Department Summary Tables*. Retrieved from http://www.cdc.gov/nchs/data/ahcd/nhamcs_emergency/2011_ed_web_tables.pdf.

Chaffin, M., & Friedrich, B. (2004). Evidence-based treatments in child abuse and neglect. *Children and Youth Services Review, 26*, 1097–1113.

Chaffin, M., Bonner, B. L., & Hill, R. F. (2001). Family preservation and family support programs: Child maltreatment outcomes across client risk levels and program types. *Child Abuse and Neglect, 25*, 1269–1289.

Chaffin, M., Bard, D., Bigfoot, D. S., & Maher, E. J. (2012). Is a structured, manualized, evidence-based treatment protocol culturally competent and equivalently effective among American Indian parents in child welfare? *Child Maltreatment, 17*(3), 242–252.

Chaffin, M., Bard, D., Silovsky, J. F., & Beasley, W. H. (2012). A statewide trial of the SafeCare home-based services model with parents in child protective services. *Pediatrics, 129*(3), 509–515.

Cordon, I. M., Lutzker, J. R., Bigelow, K. M., & Doctor, R. M. (1998). Evaluating Spanish protocols for teaching bonding, home safety, and health care skills. *Journal of Behavior Therapy and Experimental Psychiatry, 29*, 41–54.

Dachman, R. S., Halasz, M. M., Bickett, A. D., & Lutzker, J. R. (1984). A home-based ecobehavioral parent-training and generalization package with a neglectful mother. *Education and Treatment of Children, 7*, 183–202.

Dahlberg, L. L., & Simon, T. R. (2006). Predicting and preventing youth violence: Developmental pathways and risk. In J. Lutzker (Ed.), *Preventing violence: Research and evidence-based intervention strategies* (pp. 97–124). Washington, DC: American Psychological Association.

Damashek, A., Doughty, D., Ware, L., & Silovsky, J. (2011). Predictors of client engagement and attrition in home-based child maltreatment prevention services. *Child Maltreatment, 16*(1), 9–20.

Damashek, A., Bard, D., & Hecht, D. (2012). Provider cultural competency, client satisfaction, and engagement in home-based programs to treat child abuse and neglect. *Child Maltreatment, 17*(1), 56–66.

Delgado, L. E., & Lutzker, J. R. (1988). Training young parents to identify and report their children's illnesses. *Journal of Applied Behavior Analysis, 21*, 311–319.

Diaz, A., & Petersen, A. C. (2014). Institute of Medicine Report: New directions in child abuse and neglect research. *JAMA Pediatrics, 168*(2), 101–102.

Dowrick, P. W. (1999). A review of self modeling and related interventions. *Applied and Preventive Psychology, 8*, 23–39.

Dowrick, P. W. (2012). Self modeling: Expanding the theories of learning. *Psychology in the Schools, 49*(1), 30–41.

Finkelhor, D., Jones, L., Shattuck, A., & Saito, K. (2013). *Updated trends in child maltreatment, 2012*. Durham, NH: Crimes Against Children Research Center (CV203).

Finkelhor, D., Shattuck, A., Turner, H. A., & Hamby, S. L. (2014). Trends in children's exposure to violence, 2003–2011. *JAMA Pediatrics, 168*(6), 540–546.

Fixsen, D. L., Naoom, S. F., Blasé, K. A., Friedman, R. M., & Wallace, F. (2005). *Implementation research: A synthesis of the literature*. Tampa, FL: University of South Florida, Louis, de la Parte Florida Mental Health Institute, The National Implementation Research Network (FMHI Publication #231).

Fixsen, D. L., Blase, K. A., Naoom, S. F., & Wallace, F. (2009). Core implementation components. *Research on Social Work Practice, 19*(5), 531–540.

Fixsen, D. L., Blase, K. A., Metz, A., & Van Dyke, M. (2013). Statewide implementation of evidence-based programs. *Exceptional Children, 29*(2), 213–230.

Gaskin, E. H., Lutzker, J. R., Crimmins, D., & Robinson, L. (2012). Using a digital frame and pictorial information to enhance the SafeCare parent-infant interactions module with a mother with intellectual disabilities: Results of a pilot study. *Journal of Mental Health Research in Intellectual Disabilities, 5*, 187–202.

Gershater-Molko, R. M., Lutzker, J. R., & Wesch, D. (2002). Using recidivism data to evaluate Project SafeCare: Teaching bonding, safety, and health care skills to parents. *Child Maltreatment, 7*(3), 277–285.

Guastaferro, K. M., Lutzker, J. R., Graham, M. L., Shanley, J. R., & Whitaker, D. J. (2012). SafeCare®: Historical perspective and dynamic development of an evidence-based scaled-up model for the prevention of child maltreatment. *Psychosocial Intervention, 21*(2), 171–180.

Guastaferro, K. M., Lutzker, J. R., Jabaley, J. J., Shanley, J. R., & Crimmins, D. B. (2013). Teaching young mothers to identify developmental milestones. *International Journal of Child Health and Human Development, 6*(2), 223–233.

Hart, B., & Risley, T. (1995). *Meaningful differences in the everyday experiences of young American children*. Baltimore: Brookes.

Hart, B., & Risley, T. (2003). The early catastrophe: The 30 million world gap by age 3. *American Educator, 22*, 4–9.

Jabaley, J. J., Lutzker, J. R., Whitaker, D. J., & Self-Brown, S. (2011). Using iPhones™ to enhance and reduce face-to-face safety sessions within SafeCare®: An evidence-based child maltreatment prevention program. *Journal of Family Violence, 26*, 377–385.

Kaminski, J. W., Valle, L. A., Filene, J. H., & Boyle, C. L. (2008). A meta-analytic review of components associated with parent training program effectiveness. *Journal of Abnormal Child Psychology, 36*, 567–589.

Kane, G. A., Wood, V. A., & Barlow, J. (2007). Parenting programs: A systematic review and synthesis of qualitative research. *Child: Care, Health, and Development, 33*(6), 784–793.

Klevens, J., & Whitaker, D. J. (2007). Primary prevention of child physical abuse and neglect: Gaps and promising directions. *Child Maltreatment, 12*(4), 364–377.

Lundahl, B., Risser, H. J., & Lovejoy, M. C. (2006). A meta-analysis of parent training: Moderators and follow-up effects. *Clinical Psychology Review, 26*, 86–104.

Lutzker, J. R., & Chaffin, M. (2012). SafeCare®: An evidence-based constantly dynamic model to prevent child Maltreatment. In H. Dubowitz (Ed.), *World perspectives on child abuse* (10th ed., pp. 93–96). Canberra, Australia: The International Society for the Prevention of Child Abuse and Neglect.

Lutzker, J. R., McGimsey, J. F., McRae, S., & Campbell, R. V. (1983). Behavioral parent training: There's so much more to do. *The Behavior Therapist, 6*, 110–112.

Lutzker, J. R., Campbell, R. V., & Watson-Perczel, M. (1984). Utility of the case study method in the treatment of several problems of a neglectful family. *Education and Treatment of Children, 7*, 315–333.

Lutzker, J. R., Megson, D. A., Webb, M. E., & Dachman, R. S. (1985). Validating and training adult-child interaction skills to professionals and to parents indicated for child abuse and neglect. *Journal of Child and Adolescent. Psychotherapy, 2*, 91–104.

Lutzker, S. Z., Lutzker, J. R., Braunling-McMorrow, D., & Eddleman, J. (1987). Prompting to increase mother-baby stimulation with single mothers. *Journal of Child and Adolescent. Psychotherapy, 4*, 3–12.

Lutzker, J. R., Guastaferro, K. M., & Whitaker, D. W. (2014). More work needed to protect children but promising trend data on exposure to violence. *JAMA Pediatrics, 168*(6), 512–514.

MacMillan, H. L., Thomas, B. H., Jamieson, E., Walsh, C. A., Boyle, M. H., Shannon, H. S., & Gafni, A. (2005). Effectiveness of home visitation by public-health nurses in prevention of the recurrence of child physical abuse and neglect: A randomized controlled trial. *Lancet, 365*, 1786–1793.

Mandel, U., Bigelow, K. M., & Lutzker, J. R. (1998). Using video to reduce home safety hazards with parents reported for child abuse and neglect. *Journal of Family Violence, 13*, 147–162.

McGimsey, J. F., Lutzker, J. R., & Greene, B. F. (1994). Validating and teaching affective adult-child interaction skills. *Behavior Modification, 18*, 209–224.

McGimsey, J. F., Greene, B. F., & Lutzker, J. R. (1995). Competence in aspects of behavioral treatment and consultation: Implications for service delivery and graduate training. *Journal of Applied Behavior Analysis, 28*, 301–315.

Metchikian, K. L., Mink, J. M., Bigelow, K. M., Lutzker, J. R., & Doctor, R. M. (1999). Reducing home safety hazards in the homes of parents reported for neglect. *Child and Family Behavior Therapy, 3*, 23–34.

Morales, Y., Lutzker, J. R., Shanley, J. R., & Guastaferro, K. M. (2015). Parent-infant interaction training with a Latino mother. *International Journal of Child Health and Human Development, 8*(2), 135.

Olds, D. L., Kitzman, H., Knudtson, M. D., Anson, E., Smith, J. A., & Cole, R. (2014). Effect of home visiting by nurses on maternal and child mortality: Results of a 2-decade follow-up of a randomized clinical trial. *JAMA Pediatrics, 168*(9), 800–806.

Peacock, S., Konrad, S., Watson, E., Nickel, D., & Muhajarine, N. (2013). Effectiveness of home visiting programs on child outcomes: A systematic review. *BMC Public Health, 13*, 17.

Prinz, R. J., Sanders, M. R., Shapiro, C. J., Whitaker, D. W., & Lutzker, J. R. (2009). Population-based prevention of child maltreatment: The US Triple P system population trial. *Prevention Science, 10*(1), 1–12.

Rosenfeld-Schlicter, M. D., Sarber, R. E., Bueno, G., Greene, B. F., & Lutzker, J. R. (1983). Maintaining accountability for an ecobehavioral treatment of one aspect of child neglect: Personal cleanliness. *Education and Treatment of children, 6*, 153–164.

Sanders, M. R., Kirby, J. N., Tellegen, C. L., & Day, J. J. (2014). The Triple P-Positive Parenting Program: A systematic review and meta-analysis of a multi-level system of parenting support. *Clinical Psychology Review, 34*, 337–357.

Sarber, R. E., Halasz, M. M., Messmer, M. C., Bickett, A. D., & Lutzker, J. R. (1983). Teaching menu planning and grocery shopping skills to a mentally retarded mother. *Mental Retardation, 21*, 101–106.

Self-Brown, S., Whitaker, D., Berliner, L., & Kolko, D. (2012). Disseminating child maltreatment interventions: Research on implementing evidence-based programs. *Child Maltreatment, 17*(1), 5–10.

Selph, S. S., Bougatsos, C., Blazina, I., & Nelson, H. D. (2013). Behavioral interventions and counseling to prevent child abuse and neglect: A systematic review to update the U.S. Preventative Services Task Force recommendation. *Annals of Internal Medicine, 158*(3), 179–190.

Silovsky, J. F., Bard, D., Chaffin, M., Hecht, D., Burris, L., Owora, A., … Lutzker, J. (2011). Prevention of child maltreatment in high-risk rural families: A randomized clinical trial with child welfare outcomes. *Children and Youth Services Review, 33*(8), 1435–1444.

Stilwell, S. L., Lutzker, J. R., & Greene, B. F. (1988). Evaluation of a sexual abuse prevention program for abuse and neglect: The ecobehavioral imperative. *Behaviour Change, 9*, 149–156.

Strong, L. E. A., Lutzker, J. R., Jabaley, J. J., Shanley, J. R., Self-Brown, S., & Guastaferro, K. M. (2014). Training mothers recovering from substance abuse to identify and treat their children's illnesses. *International Journal of Child Health and Human Development, 7*(2), 156–166.

Sweet, M. A., & Appelbaum, M. I. (2004). Is home visiting an effective strategy? A meta-analytic review of home visiting programs for families with young children. *Child Development, 75*(5), 1435–1456.

Tertinger, D. A., Greene, B. F., & Lutzker, J. R. (1984). Home safety: Development and validation of one component of an ecobehavioral treatment program for abused and neglected children. *Journal of Applied Behavior Analysis, 17*, 159–174.

U.S. Department of Health and Human Services [DHHS], Administration for Children and Families, Administration on Children, Youth and Families, Children's Bureau. (2015). *Child maltreatment 2013*. Retrieved from http://www.acf.hhs.gov/programs/cb/research-data-technology/statistics-research/child-maltreatment.

Watson-Perzcel, M., Lutzker, J. R., Greene, B. F., & McGimpsey, B. J. (1988). Assessment and modification of home cleanliness among families adjudicated for child neglect. *Behavior Modification, 12*, 57–81.

Whitaker, D. J., Ryan, K. A., Wild, R. C., Self-Brown, S., Lutzker, J. R., Shanley, J. R., ... Hodges, A. E. (2012). Initial implementation indicators from a statewide rollout of SafeCare within a child welfare system. *Child Maltreatment, 17*(1), 96–101.

White, M. A. (1975). Natural rates of teacher approval and disapproval in the classroom. *Journal of Applied Behavior Analysis, 8*, 367–372.

Wildeman, C., Emanuel, N., Leventhal, J. M., Putnam-Hornstein, E., Waldfogel, J., & Lee, H. (2014). The prevalence of confirmed child maltreatment among US children, 2004 to 2011. *JAMA Pediatrics, 168*(8), 706–713.

Reducing the Risk of Child Maltreatment: Challenges and Opportunities

Charles A. Wilson and Donna M. Pence

The national discourse concerning child abuse and neglect that emerged in the 1960s recognized it was not sufficient to identify and respond to maltreatment of children but, as a society, we needed to seek to *prevent it* in the first place. The landmark legislation that served as the framework for the nation's child protection system, the Child Abuse Prevention and Treatment Act (CAPTA) of 1974, included prominent reference to "prevention" in its title. Prevention of child abuse and neglect, however, has proven to be an elusive goal. How can one prevent something that has such complex etiology and with such a wide array of often overlapping and interacting causes and facilitating factors, and that presents itself in so many different forms? The dynamics of neglect by an impoverished, isolated teenage mother are vastly different from the dynamics of sexual abuse of children by adults. While commonalities exist, each case is also unique, and what would potentially work to prevent one case of maltreatment may bear little relevance for others.

When one reviews the literature on maltreatment "prevention", a wide array of topics emerges. Prevention, like many other terms used in the field, is conceptualized differently by professionals, sometimes based on varying disciplines and at other times, philosophically mediated. There is, however, an overarching agreement on the desire to stop all forms of child abuse and neglect from occurring.

The use of the word ***prevention***, in and of itself, sets up expectations by both professionals and the public that we <u>can</u> truly prevent a problem before it occurs- true primary prevention (Bethea, 1999). The reality is that we have limited ability

C.A. Wilson, M.S.S.W. (✉)
Chadwick Center for Children & Families, Rady Children's Hospital, San Diego, CA, USA
e-mail: cwilson@rchsd.org

D.M. Pence
Pence-Wilson Training & Consulting, Inc., San Diego, CA, USA
e-mail: donnapence@gmail.com

© Springer International Publishing Switzerland 2017   165
D.M. Teti (ed.), *Parenting and Family Processes in Child Maltreatment and Intervention*, Child Maltreatment Solutions Network,
DOI 10.1007/978-3-319-40920-7_10

to actually prevent certain behaviors and outcomes, despite our best intentions and efforts. The community, including politicians and the media, who have supported a variety of interventions designed to "prevent" various forms of child maltreatment, may feel misled when abuse or neglect still occurs. On a micro level, the victimized child who participated in a "prevention" program at school may walk away from the training sure he or she is, indeed, somehow responsible for their own abuse because they didn't 'run, yell, or tell' as they now know they "should" have.

Prevention = Risk Reduction

With our existing knowledge and evidence, evaluating whether a program is really "preventive" of child abuse and neglect becomes challenging. In truth, much of what we call "child abuse and neglect prevention" today is really about **reducing the risk** of abuse or neglect (Pence & Wilson, 1992, 1994). The term "risk reduction" encompasses strategies at the micro, meso, and macro levels and can be used in addressing all forms of child maltreatment. To effectively "prevent" child maltreatment we must develop or adopt a wide range of risk reduction strategies, targeting the distal underlying conditions in which maltreatment festers, along with strategies that target the proximate factors that lead to abuse or neglect in individual cases.

In a traditional public health model, science seeks to isolate "the cause": the one thing or set of things that created the illness or condition that is the focus of the intervention/eradication effort, whether that be the bacteria that caused the infection, the particular genetic mutation that caused the disease, or the environmental condition that produced or exacerbated the adverse effect, such as lead in the paint of a baby's crib. In these cases, if we can isolate the 'true' or ground cause we can then seek to alter, control or eliminate it. This approach has given us clean drinking water, pasteurized milk, seat belts, "Back to Sleep" campaigns to reduce SIDS, food inspectors, environmental protection policies, immunization for many diseases, antibiotics, and a host of other preventive and early intervention measures that have transformed society into a safer place.

This concept of prevention, however, does not easily translate to child abuse and neglect. There is no single "cause" for child abuse and neglect and we don't always know why it appears in one household and not the one next door. We certainly recognize many factors that appear over and over within families where abuse and neglect occur, but many of these factors appear to *facilitate* abuse or neglect but not necessarily *cause* it. Families living under immense economic stresses of poverty are vastly over-represented among those reported to child protection authorities (Erickson & Egeland, 2002), but poverty in and of itself does not cause maltreatment. There are innumerable examples of impoverished families who don't abuse or neglect their children and many who excel at parenting. While past exposure to violence and other adverse childhood experiences, including parental history of foster care in their youth (Felitti, 2002; Vaithianathan et al., 2012) appears to be common among those who abuse or neglect children, there are many other examples of adults who experienced many adversities in childhood only to achieve great success as adults and act as strong, loving parents for their own children. Ultimately, we may find that the "cause" of child abuse and neglect rests in the complex interaction between individual genetic characteristics, environmental stress triggers, and the presence or absence of certain protective factors (Child Welfare Gateway, 2015).

The Need for Theoretical Integration

Due to the diversity of distal and proximal causes and facilitation factors, there is no unifying theory of child abuse and neglect prevention. We need to draw upon and perhaps flexibly make use of several theories of change, some of which target parental beliefs and behaviors, some which are cognitively based, some drawing from ecological models of family stress and support, and some psychodynamic. We also may need to invoke different theoretical mechanisms to help identify common factors that lead to *abuse* vs. *neglect*. Indeed, child abuse is often considered an act of "commission" while neglect is an act of "omission" (Erickson & Egeland, 2002). Reducing the risk of something harmful from being committed upon a child (abuse) may require a different strategy than reducing the risk that a parent or caregiver will fail to meet one or more of the child's primary needs (neglect).

Child neglect is the most common form of maltreatment reported to child protection authorities across the nation (USHHS/ACYF/Children's Bureau, 2015). Many in the field have long perceived that parents and caregivers who have a history of neglecting their children often simply don't know how to parent effectively. Indeed, children growing up in a neglectful home often don't learn effective parenting strategies from observing their own parents. The lack of positive parenting role models who appreciate the benefits of a physically safe environment and the critical importance of a loving, supportive, nurturing parent-child relationship leaves many new parents from neglectful homes at a loss. These parents were never taught, experienced, or observed the important aspects of being a "good" parent, so they can hardly be expected to spontaneously act as responsible parents upon the birth of their child, particularly when they are young, with few resources, and without a caring grandparent or compassionate family available for tangible support. In response to these specific factors, programs have emerged that draw on Social Learning Theory (Daro & Cohn-Donnelly, 2002) in one form or another, and seek to provide parenting education in the absence of the family's life experiences. Others have sought to prevent neglect by focusing on the common comorbid conditions such as substance use and addiction, identified nationally as early as 1998 as one of the two most common conditions seen in abusive and neglectful families (Wang & Harding, 1999). Clearly, when parents are preoccupied with meeting their own needs to acquire and use substances, the children lose out. When under the influence of drugs, the child's needs become secondary and often unattended to, leaving the child at great risk of neglect.

When inadequate knowledge of child development co-occurs with ineffective capacities to regulate negative emotions in response to normative challenges to parenting that children tend to create, risk for child abuse increases. Poor emotion regulatory capacities could in part be constitutionally based, the by-product of past traumas and being parented poorly in childhood, the result of significant cognitive limitations, a correlate of an existing affective disorder, and/or stimulated by an ongoing dependency on alcohol and substance use (Azar, 2002; Kelly, 2002). Some efforts to reduce the risk of physical abuse are built upon psychodynamic theories designed to help parents gain a better understanding of themselves and their role as parents. Other efforts have drawn on social learning theory, focused on educating parents about their role as caregiver and what to expect from their developing child. Prevention models such as Period of Purple Crying (Barr et al., 2009) and Happiest Baby (McRury & Zolotor, 2010) seek to teach caregivers what to expect as their child develops and provide them with non-abusive means of managing their own stress and the behaviors of their child. Other prevention efforts, drawing on ecological theory, have focused on reducing the stress of parental social isolation and the associated lack of social support often seen in families where abuse and neglect is present (Daro & Cohn-Donnelly, 2002; Rafael & Pion-Berlin, 2000).

We proposed that reducing the risk of child maltreatment requires a multifaceted approach that starts with broad policy initiatives that support families, creates economic opportunities, and provides mechanisms to promote child and adult mental health, sobriety, and parent education. These would include:

1. "Efforts to promote parents' basic knowledge of child development and a better understanding of what children can and can't be expected to do at particular levels of development-drawing from social-cognitive theory's premise that competence at any task requires a basic knowledge of that task (Bandura, 1989; Hess, Teti, & Hussey-Gardner, 2004)
2. Efforts to educate parents about the basic tenets of competent parenting (i.e., a healthy blend of warmth/nurturance and developmentally appropriate control).
3. Efforts to promote parents' capacities to regulate negative emotions "in the moment", particularly in response to child provocations (drawing from basic tenets of attachment theory and the growing attention being given to mindfulness parenting interventions).
4. Efforts to promote internal family supports for parenting (spousal supports, paternal involvement, co-parenting—drawing from both psychodynamic and social learning theoretical perspectives).
5. Efforts to connect external resources to parents if/when needed—drawing again from social learning theory" (Barth, 2011).

Special Considerations: Child Sexual Abuse

Prevention of child sexual abuse and exploitation represents a special case. Beginning in the 1980s, the sexual abuse of children became a topic of much public and professional conversation. A form of maltreatment that had been largely hidden or ignored by society throughout history was then being reported in growing numbers. Drawing on several theoretical approaches, numerous efforts emerged in the 1980s to reduce the risk of sexual abuse of children, initially by educating children about sexual abuse (e. g., Illusion Theater, Talking About Touching). In 1984 a simple and elegant model, around which efforts to reduce risk of child sexual abuse could be better framed, was advanced to explain the dynamics of child sexual abuse by Finkelhor (Finkelhor, 1984) at the University of New Hampshire. This model, the Four Preconditions Model of Sexual Abuse, postulates that four preconditions must exist and be aligned properly before an act of sexual abuse could occur. Altering any of these four "preconditions" could break the dynamic in a way that thwarts an incident of sexual abuse.

First, there must be a potential abuser with some *motivation to sexually abuse* (Precondition 1). Next, that motivation had to be greater than the *internal inhibitors* (Precondition 2) of the would-be abuser. These internal inhibitors are conscious awareness of the wrongness of acting on the sexual interest and the possible negative consequences of such actions. For example, an adult may know/understand that engaging in sexual behavior with a child is illegal, unacceptable to society at large and, if discovered, can result in severe sanctions and public approbation. This knowledge acts as a barrier (inhibitor) for many individuals with sexual interest in children (Precondition 1). However, a certain subset of adults with sexual interest are able to acknowledge the barrier(s) and rationalize, justify, minimize, or deny the barrier(s) and move toward acting on their interest (i.e., "I could go to jail. But only if the child tells and I get arrested. If I do—, the child won't tell and no one will find out.") This thought process may take minutes, months, or years. Once the internal inhibitors (Precondition 2) are lessened, the, *external inhibitors,* must be overcome. External inhibitors (Precondition 3) are those barriers outside of the individual, which would be active or passive impediments to acting on their sexual interest. The presence of another adult who would intervene on behalf of the child or would tell others (such as authorities) about the sexual behaviors with a child, is a frequent external inhibitor. The final precondition is the *resistance of the child.* The resistance of the child (Precondition 4) is both the most unpredictable, yet potentially effective factor. The adult has the sexual interest, has successfully mentally minimized the dangers to him or herself or harm to others, and has successfully manipulated the environment so there will be no effective intervention witnesses, but now faces the final barrier of the child's reaction to the adult's overtures/behaviors. Children's responses to all forms of maltreatment vary widely depending on age, developmental level, culture, understanding what is being proposed/happening and the short and long-term consequences of the actions, awareness of their (the child's) options for response, previous experiences when utilizing specific responses, trauma histories (including group historic trauma), and access to supportive adults. Whether the child knows the situation is one in which a decision needs to be made as to act to protect him or herself or not, whether the child is emotionally and physically capable of engaging in any form of 'resistance', and whether the child's protective actions (or inactions) will be effective, are key elements for this factor. This factor is also influenced by how adequately the adult has been able to navigate the first three factors. Skillful predatory adults will consider the possible reactions of the child and plan manipulation of the situation so as to minimize the effectiveness of any self-protection actions the child may take (or consider taking). However, an offender who believes the child will resist or report may not go forward for fear of being reported by the child, leading to negative consequences, including apprehension by law enforcement.

It is here, in the resistance of the child, that many early child sexual abuse 'prevention' efforts focus, educating children about what to do if someone has approached them with possible sexual intent or has actually abused them. For children who have not been victimized, these programs raise awareness of the issue of child sexual abuse and are primarily designed to teach children to tell if they suspect an adult of attempting to molest them. Other programs include self-protection strategies. While these programs may be categorized as "prevention", they are more accurately categorized as "target-hardening", i.e., making targets (in this case, children) more resistant to attack or difficult to maneuver into vulnerable positions. For children who have experienced victimization, these programs are perhaps better identified as a form of tertiary 'prevention', with the goal of reducing the likelihood of additional or subsequent abuse through teaching the child to "run, yell, tell" or keep away from situations where they may be victimized (risk reduction).

There are challenges to placing the burden of safety on the shoulders of the existing and potential victims of abuse or exploitation, however. Making some children who have been exposed to such programs aware that there are individuals who may seek to harm them, and aware of some of the stratagems employed by perpetrators, may be perceived by children who have already experienced victimization as holding them responsible for their abuse—if they had just said no, run away, told someone, locked the door, etc., they could have been safe. These programs do nothing to actually *prevent* an individual from developing a sexual interest in children (precondition one), little to interrupt the rationalizations used by offenders to override their internal inhibitions (pre-condition two), but may have some impact in helping children identify risky situations or environments (pre-condition three). However, an offender who believes the child will resist or report may not go forward in an attempt to molest the child for fear of public or private identification and related sanctions or consequences.

This simple paradigm is dynamic, as all four factors are fluid. For example, sexual interest (motivation) may be increased by perpetrator exposure to erotic materials; internal inhibitors increasing or diminishing based on consumption of alcohol or disinhibiting substances, or as the result of mental conditions, such as depression. The presence of external inhibitors in specific environments can vary and is subject to manipulation by the perpetrator, **but increasing the probability of the presence**

of protective adults, willing and capable of intervention, can be the focus of child abuse risk reduction strategies which can be employed by professionals working with the child and family. For example, the Child Protection Agency Safety Plan includes specific language forbidding an individual believed to be a danger to the child from having unsupervised contact with the child. Further, CPS workers, teaming with the child's family and other supportive adults, can work to develop a "safety network" of individuals who agree to watch over the child and problematic adult to maintain the safeguards designed to keep the identified external inhibitors effective (e. g., Signs of Safety). This "safety network" can also provide vital reinforcement for the resistance of the child (pre-condition 4) by overtly letting the child know who and how they can go to if they have concerns or fears.

Review of the Evidence Base on Prevention

When one thinks of child abuse and neglect prevention it is in the primary and secondary prevention arena that most efforts have focused. For decades these efforts were guided by good intentions and theoretical logic but today we have a growing body of empirical research to shed light on which efforts appears to have measurable effects. These evidence based approaches hold the promise for reducing the risk of abuse or neglect and/or addressing the related facilitating factors that are logically linked to abuse and neglect. The challenge is this literature is spread across a wide array of disciplines, and few practicing professionals have the time and resources needed to remain current on the range of possibilities. Fortunately several evidence "clearinghouses" have emerged that organize the research and classify models according to the strength of their evidence. Among these resources are the California Evidence Based Clearinghouse of Child Welfare (www.cebc4cw.org), SAMHSA's Registry of Effective Programs (www.nrepp.samhsa.gov), Blueprints for Healthy Youth Development (www.blueprintsprograms.com) and the Department of Education's What Works Clearinghouse (www2.ed.gov). The California Clearinghouse is the only one specifically designed to support child welfare decision making around child maltreatment.

The California Evidence Based Clearinghouse (CEBC) of Child Welfare identifies six "topical areas" for prevention and early intervention that generally fit the broad definition of primary and secondary prevention of child maltreatment. These include the areas Primary Prevention, Secondary Prevention, Home Visiting for Prevention of Child Abuse and Neglect, Home Visiting for Child Wellbeing, Interventions for Physical Abuse, and Interventions for Neglect. The CEBC has reviewed scores of programs purporting to address these issues and rated them on a scientific scale from "1-Well Supported" (meaning multiple randomized clinical trials and measurable sustained effect) to "5-Concerning Practices" that appear empirically to have a negative effect on the target behavior (note: no prevention related intervention has been rated a 5). The good news is that there are programs that are showing strong effects in one form of prevention or another and others that are promising in each category (see Table 1). None of these models address all forms of maltreatment but each targets a specific area and appears to reduce the risk of maltreatment.

The Clearinghouse also notes that there are some programs being marketed in each area that lack any peer reviewed published research in support of their model. That does not mean they do not work, but only that the developers have not empirically tested the efficacy of the model, or at least have not published their research in the peer reviewed literature. It is also important to note some programs are robust enough to appear in different topical areas and are represented as duplicated numbers in the table below. It is also important to note that some widely implemented programs, such as Healthy Families America, show effects in one area, home visiting *for child wellbeing*, but have not been able to show effects in another topical area, home visiting *for prevention of child abuse* and neglect.

As noted in Table 1 there are a substantial number of evidence based models relevant to prevention that communities can choose from. Given the complexity of the problem, community-wide prevention programs hold some appeal, but measuring community wide prevention efforts over time has proven difficult due to the number of interventions and providers involved and the number of variables that can influence community progress (Daro, 2005). The best example where these variables have been controlled is Triple P, a CEBC rated 2-Supported, multi-tiered system of five levels from media campaign to targeted family interventions in a variety of settings from the home to schools.

Most programs rated on the CEBC are more targeted at specific issues and service delivery strategies. Many of the highest rated of these prevention related programs have some features in common. Most of these programs draw on an integrated theoretical approach to positive parenting and share similar goals revolving around

Table 1 Assigned CEBC Scientific Rating

Topical area	Number of programs rated 1— well supported	Number of programs rated 2—supported	Number of programs rated 3—promising	Number of programs rated 4—fails to demonstrate effect	Number of programs unable to rate
Primary prevention	2	1	8		3
Secondary prevention	1	2	6		5
Home visiting child abuse & neglect	1	1	2	1	
Home visiting well-being	2	2	7		1
Interventions for neglect		3	1		2
Interventions for abuse	1	2	4		4

improved parent-child interactions, building positive, nurturing attachment, reducing harsh/coercive parenting and increasing positive parental efficacy, mixed with building external parental social supports. Those targeting neglect, such as SafeCare®, may also have components focused on improved understanding and capacity in management of the child's health care or physical environment. All evidence based prevention models are structured and task focused. Many, but not all, of the empirically strongest programs are delivered in the family's natural environment, such as the home, rather than a classroom. These include Nurse-Parent Partnerships, SafeCare®, Healthy Families, and Home Instruction for Parents of Preschool Youngsters (HIPPY) and they all resemble a structured coaching model more than traditional classroom education. Not all evidence based prevention is home based, however, as The Incredible Years achieved the highest rating in Secondary Prevention using a 14–22 session classroom model (Reid, Webster-Stratton, & Hammond, 2003; Webster-Stratton, Reid, & Hammond, 2004).Other topical areas of the Clearinghouse can inform decisions about reducing risk of child maltreatment including parent training where there are a strong set of empirically tested programs including five rated at the highest level, 1-Well Supported, and four at the 2-Supported level of evidence. Some of these parent training programs overlap with the "prevention" topical area (i.e., SafeCare®) already noted above, but parent training adds additional models that, when targeted, correctly have demonstrated reduction in risk of maltreatment, such as Child Parent Interaction Therapy (PCIT). PCIT brings the highly structured caregiver coaching approach to the clinical setting (Eyberg et al., 2001) where the parent can practice new skills in a structured environment live while the therapist typically coaches the parent through a one way mirror and a 'bug in the ear' communication system. Researchers have also demonstrated the power of marrying evidence based interventions like PCIT and the primary prevention model, SEEK, with the evidence based engagement model, Motivational Interviewing (Chaffin, Funderburk, Bard, Valle, & Gurwitch, 2011; Dubowitz, Lane, Semiatin, & Magder, 2012).

Another trend in prevention is to bring a short term intervention into the health care setting where parents are seeking prenatal, obstetrics, or pediatric care. Several leading physicians have developed primary prevention models to reduce the risk of inflicted infant injury, particularly around abusive head trauma. Some of these short term educational models, such as Period of Purple Crying (Barr, 2012) and the Upstate New York Shaken Baby Syndrome Education Program (Dias, Smith, Mazur, Li, & Shaffer, 2005), have shown promise in empirical studies and rated a 3 on the CEBC. Dr. Howard Dubowitz developed Safe Environment for Every Kid (SEEK) model that instructs physicians caring for children 0–5, in a primary pediatric care setting to identify issues within the family which impact the safety of the child and then connects the parents with community resources. (Dubowitz, Feigelman, Lane, & Kim, 2009). SEEK has shown significant reductions in child maltreatment reports and has earned it a "1-Well Supported" rating on the CEBC. As the body of evidence grows, some observers have begun to look across evidence based practices and identify the "common elements" (Chorpita, Daleiden, & Weisz, 2005) or "common components", (Barth, 2012) that are seen in multiple named brand evidence based practices. Advocates for the "common elements" argue that certain components appear repeatedly in different empirically supported manualized treatments and interventions and that the best course may be to spread those common elements or components among the professional provider base. This was first explored with mental health treatments focused on youth depression, anxiety, and disruptive behavior (Chorpita et al., 2002). Closer to the topic of prevention, Barth and Liggett-Creel examined seven highly regarded parent training models and found that they had a number of components in common, from the incorporation of social learning theory elements such as role play, feedback, and in vivo or video recorded coaching, to the use of homework (in 85 %), and the power of positive peer group influence (in 71 %). While their conclusions have not been universally accepted, the authors suggest that the use of the common components of evidence based parenting interventions, especially for children ages 4–8, is likely to achieve benefits even without use of a name brand evidence based parenting intervention (Barth & Liggett-Creel, 2014).

One area of prevention that has not been as well researched are efforts that seek to decrease the risk of child sexual abuse. These efforts tend to fall into four categories addressing the different preconditions, as Finkelhor characterized them in his 4 Preconditions Model described earlier, and are focused on different audiences. Traditionally, a great deal of early effort focused on educating children about what sexual abuse is and using a variation of the touch continuum ("good touch-bad touch-confusing touch") developed by Cordelia Anderson (Kenny & Wurtele, 2012) to instruct children what to do if they perceive someone was engaging in abusive or threatening behavior. This type of program is designed for children and is focused on enhancing the possibility that a child exposed to the information will be better able to recognize and avoid potentially dangerous situations or effectively resist and/or report attempts by adults to sexually assault them (Precondition 4-Resistence of the Child). Early examples of this thinking produced programs such as Talking About Touching (Madak & Berg, 1992) and Stop Child Abuse and Neglect (SCAN) at the National Children's Advocacy Center (NCAC, 2015), a school-based program designed to provide child abuse prevention and safety information to school children. By the 1990s some form of school- based child sexual abuse education was common across the nation (Kenny & Wurtele, 2012). Some of these models have now been studied and while none have achieved the highest rating on the CEBC, four now have enough published research to be classified as a 3-Promising on the Clearinghouse including "Who Do You Tell?"™ (Tutty, 1997), Body Safety Training Workbook (BST) (Wurtele, Kast, Miller-Perrin, & Kondrick, 1989), The Safe Child Program (Fryer, Kraizer, & Mlyoshi, 1987), and Darkness to Light's Stewards of Children (Paranal, Washington Thomas, & Derrick, 2012).

More recently others have approached child sexual abuse prevention more broadly seeking to increase internal and external inhibitors and enhance the willingness of bystanders to act as external inhibitors through broad awareness such as Stop It Now! (www.stopitnow.org). Peer reviewed published evidence is not yet available to classify these efforts. Even more broadly, many who seek to prevent child sexual abuse focus on wider societal changes from greater public awareness, to redefining children and youth involved in sexual trafficking as "victims" rather than delinquents, to increasing the willingness of all persons to act as external inhibitors to sexual abuse (National Coalition to Prevent Child Sexual Abuse and Exploitation, 2012). Youth serving organizations have also sought to reduce the risk of abuse within their systems through organizational policy initiatives and enhancing internal and external inhibitors and increasing the resistance of the children they serve (CDCP, 2007; Darkness to Light, 2015). These efforts include improved screening of staff and volunteers, guidelines for staff/child interactions, interaction monitoring (Precondition 3-External Inhibitors), environmental strategies (Precondition 3-External Inhibitors), organizational response to questionable behavior, and child education (Precondition 4-Increasing Resistance of the child) and staff training (National Children's Advocacy Center, 2014). At least one major children's hospital has taken this notion of strengthening the external inhibitor role to very formal levels by training every single employee to be alert for potential sexual abuse and concerning high risk behavior, even by coworkers, within a large 400 plus bed children's hospital. (Sadler, 2011).

Whether through the effectiveness of these type efforts or a combination of sexual abuse prevention and wider societal changes, authorities have noted a consistent decrease in the number of reports of child sexual abuse since the1990s. The trend was scrupulously analyzed by David Finkelhor and colleagues at the University of New Hampshire National Crimes Against Children Research Center. Finkelhor and colleagues tested a number of theories for the drop in reports from a reduction in the intensity of media attention, to actual declines in the prevalence of abuse, to changes in CPS reporting procedures or legal definitions. In the end, they concluded that there appeared to be an actual reduction in sexual abuse of children over a 20 year period (Finkelhor & Jones, 2006). Something was working to reduce the likelihood of children being sexually abused. Now the challenge is to continue and accelerate the trend and achieve similar or greater reductions in others forms of abuse and neglect.

Cultural Influences

When discussing reducing the prevalence of child maltreatment, there are a number of complicating factors which cross different types of abuse and neglect. One of the most challenging in contemporary society is that of 'culture'. We do not live in a monocultural society. People may identify with more than one culture or subculture, and thus may receive conflicting or competing messages concerning acceptable or appropriate parenting techniques or child rearing norms. Considering that the term "culture" can be both broadly (culture of poverty, military culture, Muslim, Jewish, or Christian culture, Western or Southern culture, Native American culture, etc.) and narrowly defined (African-American families residing in Southern California, first generation female refugees from Darfur, etc.) adds to the difficulty of conceptualizing effective risk reduction efforts. Within this framework, addressing cultural attitudes and behaviors which run counter to our (Westernized professional) concept of child well-being is complex. "Attitudes about the role of children, their discipline, the authority of parents, and the utility of violence—these may be among the most important elements of creating safe environments for children. But the methods for promoting nurturing values—and promoting them in different cultural environments—have not been formally conceptualized." (Finkelhor & Lannen, 2014). Even defining what is or is not culture is ever evolving. "The many meanings of culture in terms of their social constructions, adaptiveness, intergenerational transmission, and variations across time, generations, and sociopolitical contexts reflect the illusiveness of the boundedness of culture." (Ortega & Faller, 2011). The issue of specific groups within a culture defining certain practices or beliefs as an intrinsic part of that culture is also relevant, as they may or may not be an accurate interpretation of actual perspectives (Narayan, 1997).

The desire to be respectful of cultural differences in parenting values and behaviors can, and seemingly does, impede establishing and promoting universal methods of protection and safety for children, particularly if child safety and well-being is considered from an adult-centric point of view. Is there a cultural presumption that children have the right to be safe from abuse and neglect as distinct from unlimited parental and family authority to exercise prerogatives 'necessary' to support "cultural" values? (Finkelhor & Lannen, 2014) Recognizing the wide range of child rearing practices seen in the United States, based on differing histories, values and norms, leaves simple risk reduction messages and programs open to misinterpretation, misapplication, or misperception as microinsults/microaggressions. Not to be underestimated is the recognition that there are cultural variations in expressing affection with their children as well as acceptable ways of administering discipline (and what child behaviors are seen as positive—and by which gender). As noted by Nadan, Spilsbury, and Korbin (2015), "culture expresses itself in numerous ecological contexts, from the interactions of child and parent to macro-level societal factors." When one expands the consideration of culture using an intersectionality perspective, understanding how multiple identities such as gender, race and socioeconomic status, age, mental health, disability, sexual orientation, religion, and geographic location (Nadan et al., 2015) effect values, beliefs and behaviors towards children and parenting, the challenge of effective primary, secondary, and/or tertiary intervention becomes more problematic.

The intersectional perspective approach towards risk reduction or target hardening efforts and initiatives requires involving individuals who have a variety of cultural perspectives and can speak not only to traditional cultural norms, but also existing common variations of those norms. An important role for individuals acting as cultural brokers, aside from informing developing prevention efforts, is to use their cultural 'lens' to assess the variety of (realistic) interpretations that members within that culture might read into the messages (Sue, 2010). Involving individuals from differing cultures in discussions of existing protective institutions and practices, risk reduction and target hardening strategies or activities within their culture which have been effective before imposing the adoption of 'new' programs should be critically evaluated. This proactive scrutiny can help reduce the possibility of hidden messages of prejudice, stereotypes and biases thus enhancing program reception and the probability of meeting anticipated outcomes.

Future Directions

The future of prevention efforts is embedded in a complex web of interacting policy and practices playing out at national and state political levels far removed from focused discussions about prevention of child maltreatment. Decisions about the future of health care, family leave policies to care for ill children or maternity/paternity leave, access to child care and early childhood education, and social service spending policies will have immense impact on the community and family environments in which children are raised and upon which they depend.

While adequately addressing these core social issues will not prevent child maltreatment across the board, removing these social supports will surely increase the pressures on families in ways that facilitate maltreatment.

On a more focused level, there is much work left to be done in spreading and taking to scale what we already know works, those highest rated evidence based interventions designed to reduce the risk of abuse and neglect. We can also expect some current promising practices to be elevated to higher levels of evidence once they have been properly studied and released through the peer review literature, adding to the menu of quality programs for communities to choose from. But more evidence based practices are of little value if they are not available for those who need them. In that arena we are learning more about how to spread and effectively implement evidence based practices with the advent of "Implementation Science." There are a growing number of research-based approaches to implementation (Walsh, Rolls, & Williams, 2015) and new web based resources to support community efforts to effectively introduce new evidence based practices (i.e., National Implementation Research Network (www.nim.fpg.unc.edu) and the implementation web resources of the California Clearinghouse (www.cebc4cw.org)). This emerging field of science helps communities to select the right model to address the core issues they face in preventing maltreatment and then guides them through the steps of implementation to sustainment.

Another trend we will likely see more of is the clustering of a suite of evidence based models together designed to reduce the risk of maltreatment by giving families multiple options, intensity levels, and entry points for services. This has already been done successfully in the treatment of depression, anxiety, and conduct problems in youth (Chorpita et al., 2013). Likewise, the evidence based engagement strategy of Motivational Interviewing has already been paired with prevention and early intervention models. Other combinations of evidence based models are likely to follow producing a "cocktail approach" and combining common elements in new ways.

Another direction that may emerge is the use of so called "Big Data" to produce predictive modeling (Wilson, Tumen, Ota, & Simmons, 2015) in ways that refine the targeting of secondary prevention efforts. This has already been introduced in New Zealand (Vaithianathan et al., 2012) and is gaining traction in Los Angeles, Tampa, Florida, and Pittsburgh, Pennsylvania (Slattery, 2015). In California, Emily Putnam-Hornstein, at the University of Southern California, School of Social Work has analyzed cross system data on two million children born in California between 1999 and 2002 to identify characteristics of children who later are the subject of a substantiated child abuse and neglect complaint. She has identified six high risk birth factors (late prenatal care, three or more children in the family, mothers 24 or younger, mother with no more than a high school education, low income and Medicaid eligible, and no father listed on the birth certificate) that predict higher risk of subsequent substantiated maltreatment report (Putnam-Hornstein & Needell, 2011). This type of use of large data analysis and similar efforts at Chapin Hall at University of Chicago (FCDAchapinhall.org) can be used in the future to better determine who should be offered secondary prevention services so the most at risk are served and where the investment is more likely to pay dividends in maltreatment reduction.

Perhaps Predictive Analytics and "Big Data" can be effectively integrated with an ever more sophisticated use of Positive Social Deviance concepts (Pascale, Sternin, & Sternin, 2010) in the child maltreatment field to produce a refined understanding of protective factors. With this wisdom in hand we may be able to use complex social systems to spread effective parenting in ways that are uniquely suited for needs of individual communities.

In the years to come we may also learn much more about the role genetics plays as the science of Epigenetics turns its attention to trauma and toxic stress (Mehta et al., 2013), but for now prevention efforts tend to focus on underlying environmental conditions and facilitating factors that are commonly seen in maltreatment and building the protective capacity of children, families, and communities. Today one in five children live in poverty and almost one in two live in families considered low income (National Center for Children in Poverty, 2015). Until we address the underlying stresses of poverty on families it is hard to imagine we can see dramatic reduction in child neglect and even physical abuse. In the long run, progress in child maltreatment prevention will be linked not only to advances in prevention science and development of evidence based services arrays but also to progress in social equality, financial security, management of substance abuse, improved housing, and broad reductions in the use of violence in the home and society.

References

Azar, S. T. (2002). Parenting and child maltreatment. In M. H. Bornstein (Ed.), *Handbook of parenting volume four: Social conditions and applied parenting* (pp. 361–388). Mahwah, NJ: Lawrence Erlbaum.

Bandura, A. (1989). Human agency in social cognitive theory. *American Psychologist, 44*(9), 1175–1184.

Barr, R. G. (2012). Preventing abusive head trauma resulting from a failure of normal interaction between infants and their caregivers. *Proceedings of the National Academy of Sciences, 109*(2), 17294–17301.

Barr, R. G., Rivara, F. P., Barr, M., Cummings, P., Taylor, J., Lengua, L. J., & Meredith-Benitz, E. (2009). Effectiveness of educational materials designed to change knowledge and behaviors regarding crying and shaken-baby syndrome in mothers of newborns: A randomized, controlled trial. *Pediatrics, 123*(3), 972–980.

Barth, R. P., Lee, B. R., Lindsey, M. A., Collins, K. S., Strieder, F., Chorpita, B.F., Becker, K & Sparks, J. A. (2011). Evidence-based practice at a crossroads: The emergence of common elements and factors. Research on Social Work Practice, 1049731511408440.

Barth, R. P., & Liggett-Creel, K. (2014). Common components of parenting programs for children birth to eight years of age involved with child welfare services. *Children and Youth Services Review, 40*, 6–12.

Bethea, L. (1999). Primary prevention of child abuse. *American Family Physician, 59*(6), 1577–1585.

Centers for Disease Control and Prevention (2007). *Preventing child sexual abuse within youth-serving organizations*. Atlanta, GA: USHHS, Centers for Disease Control and Prevention.

Chaffin, M., Funderburk, B., Bard, D., Valle, L. A., & Gurwitch, R. (2011). A combined motivation and parent–child interaction therapy package reduces child welfare recidivism in a randomized dismantling field trial. *Journal of Consulting and Clinical Psychology, 79*(1), 84.

Child Welfare Gateway. (2015). Retrieved from https://childwelfare.gov/topics/can/factors/?hasBeenRedirected=1.

Chorpita, B. F., Daleiden, E. L., & Weisz, J. R. (2005). Identifying and selecting the common elements of evidence based interventions: A distillation and matching model. *Mental Health Services Research, 7*(1), 5–20.

Chorpita, B. F., Weisz, J. R., Daleiden, E. L., Schoenwald, S. K., Palinkas, L. A., Miranda, J., … Gibbons, R. D. (2013). Long-term outcomes for the Child STEPs randomized effectiveness trial: A comparison of modular and standard treatment designs with usual care. *Journal of Consulting and Clinical Psychology, 81*(6), 999.

Chorpita, B. F., Yim, L. M., Donkervoet, J. C., Arensdorf, A., Amundsen, M. J., McGee, C., & Morelli, P. (2002). Toward large-scale implementation of empirically supported treatments for children: A review and observations by the Hawaii empirical basis to services task force. *Clinical Psychology: Science and Practice, 9*(2), 165–190.

Darkness to Light. (2015). Retrieved from www.d2l.org/site/c.4dICIJOkGcISE/b.6069257/k.CBE3/Preventing_Child_Sexual_Abuse_is_an_Adult_Responsibility.htm.

Daro, D. (2005). *Creating community responsibility for child protection: Findings and implications from the evaluation of the Community Partnerships for Protecting Children Initiative*. Chapin Hall Center for Children.

Daro, D., & Cohn-Donnelly, A. (2002). Child abuse prevention. In *APSAC handbook on child maltreatment* (pp. 431–448). Newbury Park, CA: Sage.

Dias, M. S., Smith, K., Mazur, P., Li, V., & Shaffer, M. L. (2005). Preventing abusive head trauma among infants and young children: A hospital-based, parent education program. *Pediatrics, 115*(4), e470–e477.

Dubowitz, H., Feigelman, S., Lane, W., & Kim, J. (2009). Pediatric primary care to help prevent child maltreatment: The Safe Environment for Every Kid (SEEK) model. *Pediatrics, 123*(3), 858–864.

Dubowitz, H., Lane, W. G., Semiatin, J. N., & Magder, L. S. (2012). The SEEK model of pediatric primary care: Can child maltreatment be prevented in a low-risk population? *Academic Pediatrics, 12*(4), 259–268.

Erickson, M. F., & Egeland, B. (2002). Child neglect. *The APSAC Handbook on Child Maltreatment, 2*, 3–20.

Eyberg, S. M., Funderburk, B. W., Hembree-Kigin, T., McNeil, C. B., Querido, J., & Hood, K. K. (2001). Parent-child interaction therapy with behavior problem children: One- and two-year maintenance of treatment effects in the family. *Child & Family Behavior Therapy, 23*, 1–20.

Felitti, V. J. (2002). The relation between adverse childhood experiences and adult health: Turning gold into lead. *Permanente Journal, 6*(1), 44–47.

Finkelhor, D. (1984). *Child sexual abuse: New theory and research*. New York: Free Press.

Finkelhor, D., & Jones, L. (2006). Why have child maltreatment and child victimization declined? *Journal of Social Issues, 62*(4), 685–716.

Finkelhor, D., & Lannen, P. (2014). Dilemmas for international mobilization around child abuse and neglect. *Child Abuse & Neglect.*

Fryer, G. E., Kraizer, S. K., & Mlyoshi, T. (1987). Measuring actual reduction of risk to child abuse: A new approach. *Child Abuse & Neglect, 11*(2), 173–179.

Hess, C. R., Teti, D. M., & Hussey-Gardner, B. (2004). Self-efficacy and parenting of high-risk infants: The moderating role of parent knowledge of infant development. *Journal of Applied Developmental Psychology, 25*(4), 423–437.

Kelly, S. (2002). Child maltreatment in the context of substance abuse. *The APSAC handbook on child maltreatment*. Sage.

Kenny, M. C., & Wurtele, S. K. (2012). Preventing childhood sexual abuse: An ecological approach. *Journal of Child Sexual Abuse, 21*(4), 361–367.

Madak, P. R., & Berg, D. H. (1992). The prevention of sexual abuse: An evaluation of talking about touching. *Canadian Journal of Counseling, 26*(1), 29–40.

McRury, J. M., & Zolotor, A. J. (2010). A randomized, controlled trial of a behavioral intervention to reduce crying among infants. *Journal of the American Board of Family Medicine, 23*(3), 315–322.

Mehta, D., Klengel, T., Conneely, K. N., Smith, A. K., Altmann, A., Pace, T. W., … Binder, E. B. (2013). Childhood maltreatment is associated with distinct genomic and epigenetic profiles in post-traumatic stress disorder. *Proceedings for the National Academy of Sciences, 110*(20):8302–8307.

Nadan, Y., Spilsbury, J. C., & Korbin, J. E. (2015). Culture and context in understanding child maltreatment: Contributions of intersectionality and neighborhood-based research. *Child Abuse & Neglect, 41*, 40–48.

Narayan, U. (1997). *Dislocating cultures: Identities, traditions, and third world feminism*. New York: Routledge Press.

National Center for Children in Poverty. (2015). Retrieved from http://nccp.org/publications/pub_1097.html.

National Children's Advocacy Center. (2014). Retrieved from www.nationalcac.org/online-training/web-deborah-callins-04-23-2014.html.

National Children's Advocacy Center. (2015). Retrieved from www.nationalcac.org/prevention/scan.html.

National Coalition to Prevent Child Sexual Abuse and Exploitation. (2012). *The National Plan to Prevent the Sexual Abuse and Exploitation of Children*. Retrieved October 6, 2015 from http://preventtogether.org/.

Ortega, R. M., & Faller, K. C. (2011). Training child welfare workers from an intersectional cultural humility perspective: A paradigm shift. *Child Welfare, 90*(5), 223–228.

Paranal, R., Washington Thomas, K., & Derrick, C. (2012). Utilizing online training for child sexual abuse prevention: Benefits and limitations. *Journal of Child Sexual Abuse, 21*(5), 507–520.

Pascale, R., Sternin, J., & Sternin, M. (2010). *The power of positive deviance*. Boston: Harvard Business School Publishing.

Pence, D. M., & Wilson, C. (1992). *The role of law enforcement in the response to child abuse and neglect*. U.S. Department of Health and Human Services Administration for Children and Families Administration on Children, Youth and Families National Center on Child Abuse and Neglect.

Pence, D. M., & Wilson, C. (1994). *Team investigation of child sexual abuse: The uneasy alliance*. Thousand Oaks, CA: Sage.

Putnam-Hornstein, E., & Needell, B. (2011). Predictors of child protective service contact between birth and age five: An examination of California's 2002 birth cohort. *Children and Youth Services Review, 33*(8), 1337–1344.

Rafael, T., & Pion-Berlin, L. (2000). Parents anonymous®: Strengthening families. In H. Henderson (Ed.), *Domestic violence and child abuse sourcebook* (pp. 372–397). Health reference series, 1st edition. Detroit, MI: Omnigraphics.

Reid, M. J., Webster-Stratton, C., & Hammond, M. (2003). Follow-up of children who received the incredible years intervention for oppositional-defiant disorder: Maintenance and prediction of 2-year outcome. *Behavior Therapy, 34*(4), 471–491.

Sadler, B. (2011). How a Children's Hospital Discovered child pornographers in its midst. *Health Affairs, 30*, 91795–91798.

Slattery, H. (2015). Big data wave breaks on child protective services. *The Chronicle of Social Change, 1*, 2015.

Sue, D. W. (2010). *Microaggressions in everyday life: Race, gender, and sexual orientation.* Hoboken, NJ: Wiley.

Tutty, L. M. (1997). Child sexual abuse prevention programs: Evaluating who do you tell. *Child Abuse & Neglect, 21*(9), 869–881.

USHHS/ACYF/Children's Bureau. (2015). *Child Maltreatment 2013*. Retrieved from www.acf. hhs.gov/programs/cb/resource/child-maltreatment-2013.

Vaithianathan, R., Maloney, T., Jiang, N., De Haan, I., Dale, C., Putnam-Hornstein, E., … Thompson, D. (2012). Vulnerable children: Can administrative data be used to identify children at risk of adverse outcomes. *Report Prepared for the Ministry of Social Development. Auckland: Centre for Applied Research in Economics (CARE), Department of Economics, University of Auckland.*

Walsh, C., Rolls, R. J., & Williams, R. (2015). *Selecting and implementing evidence-based practices: A guide for child and family serving systems* (2nd ed.). San Diego, CA: California Evidence-Based Clearinghouse for Child Welfare.

Wang, C. T., & Harding, K. (1999). *Current trends in child abuse reporting and fatalities: The results of the 1998 annual fifty state survey.* Chicago: National Committee to Prevent Child Abuse.

Webster-Stratton, C., Reid, M. J., & Hammond, M. (2004). Treating children with early-onset conduct problems: Intervention outcomes for parent, child, and teacher training. *Journal of Clinical Child and Adolescent Psychology, 33*(1), 105–124.

Wilson, M., Tumen, S., Ota, R., & Simmons, A. (2015). Predictive modeling: Potential application in prevention sciences. *American Journal of Preventive Medicine, 48*(5), 509–519.

Wurtele, S. K., Kast, L. C., Miller-Perrin, C. L., & Kondrick, P. A. (1989). Comparison of programs for teaching personal safety skills to preschoolers. *Journal of Consulting and Clinical Psychology, 57*(4), 505.

Meeting at the Midway: Systems, Partnerships and Collaborative Inquiry to Generate Practice Based Evidence

Sharon M. Wasco

The chapters in this edition start from a premise that we can do better for our children. We acknowledge both the problem of child maltreatment and the possible solutions. We know that adverse childhood events, including acts of maltreatment and abuse, are significantly correlated with many unhealthy behaviors and leading causes of death in the U.S. (Edwards, Anda, Felitti, & Dube, 2003; Felitti et al., 1998) including heart disease (Dong et al., 2004), cancer (Brown et al., 2010), chronic obstructive pulmonary disease (COPD) (Anda et al., 2008), and suicide (Dube et al., 2001). We also come from a place of having observed success in efforts to help children and families (Cohen & Mannarino, this volume; Kellogg, this volume; Wilsie, Campbell, Chaffin, & Funderburk, this volume) that have suffered from harm done by child maltreatment. More germane to this chapter, perhaps, is that the field has moved enough of resources "upstream" from the point of outcry to develop preventive interventions that show some promise that we can stop child maltreatment before it occurs (Guastaferro & Lutzger, this volume; Wilson & Pence, this volume). Today there exist a number of preventive interventions for a variety of child maltreatment issues. In addition, although I have no published study to cite, there seems to be a growing belief that child maltreatment is not inevitable and an emerging sense of collective efficacy that we can, in fact, make things better for children.

Evidence has been, and will always remain, central to child maltreatment prevention efforts. Each of the four steps in a public health model of prevention—(1) defining and monitoring the problem, (2) identifying risk and protective factors, (3) developing and testing prevention strategies, and (4) assuring widespread adoption—relies on systematically-collected evidence. As child maltreatment prevention work progresses, an expanded scope of what is considered

S.M. Wasco, Ph.D. (✉)
142 North Hayden Parkway, Hudson, OH 44236, USA
e-mail: Sharon.Wasco@gmail.com

© Springer International Publishing Switzerland 2017   183
D.M. Teti (ed.), *Parenting and Family Processes in Child Maltreatment
and Intervention*, Child Maltreatment Solutions Network,
DOI 10.1007/978-3-319-40920-7_11

evidence has become a strong driving force toward the end goal of the model: widespread prevention adoption. A trending concept in these discussions — especially among community-based prevention program coordinators and evaluators — is *practice-based evidence*.

What is Practice Based Evidence?

Practice based evidence, or PBE, is part of a movement towards "real world" data collection that puts actionable results directly into the hands of the end-user. Decades into the Information Age, the lexicon related to data and evidence continues to expand as we describe, with increasing nuance, information-related activities that fill our daily lives. Almost every profession has made significant strides to incorporate data use into their organizational practices: big data, cellular data, data utilization, data dashboards. In community-based programming to address child maltreatment and respond to violence — and elsewhere — there is value placed on evidence-driven decision-making; and time is spent parsing the difference between evidence-based and evidence-informed prevention strategies. Technology has opened new avenues for collecting and analyzing data, and prevention program staff and evaluators allocate larger amounts of resources to explicate goals, objectives, inputs, outputs, outcomes, impacts, indicators — all in the interest of measuring differences and monitoring change.

Differences in language are not just semantical. New typologies and uses of evidence are made necessary by tougher problems, deeper understandings, evolving values, shifting conceptualizations — and, of course, doing increasingly better work. In 2011 the United States Centers for Disease Control and Prevention (CDC) began disseminating a framework for thinking about evidence in the context of prevention work (Puddy & Wilkins, 2011). The three types of evidence are *best available research evidence, contextual evidence,* and *experiential evidence.* Best available research evidence is used to determine the extent to which, and the ways in which, any given strategy achieves desired outcomes. The strength of the evidence is based on the rigor of the research design. Contextual evidence refers to information about strategy "fit" with local context and is used to assess the likelihood that a particular community will find an intervention strategy feasible, useful, and acceptable (Victora, Habicht & Bryce, 2004). Experiential evidence, sometimes considered intuitive or tacit knowledge (Orleans, Gruman & Anderson, 1999), accumulates over time and represents the collective experience and expertise of those who have practiced or lived in a particular setting. The Venn diagram shown in Fig. 1 suggests that best practice occurs at the point of overlap at the center of the model, when all three types of evidence are considered concurrently.

One way to think about PBE is that it is knowledge that emerges from systematically documenting the overlapping section of Fig. 1. This can be done by collecting and synthesizing contextual and experiential evidence in the context of implementing real-world programs that have informed by the best available

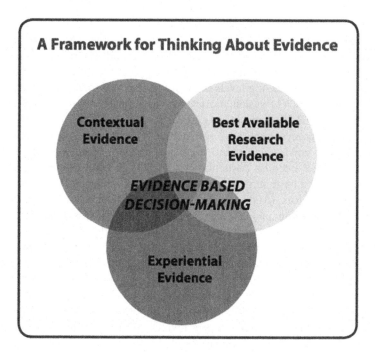

Fig. 1 A framework for thinking about evidence. Reprinted with permission from the Centers for Disease Control

research. Generating PBE may be a particularly worthy activity for professional program evaluators, who build upon data collection and data analysis skills by applying data visualization and data utilization skills to help program staff use empirical results to navigate, adjust, and make data-driven decisions in the communities they serve. In making the case for an increased emphasis on PBE to more effectively and efficiently prevent child maltreatment, I'd like place it as complementary to evidence-based practice (EBP). After drawing the distinctions between the two concepts, I will then offer a set of important considerations in generating PBE and using it to do better prevention work.

Consider the following statement on EBP, approved as policy within the American Psychological Association, in 2005:

> *Evidence-based practice in psychology (EBPP) is the integration of the best available* research *with clinical expertise in the context of patient characteristics, culture, and preferences. (emphasis mine)*

The definition of evidence-based practice in psychology described above was altered from the Institute of Medicine's (2001) influential report, Crossing the Quality Chasm: A New Health System for the Twenty-First Century: "*Evidence-based practice is the integration of best research evidence with clinical expertise and patient values*" (p. 147), which was, in turn, adapted from Sackett, Straus, Richardson, Rosenberg, and Haynes (2000). This definition raises a first question of what is research? What is *best* research?

Within the research world, hierarchies do exist. The CDC guidance document mentioned above (Puddy & Wilkins, 2011), for example, places evidence on a continuum that defines a set of clear and universal standards for what is best available research evidence for the field of violence prevention (p. 4). Generally, researchers place decreasing levels of credibility on the evidence produced by the following activities: (1) systematic reviews and meta-analyses, (2) randomized controlled trials (RCTs) and other experimental research, (3) non-experimental research (e.g., surveys, qualitative research), (4) conference and seminar reports, (5) examples of good practice, and (6) expert opinion. More specifically, a strict definition of EBP includes particular criteria: (1) at least two controlled group design studies or a large series of single-case design studies, (2) a minimum of at least two investigators, (3) the consistent use of a treatment manual, (4) clinicians with uniform training and adherence, and (5) long-term outcomes measured beyond the end of the treatment intervention (Hoagwood, 2003, p. 555). The point being made here is that most formulations of EBP require researcher driven activity—such as randomized controlled trials (RCT)—and clinical experts to answer questions like: *"Is the right person doing the right thing, at the right time, in the right place in the right way, with the right result?"* (Sackett, Rosenberg, Gray, Haynes, & Richardson, 1996). These are important questions for which the research model, heavily reliant on peer review (from IRB approval to acceptance for publication) and the scientific process, is well suited to answer.

These answers are a necessary component in child maltreatment prevention, but they are not enough. Particularly as we move out of the realm of person-/client-/family- based psychological interventions aimed at individual and behavioral outcomes and move towards public health initiatives aimed at changing norms held at the community or societal levels, we need to maximize the "real world" element—sometimes conceived of as external, ecological, psychopolitical (v. internal) validity and/or clinical/practical (v. statistical) significance (Jacobson & Truax, 1991). In an editorial introduction to a volume on PBE, Swisher (2010) offers this contrast to the questions asked in the previous paragraph:

> "In the concept of practice-based evidence, the real, messy, complicated world is not controlled. Instead, real world practice is documented and measured, just as it occurs, "warts" and all. It is the process of measurement and tracking that matters, not controlling how practice is delivered. This allows us to answer a different, but no less important, question than 'does X cause Y?' This question is: 'how does adding X intervention alter the complex personalized system of patient Y before me?' " (p. 4)

There are, indeed, many empirical questions to be asked about the quality of practitioner expertise and the context and characteristics of settings and communities that host prevention programs. Advocates of PBE make a good case that *"evidence supporting the utility, value, or worth of an intervention...can emerge from the practices, experiences, and expertise of family members, youth, consumers, professionals and members of the community"* (Lieberman et al., 2010, p. 2).

None of this is necessarily new; for social scientists who have strived to responsibly understand and mix quantitative and qualitative methods, additional classifications of evidence reignite long-standing discussions within the philosophy of science about the nature of being (i.e., ontology) and the meaning of knowledge (i.e., epistemology). At the core of the movement towards practice-based evidence are philosophical questions about how to do science: What is reality?, and its corollaries What can be known? What is knowledge? How is knowledge produced? Who is qualified to produce evidence? These questions have been tackled by many groups looking to expand the realm of credibility in science, including qualitative (Creswell, 2009; Guba & Lincoln, 1994) and feminist (Campbell & Wasco, 2000) researchers.

Keeping in mind that prevention messaging is often a combination of psychological or public health services, educational programming, and social marketing efforts; PBE can answer practical questions: What is useful about our program? What does success look like? What evidence will demonstrate that this program is working? What constitutes a "win" for the practitioners implementing the strategy? PBE can provide answers to questions about the robustness of prevention programs across different delivery modes, feasibility of prevention implementation in real world settings, and the cost in terms of time, materials, and social capital/interpersonal connection associated with prevention work. Efforts can focus on studying the practices of prevention programs who obtain the best outcomes in the community, identifying technical skills utilized by practitioners when implementing successful programs, studying conditions that maximize prevention practitioners' expertise, determining the extent to which errors and biases compromise fidelity to implementation, and providing prevention practitioners with real-time participant feedback. Similarly, answers to questions about the characteristics of communities can result in PBE that complements best available research. For example, what are the critical features of a setting—sometimes called climate—that moderate prevention program effectiveness? Are interventions found to be effective in clinical trials with one population effective with other populations? How should prevention work be implemented with traumatized communities or communities in crisis? How can one address the gendered or racialized qualities of settings? What are ways to make information about cultural and community difference more accessible to prevention practitioners? How can one maximize prevention practitioners' cognitive, emotional, and role competence with diverse kinds of community settings?

These questions do not need to be answered by researchers and written up as reports for publication in academic journals; rather these questions can be the subject of collaborative inquiry, and the findings that result can be considered practice-based evidence. The activity that generates practice-based evidence may take forms a bit different than typical university-sponsored research. As mentioned above, PBE is sometimes understood to be the "clinical expertise" piece of the IOM definition for EBP, but outside of the medical model, contemporary articulations of PBE include formative or summative program evaluation, reflective practice, clinical audit, and implementation studies.

In fact, EBP and PBE are actually complementary; and prevention evaluators and science practitioners *can be transformative in the melding of the approaches.* Some suggest a "new normal" for evidence *informed* practice (Nevo & Slonim-Nevo, 2011) which integrates best available (external) evidence from systematic research with practice-based evidence generated by documenting real-world implementation conditions and taking into account the community being served: their needs and expectations. What seems most critical at this point in the evolution of prevention is creating feedback loops that allow PBE to flow out from one community that so that it can be used in other communities. This first section of the chapter has classified and codified evidence—making a case for the importance of best available research evidence in guiding prevention strategy decisions as well as PBE for the purpose of improving prevention service delivery—the remaining comments "zoom out" to address big-picture issues regarding the crazy nature of preventing child maltreatment. First, child maltreatment may very well be a "wicked problem" (defined below); second, communities are dynamic, multidimensional places—full of noise, statistical and otherwise.

Wicked Problems and Systems Thinking

Moving forward, it may be helpful to understand child maltreatment as a *wicked problem*. Rittel and Webber (1973) temper our confidence that we can find scientific bases for confronting problems of social policy. In seminal work that has inspired a generation of problem-solving social innovators, they contrast "wicked" problems with the "tame" problems for which "science has developed to deal" (p. 155). Most social or cultural problems are wicked in nature: interconnected, such that one wicked problem is a symptom of another; with more than one explanation; and having no universal template to solve them because, for example, the problem of inequality in my U.S. community is similar yet different from child inequality in India (Kolko, 2012). If child maltreatment is correctly identified as a wicked problem, one corollary is that science and practice alone are not enough to address this harm done to our children. Prevention initiatives may need design and marketing expertise as much as they need science. Additional corollaries are that there are no "stopping rules" and that solutions are not true-or-false, but good-or-bad. Those working on wicked problems use values, not logic, to decide when to terminate work—and usually for context-driven reasons. As Rittel and Webber (1973) noted, someone tackling a wicked problem "finally says, 'That's good enough,' or 'This is the best I can do within the limitations of the project,' or 'I like this solution'" (p. 162). Public will plays a huge role in this type of reasoning.

The prevention programs that will evolve as "solutions" to the wicked problem of child maltreatment will be implemented within communities, which always consist of complex sets of interconnected systems. Thus, systems thinking is necessary. Although science alone is not a *sufficient* approach to wicked problems, it is a *necessary* component of child maltreatment prevention designs. The fields of implementation science and complexity science (Phelen, 2001) are particularly well-positioned to shape twenty-first century change strategies that can increase the sustainable prevention implementation in communities (Foster-Fishman & Watson, 2012; Olson & Eoyang, 2001; Relyea, 2015). A particularly helpful systems model is the Interactive Systems Framework (ISF) for Prevention Innovation and Dissemination (Wandersman, Chien, & Katz, 2012; Wandersman, Duffy, et al., 2008) shown in Fig. 2.

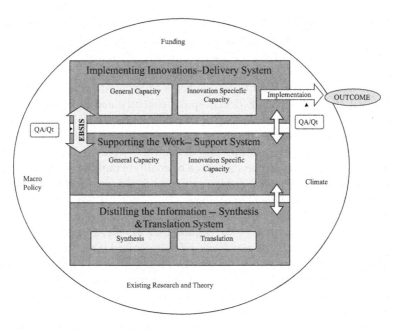

Fig. 2 The interactive systems framework for prevention dissemination and implementation. Reprinted with permission from Abraham Wandersman

As depicted in the ISF, multiple systems are involved in successful prevention efforts and are situated in the context of funding, climate, existing research, and theory. Importantly, the process of implementation—in the upper right of the model—carries prevention work out of the systems designed by prevention-minded professionals. The desired outcomes in this model, for example happy and healthy children, extend outside of the realm of the bounded prevention systems. This notion, that the end result of prevention work is drawn into a location outside of researchers' control, is important. A metaphor can be used to stimulate thinking about how to prevent child maltreatment in the twenty-first century. It starts with a visualization of the area, or gap, between science and practice. How we see "science-practice gaps," and what we do in those spaces, provide unique opportunities for prevention. Metaphorically, EBP can be understood as a bridge, while PBE is more of a county fair midway (Wasco, 2014).

Envision a landscape with two plateaus built up over time upon separate foundations and with slightly different surfaces; and mentally label one of these plateaus "research" and the other "practice." One way to connect the plateaus is to build a bridge from one high point (i.e., research) to the other (i.e., practice). Mentally label this bridge EBP. Bridges, like rocket engines, are fairly straightforward scientific solutions; although they may be complicated, they are not considered complex. Below the bridge, though; and in between the plateaus, there is an open space in the middle. Drawing my inspiration from Bernice Johnson Reagon's (1983) take on coalition building and working across difference, I ask you to envision an entire county fair midway—complete with concessions, games of chance, and carnival rides—in the space below the bridge. This county fair midway is one way to think about PBE. The people in the shared space of the midway are not only stakeholders from the two plateaus of practice and research, but are also leaders from the policy realm, and sponsors, and donors, and consumers. Coalition building—not just engineering—is needed to organize the midway.

While addressing the West Coast Women's Music Festival in 1981, longtime activist and musician Reagon (1983) spoke cogently and movingly about the challenges of coalition work. Among other points, she drew an important distinction between the safe, home-like space that those challenging the status quo may need to bolster themselves and to help define their work, and the challenging, stretching, and often uncomfortable space of coalition building. Her remarks are just as relevant for advocates in this century as they were for those in the last, *"Coalition work is not done in your home. Coalition work has to be done in the streets... And you shouldn't look for comfort. Some people will come to a coalition and the rate the success of the coalition on whether or not they feel good when they get there. They're not looking for a coalition; they're looking for a home!* (p. 356). The message of the midway metaphor is: while there is value in engineering sophisticated "bridges" to transport innovation (i.e., EBP) between the worlds of research and practice, there are also good reasons to expand notions of feedback loops to include a much more inclusive set of prevention stakeholders who should be sharing their successes and lessons learned from working with prevention innovations. The feedback that gets looped within the complexity of the "midway" system is another way to think about PBE.

The Art and Science of Responding to Child Maltreatment

Coalition Building & Prevention Partnerships

Because violence and trauma harm men, women, and children of all ages, races, and ethnicities across time, community, and culture, our prevention efforts must include a diverse array of stakeholders. As Reagon would say, "And watch that "our"—make it as big as you can... the "our" must include everybody you have to include in order for you to survive. That's why we have to have coalitions" (p. 365). Multiple groups will need to work together to measure and demand effectiveness in future prevention work; and this is part of the move towards practice-based evidence. The focus is not just connection between research-practice (i.e., as depicted by the "controlled" solution of the two-way bridge). This is now the age of researcher-practitioner-funder-consumer partnerships (i.e., as depicted by the more complex situation of multiple events and contributors at the county fair midway); and for a future without child maltreatment, the emphasis must be to figure out how multiple partners can work in coalition to achieve outcomes *together* that no single entity could achieve on their own.

In violence prevention work, the CDC has defined coalition building as a strategy that increases the ability of two or more organizations to work collaboratively, which begs the question of what is meant, exactly, by collaboration. The short answer is: collaboration is the gold standard of *partnership functioning* (Weiss, Anderson, & Lasker, 2002). Besides coalition, a primary way to think about working together is to consider prevention partnerships, which are the foundational relationship mechanisms by which trust, shared vision, and aligned goals—all necessary to sustain the long-term nature of prevention programs aimed at unraveling deep-rooted causes of violence—can be generated. The prevention partnership seems key to prevention efforts in the same way that therapeutic alliance facilitates individualized treatments. That is, research that has looked at "what works" in treatment suggests that it is not only the treatment approach itself (e.g., psychotherapy A vs. psychotherapy B), but also the relationship between the client and change agent (Martin, Garske & Davis, 2000). The concept that extends therapeutic alliance out of the therapist-client setting into a broader community context is partnership functioning.

Not all partnerships function the same way. Huxham (1996) suggests different levels of functioning from *networking*, which is when partners share information for the benefit of all parties; to *coordinating*, when partners not only share information, but also change their activities to achieve a stated goal; to *cooperating* where partners share information, change activities, and divide resources for the benefit of all parties and to achieve a stated goal; and finally, *collaborating* which includes all of the previously stated elements, *plus* partners improve the capacity of another for the benefit of all parties and to achieve a stated goal. According to Lasker, Weiss, & Miller (2001) the output of a partnership functioning at a collaborative level is *synergy*—or combining power—which is theorized to lead to partnership effectiveness in reaching the stated goal.

In navigating the complex nature of prevention systems—the ISF in Fig. 2 collaborative partnerships become critical in two ways. First, collaboration becomes the operative mechanism for building the partnership's capacity. Both the prevention delivery system and the prevention support system require general capacity and innovation-specific capacity; and partners—for example, a community-based task force that includes local university-based researchers, members of the press, victim advocates, the district attorney's office and meets regularly—can, through shared work and collective action, build each other's capacity. Secondly, partnerships, especially partnerships that include program evaluators, can force accountability. Wandersman (2011) suggests that the remedy to the mediocrity of current prevention practice will not be choosing between EBP or interventions "homegrown" in the community, but rather developing shared vision for outcomes and methods for accountability. Coalitions are a mechanism for creating shared vision and developing authentic community accountability. In working with other groups who are inspired by different leaders—and who may not necessarily share organizational practices, values, or beliefs—partners become accountable for overcoming jargon to articulate ideas and specify the meaning of success that allows stakeholders to take collective action. The concept of practice-based evidence returns, because those partnerships that include a program evaluator as a partner, or use methods of program evaluation, have an opportunity to document the real-world conditions of preventive intervention implementation and share evidence about what, if anything, was significant or worthy about that work.

Participatory Methods and Collaborative Inquiry

The purpose of this chapter, again, is to illustrate the value of PBE in taking evidence-based prevention programs to scale. To this point, the stated case is: given the wicked nature of child maltreatment and the complexity of the interactive systems of community-based prevention, collaborative partnerships are a precondition for successful efforts in the twenty-first century. What, then, should these partnerships be doing? Implementing, documenting, learning, and sharing. Collectively. As a feminist scholar, community psychologist, and utilization-focused evaluator, I support diverse forms of evidence and pluralistic processes of evidence production. One such process is *collaborative inquiry*.

Collaborative inquiry is primarily a process to support professional learning. It is a means for learning communities "to deconstruct knowledge through joint reflection and analysis, reconstructing it through collaborative action, and co-constructing it through collective learning from their experiences" (Stoll, 2010, p. 474). Since it is contextual in nature, it is not expected that findings are generalized to a larger population. The four stages of collaborative inquiry include: framing the problem; collecting evidence; analyzing the evidence; and finally, documenting, celebrating, and sharing. The infrastructure for sharing is underdeveloped. How does knowledge get transferred from one community's midway to another? Margison, et al. (2000) recommend *practice research networks* (PRNs) as the mechanism for using practice-based evidence to improve the effectiveness of routine practice. Another option, especially for relatively new prevention programs, is for prevention practitioners to partner with an evaluator and collaborate to conduct formative evaluation (performance measurement)—and then later continuous quality assurance and quality improvement (performance monitoring). This professional relationship between evaluator and program stakeholders may be a platform for collaborative inquiry.

Collaborative inquiry is a PBE-generating activity that can be applied within many models of participatory evaluation and action research. Participatory evaluation is applied systematic inquiry that involves trained evaluators working in partnership with non-evaluator stakeholders for the purposes of making judgements about the merit and worth of programs or supporting organizational decision-making (Cousins & Earl, 1992). Participatory evaluation may be practical, which is utilization-oriented and problem solving (Practical-Participatory Evaluation), or transformative, which is democratic, emancipatory, and empowerment-oriented (Tranformative-Participatory Evaluation)) (Cousins & Whitmore, 1998). Other models include action research (in the tradition of Lewin, 1951), participatory action research (Greenwood, Whyte, & Harkavy, 1993), empowerment evaluation (Fetterman, 1994a, 1994b) and others.

Within the fields of prevention and evaluation, the value of practice-based evidence is not just in generating knowledge, but in *using* it. Forces driving the utilization of PBE include not just the range of models for participatory evaluation, and interest in collaborative inquiry as a process to support professional learning, but also more internal evaluators hired by organizations to contribute to organizational learning and growth, and a shared value for culturally competent evaluation. The key to use is getting the PBE in front of individuals with their hands on the levers for change— whether a principal in a school, or a chief of police. It is critical that these individuals are intentionally involved in formulating the questions that will be answered with data. Expert change agents can ask the questions that prompt prevention practitioners to update their programming, opinion leaders and champions can raise awareness for the need to change prevention practices, public opinion can influence health policy or organizational commitment.

All this matters because rates of prevention program adoption are lower than ideal. Although systematic research reviews and program registries have facilitated the implementation of evidence-based programs (e.g., Cochrane Collaboration since 1993), still relatively few programs are taken to the scale necessary to create broad-based change to end child abuse in our lifetime (Baum, Blakeslee, Lloyd & Petrosino, 2013). In meeting the challenge of how to increase use of effective programs, a delicate rhythm must play out in which practitioners adapt or modify a program to meet needs of a specific population while also preserving the core program components. Within three alternative implementation approaches—direct adoption, adaptation, or community-driven implementation (Baum et al., 2013) — multidisciplinary partnerships, collaboration, and participatory evaluation methods seem to be increasingly relevant mechanisms for problem-solvers who are "meeting at the midway." The resulting practice-based evidence may better describe complexity, catalyze action, inform new strategy design, and sustain prevention until child maltreatment is, hopefully, a problem no more.

References

Anda, R. F., Brown, D. W., Dube, S. R., Bremner, J. D., Felitti, V. J., & Giles, W. H. (2008). Adverse childhood experiences and chronic obstructive pulmonary disease in adults. *American Journal of Preventive Medicine, 34*(5), 396–403.

Baum, K., Blakeslee, K.M., Lloyd, J., & Petrosino, A. (2013). *Violence prevention: Moving from evidence to implementation.* A Discussion Paper published by the Institute of Medicine of the National Academy of Sciences.

Brown, D. W., Anda, R. F., Felitti, V. J., Edwards, V. J., Malarcher, A. M., Croft, J. B., & Giles, W. H. (2010). Adverse childhood experiences and the risk of lung cancer. *BMC Public Health, 10*, 20.

Campbell, R., & Wasco, S. M. (2000). Feminist approaches to social science: Epistemological and methodological tenets. *American Journal of Community Psychology, 28*, 773–791.

Cousins, J. B., & Earl, L. M. (1992). The case for participatory evaluation. *Educational Evaluation and Policy Analysis, 14*, 397–418.

Cousins, J. B., & Whitmore, E. (1998). Framing participatory evaluation. *New Directions for Evaluation, 80*, 5–23.

Creswell, J. (2009). *Research design: Qualitative, quantitative, and mixed methods approaches.* London: Sage.

Dong, M., Giles, W. H., Felitti, V. J., Dube, S. R., Williams, J. E., Chapman, D. P., & Anda, R. F. (2004). Insights into causal pathways for ischemic heart disease: Adverse childhood experiences study. *Circulation, 110*, 1761–1766.

Dube, S. R., Anda, R. F., Felitti, V. J., Chapman, D., Williamson, D. F., & Giles, W. H. (2001). Childhood abuse, household dysfunction and the risk of attempted suicide throughout the life span: Findings from adverse childhood experiences study. *JAMA, 286*, 3089–3096.

Edwards, V. J., Anda, R. F., Felitti, V. J., & Dube, S. R. (2003). Adverse childhood experiences and health-related quality of life as an adult. In K. Kendall-Tackett (Ed.), *Health consequences of abuse in the family: A clinical guide for evidence-based practice* (pp. 81–94). Washington, DC: American Psychological Association.

Felitti, V. J., Anda, R. F., Nordenberg, D., Williamson, D. F., Spitz, A. M., Edwards, V., ... Marks, J. S. (1998). Relationship of childhood abuse and household dysfunction to many of the leading causes of death in adults: The Adverse Childhood Experiences (ACE) Study. *American Journal of Preventive Medicine, 14*, 245–258.

Fetterman, D. M. (1994a). Steps of empowerment evaluation: From California to Cape Town. *Evaluation and Program Planning, 17*(3), 305–313.

Fetterman, D. M. (1994b). Empowerment evaluation. *Evaluation Practice, 15*, 1–15.

Foster-Fishman, P. G., & Watson, E. R. (2012). The ABLe change framework: A conceptual and methodological tool for promoting systems change. *American Journal of Community Psychology, 49*, 503–516.

Greenwood, D. J., Whyte, W. F., & Harkavy, I. (1993). Participatory action research as a process and as a goal. *Human Relations, 46*, 175.

Guba, E. G., & Lincoln, Y. S. (1994). Competing paradigms in qualitative research. In N. K. Denzin & Y. S. Lincoln (Eds.), *Handbook of qualitative research* (pp. 105–117). Thousand Oaks, CA: Sage.

Hoagwood, K. (2003). The evidence for (or against) the evidence: State of science, practice, and policy on children's mental health. In H. Hair (Ed.), *Outcomes for children and adolescents after residential treatment: A review of research from 1993 to 2003. Journal of Child and Family Studies, 14*(4), 551–575.

Huxham, C. (1996). The search for collaborative advantage. In C. Huxham (Ed.), *Creating collaborative advantage* (pp. 176–180). London: Sage.

Jacobson, N. S., & Truax, P. (1991). Clinical significance: A statistical approach to defining meaningful change in psychotherapy. *Journal of Consulting & Clinical Psychology, 59*, 12–19.

Kolko, J. (2012). *Wicked problems: Problems worth solving*. Austin, TX: Austin Center for Design

Lasker, R. D., Weiss, E. S., & Miller, R. (2001). Partnership synergy: A practical framework for studying and strengthening the collaborative advantage. *Milbank Quarterly, 79*, 179–205.

Lewin, K. (1951). *Field theory in social science*. New York: Harper and Row.

Lieberman, R., Zubritsky, C., Martinez, K., Massey, O., Fisher, S., Kramer, T., Koch, R., & Obrochta, C. (2010). *Issue brief using practice-based evidence to complement evidence-based practice in children 's behavioral health*. Atlanta, GA: ICF Macro, Outcomes Roundtable for Children and Families.

Margison, F. R., Barkham, M., Evans, C., McGrath, G., Clark, J. M., Audin, K., & Evans, C. (2000). Measurement and psychotherapy: Evidence-based practice and practice-based evidence. *British Journal of Psychiatry, 177*, 123–130.

Martin, D., Garske, J., and Davis, M. (2000). Relation of the therapeutic alliance with other outcome and other variables: a meta-analytic review. *Journal of Consulting and Clinical Psychology, 68*, 438–450.

Nevo, I., & Slonim-Nevo, E. (2011). The myth of evidence-based practice: towards evidence informed practice. *British Journal of Social Work, 22*, 1–22.

Olson, E. E., & Eoyang, G. H. (2001). *Facilitating organization change: Lessons from complexity science*. San Francisco: Jossey-Bass/Pfeiffer.

Orleans, Gruman, & Anderson, 1999 (March 4, 1999). *Roadmaps for the next frontier: Getting evidence-based behavioral medicine into practice*. Paper presented at Society of Behavioral Medicine, San Diego, CA.

Phelen, S. E. (2001). What is complexity science: Really? *Emergence, 3*(1), 120–136.

Puddy, R. W., & Wilkins, N. (2011). *Understanding evidence part 1: Best available research evidence. A guide to the continuum of evidence of effectiveness*. Atlanta, GA: Centers for Disease Control and Prevention.

Reagon, B. J. (1983). Coalition politics: Turning the century. In B. Smith (Ed.), *Home girls: A black feminist anthology*. New York: Kitchen Table Press.

Relyea, M. (2015). *Treating bystander intervention as systems change*. Unpublished manuscript.

Rittel, H. W. J., & Webber, M. M. (1973). Dilemmas in a general theory of planning. *Policy Sciences, 4*, 155–169.

Sackett, D. L., Rosenberg, W. M., Gray, J. A., Haynes, R. B., & Richardson, W. S. (1996). Evidence based medicine: What it is and what it isn't. *British Medical Journal, 312*(7023), 71–72.

Sackett, D. L., Straus, S. E., Richardson, W. S., Rosenberg, W., & Haynes, R. B. (2000). *Evidence based medicine: How to practice and teach EBM* (2nd ed.). London: Churchill Livingstone.

Swisher, A. K. (2010). Practice-based evidence. *Cardiopulmonary Physical Therapy Journal, 21*(2), 4.

Victora, C., Habicht, J. P., & Bryce, J. (2004). Evidence-based public health: Moving be- yond randomized trials. *American Journal of Public Health, 94*, 400–405.

Wandersman, A. (2011). *Accountability and going to scale with quality*. Presentation at the Emphasizing Evidence Based Programs for Children and Youth Forum. Washington, DC.

Wandersman, A., Chien, V. H., & Katz, J. (2012). Toward an evidence-based system for innovation support for implementing innovations with quality: Tools, training, technical assistance, and quality assurance/quality improvement. *American Journal of Community Psychology, 50*, 445–459.

Wandersman, A., Duffy, J., Flaspohler, P., Noonan, R., Lubell, K., Stillman, L., ... Saul, J. (2008). Bridging the gap between prevention research and practice: The interactive systems framework for dissemination and implementation. *American Journal of Community Psychology, 41*, 171–181.

Wasco, S. M. (2014). *Sharon Wasco on practice-based evidence: Another frame for evaluation* [Weblogpost].Retrievedfromhttp://aea365.org/blog/sharon-wasco-on-practice-based-evidence-another-frame-for-evaluation/

Weiss, E.S., Anderson, R.M., Lasker, R.D. (2002) Making the most of collaboration: Exploring the relationship between partnership synergy and partnership functioning. *Health Education & Behavior, 29*, 683–698.

Index

© Springer International Publishing Switzerland 2017
D.M. Teti (ed.), *Parenting and Family Processes in Child Maltreatment
and Intervention*, Child Maltreatment Solutions Network,
DOI 10.1007/978-3-319-40920-7

CPSIA information can be obtained
at www.ICGtesting.com
Printed in the USA
LVOW13*2121261216
518713LV00003B/34/P